HERRYMON MAURER is the author of two books on China and co-editor of *Fortune's* single-subject issue, *Japan and the Japanese*. He was formerly Instructor in English in the University of Nanking at Chengtu, Szechwan, China, and later member of the Board of Editors of *Fortune* Magazine. He is now a lecturer at Pendle Hill, the Quaker graduate-study center, and a contributor to *Fortune, Commentary,* and other periodicals.

Does anyone want to take the world and do what he wants with it?

I do not see how he can succeed.

The world is a sacred vessel, which must not be tampered with or grabbed at.

To tamper with it is to spoil it, and to grab at it is to lose it.

—LAO-TZE

Collision
of EAST and WEST

by

HERRYMON MAURER

with an Introduction
by HU SHIH

HENRY REGNERY COMPANY
CHICAGO, 1951

Manufactured in the United States of America
by The Colonial Press Inc., Clinton, Mass.

Author's Note

IN AN INCREASING NUMBER OF COUNTRIES HISTORY IS NOWA-
days written by a conqueror, and that conqueror tells lies.
This project grew out of an urgent sense that history would
have to be written currently or it could not be written at all,
and out of a concern over current conflicts between persons
and peoples. But as research for the project continued and the
writing of this book progressed, it became clear that what happens now has such tenacious lodgement in what has happened
in the past that it would be misleading to describe either the
fall of states or the price of fish except in terms of age-old
cultural drives and urges. Seen in these terms, the present
itself looms increasingly large. It is not enough to detail some
part of it; it is necessary to try to hold all of it in mind, which
is impossible, and failing that to hold as much of it as possible: books and businesses, strategies of war and beliefs of
religion, ways of raising children or building homes, types of
humor, devices of diplomacy, and what not.

As facts accumulated for this somewhat forbidding pano-
rama, the conviction grew upon the writer that the facts,
copious as they were, were embraced by one great fact—the
inward, persistent, cultural collisions of individuals and peoples. Hence the scope of the project and the form of the
present volume, the first of a series of accounts of current

cultural collisions. Persuaded that observed events include the observer, the writer has felt it preferable to shape the book consciously around the conviction that the events have aroused in him rather than to let the events be shaped and selected after some subconscious pattern. Attempt has therefore been made to keep the narrative of the collision of the Far East and the West as direct as possible, letting detail spill over into notes. Attempt has been made not to argue the theory of cultural collisions philosophically—that will require another book—but to let it argue itself so far as possible pragmatically. The writer plans to use the method of this book in a series of other books: collision with Russia, India's collision with the West, the internal collision of the West and, finally, the theory of cultural collisions.

Sources of historical data are indicated in the notes. The greater part of the data of recent events has come either from the writer's direct observation or—more important—from extended interviews with persons who were prominent in the events themselves. These interviews, somewhat more than a hundred in number, were by their nature not-for-attribution. They were conducted mainly for articles that appeared in *Fortune* Magazine, and the data that was gained from them were subjected to *Fortune's* regular checking procedures.

Since much of the material in the book is based upon articles on the Far East written for *Fortune* from 1942 to 1948, the writer wishes to express his appreciation to the Editors for permission to make use of the material. The writer's views, of course, are his and not *Fortune's*. He would like further to express gratitude for the opportunity to carry on continuing and detailed research, without which this book could not have been attempted. He owes special gratitude to researchers who worked with him on particular articles: Alberta Conway, Anna De Cormis, Mia Fritsch, Elida Griffin, Elsieanna Graff, Florence Horn, Jean Krummes, Józefa Malinowska, Elsa Wardell, Selma Wolff, and Betty Youngstrand,

and to copy chief Mary Grace. He wishes to express warm personal appreciation to Albert L. Furth, Henry R. Luce, and Ralph D. Paine, Jr., editors of the various articles, and to Helen S. Maurer, who has given both labor and light to all phases of the project.

The writer wishes also to indicate his very great indebtedness to R. O. Joliffe, Hu Shih, and the late James S. Y. Tang, to whom he owes such understanding of the Far East as he has. Thanks are due for permission to quote from the following books: *The Russian Idea,* copyright 1947 by Nicholas Berdyaev, The Macmillan Company; *Peking Diary,* Derk Bodde, copyright 1950 by Henry Schuman, Inc.; *China's Destiny* and *The Collected Wartime Messages of Generalissimo Chiang Kai-shek,* Chiang Kai-shek, copyright 1947 and 1943–46 by Central News Service; *The Rise of Russia in Asia,* David J. Dallin, copyright 1949 by Yale University Press; *Musings of a Chinese Mystic,* Herbert Giles ("Wisdom of the East Series"), John Murray, London, 1920; "China in Stalin's Grand Strategy," Hu Shih, *Foreign Affairs,* copyright 1950 by the Council on Foreign Relations, Inc.; *The Chinese Renaissance,* Hu Shih, copyright 1934 by the University of Chicago; *The Invasion of China by the Western World,* E. R. Hughes, copyright 1938 by The Macmillan Company; *The Wisdom of China and India* (1942) and *The Wisdom of Confucius,* Lin Yutang (1938, 1942), copyright by Random House, Inc.; *The Gay Genius, The Life and Times of Su Tungpo,* Lin Yutang, copyright 1947 by The John Day Company; *Mao Tse-tung, Ruler of Red China,* copyright 1950 by Robert Payne, Henry Schuman, Inc.; *Japan, A Short Cultural History,* G. B. Sansom, copyright 1943 by D. Appleton-Century, Inc. (by permission of Appleton-Century-Crofts, Inc.); *Roosevelt and Hopkins,* copyright 1948 by Robert E. Sherwood, Harper and Brothers; *A Daughter of the Samurai,* Etsu Inagaki Sugimoto, copyright 1926 by Doubleday Page and Company (by permission of Doubleday and Company); *Seven Decisions That*

Shaped History, copyright 1950, 1951 by Sumner Welles, Harper and Brothers.

Special thanks are due also to John C. H. Wu for his translation of the *Tao Teh Ching.* The writer is indebted also to the authorities mentioned in the notes and to the persons whom he has interviewed. To all of these persons whatever is of value in the book is largely owing. The writer hopes that errors and misjudgments, for which he is responsible, will not stand too greatly in the way of their contribution.

In romanizing Chinese and Japanese words and names, the writer has omitted all diacritical marks and has made use of other simplifications in an attempt to make reading easier for readers who are not familiar with Oriental languages. Whenever this system of romanization results in names different from those in the cutsomary Wade and Hepburn systems, the customary form appears in parentheses in the Index.

April 15, 1951

H.M.

Contents

Introduction

My friend Mr. Herrymon Maurer has written a very good book on a tragic theme: the collision of East and West during the years 1937–1947 and the frightening consequences of that collision during the years that followed. It deals with the tragedy of the four-cornered war between China and Japan, between Japan and the United States, between Japan and Russia, between China and Russia, and the cultural and political war between China and the United States. It is an excellent historical and psychological study of the failure of statesmanship to avert the century-old collision in the Far East, a collision which "finally blew up [a quarter of the world] so violently in the space of ten short years that it set the West itself on fire, overwhelmed four-thousand-year-old China, and involved East, West, and Russia perhaps fatally with each other."

The book exemplifies a new method for the study of current history. It is an evaluation of present events through the use of psychological and historical tools, whereby the present is seen as the outgrowth of the cultural past. It is an attempt to understand the collisions between peoples through a study of the reactions of the human mind to the events, ideas, and experiences that have passed through it.

Mr. Maurer is a thoughtful writer who interprets world events with the sympathetic understanding of the true philosopher. For he is a philosopher who lives his philosophy. He is a Quaker. He is the author of two philosophical books: *The Old Fellow,* an interpretation of the Chinese philosopher Lao-tze in the form of a novel, and *Great Soul,* a book on Gandhi. He is deeply attracted by Lao-tze, who taught non-resistance five centuries before Jesus of Nazareth, and by Gandhi, who achieved the great miracle of modern times in winning the independence of India by nonviolence.

Mr. Maurer does not explain the failure of the tyrannous decade by means of the doctrine of nonresistance or nonviolence, although he does say that "from the standpoint of timeless truth and its growth in the affairs of men, it may well have been that China should not have been aided and encouraged in violent resistance," and that "it may have been that, given suitable encouragement, the Chinese, instead of waging a half-violent war, could have waged one that was nonviolent and thereby have prevented a bitter aftermath to the struggle with Japan."

The philosophical or moral standpoint with which Mr. Maurer seeks to view the collisions of those ten years comes very near Immanuel Kant's doctrine of the Categorical Imperative: "So act," Kant said, "as to treat humanity, whether in thine own person or in that of any other, in every case as an end in itself, never as a means only."

"It is," says Mr. Maurer, "the attempt of this book to press urgently the conviction that the world of men . . . is of such nature that outward activity, however well-intentioned, invites personal and international disaster whenever it is not based on a profound inner awareness of other persons, other nations, other cultures." In his concluding chapter, he says: "In short, the mistake that threw the cultural meeting of East and West into an intense cultural collision was the mistake of treating Eastern peoples not straightforwardly as persons who are valuable in themselves but rather as units of population which can be used as means to some greater end. . . . It was assumed, for instance, that it was to the advantage of China to be treated not simply as a country in itself, as a country of special needs, sufferings, and hungers, but as an adjunct to the American war effort and to the American plan for peace, which for some years centered on the hope of Russo–American co-operation. It was assumed also that it was to the advantage of Japan and Korea to be treated as adjuncts to American foreign policy. . . ."

And, being a Quaker and a true philosopher, he leaves with us this message of admonition and hope: "The attitude will change finally when a sufficient number of persons grasp a profound, simple, but very taxing fact of human experience: the use of other persons or other peoples as devices to make oneself feel superior provokes hostility and leads to emotional or cultural collision. Other persons, whether they be of one culture or another, must be treated as ends in themselves, not as means to some other end."

As a Chinese heathen, I confess that I find Mr. Maurer's central theme morally refreshing and historically illuminating. I am inclined to think that this Kantian principle of always treating anyone as an end in himself and never as a means, may yet prove to be a more satisfactory hypothesis for the explanation of the tragic history of our times than any other theory proposed so far. It seems to me that this principle at least offers a more satisfactory explanation of what happened between China and the United States in those years. As Mr. Maurer has put it, "For some years the United States had been fond of China to the point of sentimentality, and for one year it had been planning and promising a great program of affectionate aid. Yet almost as soon as the United States and the Chinese Government became allies, the United States began to dislike the Chinese Government as emotionally as it once used to applaud it."

What provoked this shift was the unfortunate historical fact that China was promoted (or, shall I say, degraded) from "a friend" to "an ally." For nearly a century, China and the

United States were mere friends, separated by the greatest
ocean between them, and with no aggressive designs toward
each other. It was possible for the United States to cherish
a truly disinterested friendship and even fondness for the
"China of blue porcelain bowls and exquisite silk scrolls,"
for the China of Lao-tze and Confucius, of Li Po, Tu Fu and
Po Chu-i, of Li Lung-mien, Ma Yuan and Hsia Kwei. This
genuine and disinterested friendship was fully appreciated
and requited by China, which was sending every year thousands of her young men and women to American universities
and graduate schools in a sincere desire to understand this
great nation which had tremendous strength but was disciplined not to use it for aggression. There was sincere friendship and real appreciation of each other's cultural achievements.

But China's woe began on that memorable day in January
1942, when she was invited by the United States Government
to sign the United Nations' Declaration, together with the
United Kingdom, the United States, and the U.S.S.R., one day
before the other nations, which were to sign the next day
according to the alphabetical order. By that act of well-intentioned courtesy, China was made, not only an ally of the three
greatest powers fighting German and Japanese aggression, but
a member of the Big Four! From that time on, China's relations with her powerful allies became more and more difficult.

As a "poor relation" of the mighty three, China could be
forgiven for having acquired certain airs not unusual for the
equals of the gods. She aspired to play the part of the leader
of the Asiatic continent; she remembered the pledge of Sun
Yat-sen and his party to give aid to every Asiatic people seeking freedom from the yoke of imperialism; and Chiang Kai-
shek even dared to lecture Great Britain on India and Burma.
Indeed he even dared to say No to some of the plans proposed
by General Stilwell or by President Roosevelt.

But China's greatest difficulty was her failure to live up to
her American ally's great expectations of her. As a great ally

still claiming control over a population of two hundred million, China was expected not only to hold her own in the China theater, but rapidly to train her manpower in preparation for effective participation in the great Allied offensive to come. China should have been able to fulfill such reasonable and minimum expectations if she could have received even a small fraction of the material aid that Soviet Russia was then receiving from Britain and America. But the Japanese military saw the threat of Free China being adequately aided and armed by her allies. Japanese strategy on the Asiatic continent —the rapid conquering of Siam and Burma, the disabling of the Burma road, the increasing effectiveness of the almost absolute economic blockade against Free China—was clearly directed toward preventing China from receiving adequate military and material aid from the outside. It was the one Japanese strategy which the Allied Powers did not break up.

And there were other expectations, probably equally natural and reasonable. Nationalist China was asked to patch up its political differences with the Chinese Communists, to consent to American proposals to arm the Chinese Communist armies, to give the Chinese Communists greater share in the Central Government, and so on. President Roosevelt was saying to Chiang Kai-shek, in discussing the latter's refusal to accept General Stilwell's plan to arm the Chinese Red Army: "When the enemy is pressing us toward possible disaster, it appears unsound to reject the aid of anyone who will kill Japanese." At a time when Great Britain and the United States were giving every possible military aid to Soviet Russia, thereby making her the greatest military power in European history, it did seem so "unsound" and so unreasonable for Chiang Kai-shek to persist in his refusal to arm and supply the Chinese Reds. Could the Chinese Red Army be possibly more dangerous than the mighty Red Army of the U.S.S.R.?

In short, it was China the new ally, the weakest member of the "Grand Alliance," that had to be somehow reconstructed and reformed so that she might be better fitted to play her part in the allied war strategy. And when she sometimes failed to comply with any particular line or plan in this "reconstruction," she came to be more and more disliked by her fond friend of an earlier age.

I am therefore inclined to agree with Mr. Maurer that the fundamental mistake underlying this great collision in Asia was the attitude of treating a nation, a people, a culture, not as an end valuable in itself, but only as a means to some greater good. China came to be disliked because she was found to be not fully satisfactory "as an adjunct to the American war effort and to the American plan for peace," although it was a matter of historical record that China did try hard to play her role in both of those capacities, even to the extreme extent of negotiating and signing, under most humiliating conditions, the Sino–Soviet Treaty, which legalized the secret Yalta Agreement.

To those readers who may find the Kantian "Categorical Imperative" too austere or moralistic, I would like to suggest a Chinese principle of common sense as taught by the humanist and democratic philosopher Mencius. Mencius once said: "Between father and son there should be no reproving admonitions as to what is good. Such reproving admonitions lead to alienation, and there is nothing more inauspicious than alienation [between father and son]." What Mencius did not wish to find existing between father and son, was actually practiced with vehement pressure by the government of one great power on the government of a weak power. The inevitable result was dislike, recrimination, and cataclysmic collision.

May not this Chinese warning of twenty-three centuries ago help us to understand the historical lesson which Mr. Maurer has tried to make us all learn from the tragedies of the tyrannous decade?

Hu Shih

March 27, 1951

Collision of EAST *and* WEST

The Fact of Collision

IF ONE PEOPLE ANY LONGER SHARE ANYTHING WITH AN-
other, it may perhaps be a common expectation of doom.
The Far East, certainly, is made one with the West only
through insistent and unpleasant facts: many persons are
sunk in a misery that involves them in hunger, slavery, and
violence. Other persons are set upon by fear that these pesti-
lences will spread and engulf them. It is the dark dream of
men that if somehow they stave off the despoiling of the resources of the earth, somehow escape the breakup of their
own minds, and somehow postpone the collapse of their systems of livelihood, they will still face the end of life as they
know it. There is a secret and uneasy sense that the virulence
of discord will call out weapons of mass annihilation, and
that salvation is possible only by some great political scheme
or by some great economic plan or by some overwhelming
military advantage.

This book aims to show that not for Asia, not for the West,
and not for the persons in them, are there any political solutions to these unpleasant facts, nor yet any economic or military solutions; that all the outward efforts of men to seek
salvation from the evil around them only damn them in the
long run to an increase of that evil. There are no panaceas.

There are only the hidden and dynamic forces of men's inward minds, but these forces, potent of growth when put to use, are prolific of destruction when overlooked.

Thus to state good and evil is to state a belief occasionally accepted but very seldom acted upon. Ambassadors and soldiers, merchants, missionaries, and citizens are wont to agree that good will and sound principle should be the inward forces alike in foreign policy and in personal living. But this inclination shatters against the hard psychological fact of the strangeness and hostility with which men now confront other men. When person meets person, each thinks he sees something that is outward to him, something that is uncertainly and vaguely threatening, something with which he can get along only on terms of common participation in some big and overriding purpose of earning a living, building a dam, watching a ball game, working on a committee, or forming a government.

When group meets group, it is still individuals who meet, only the individuals are the more strange to each other and the more hostile in the hidden levels of their minds. The sense of community, of one person being to some degree part of another, is absent, for there is no common inward understanding on which such community could be built. The dealings of large groups like nations and cultures are increasingly economic and political, at least at such times as they are not brutally and frankly military.

It is therefore the attempt of this book to press urgently the conviction that the world of men, the world of history, the world of the ordinary daily activity alike of persons in their homes and persons in their governments—that this world is of such nature that outward activity, however well-intentioned, invites personal and international disaster whenever it is not based on a profound inner awareness of other persons, other nations, other cultures. It is the aim of the book not to argue this conviction in an effort to prove it

formally, but to let it argue itself in an account of a few passing instants in the stretch of human history.

These few instants have to do with the dealings of the Far
East and the West. Other instants could serve as well. The
account could be written in terms of Russia and Europe and
America, in terms of Britain and Palestine, in terms of capital and labor in France, in terms of American citizens and
politicians, black and white, rich and poor, and in terms
everywhere of man and his neighbor and man and himself.
It could be documented with notes on everything from the
raising of children to the fragmentation of space in twentieth-century painting and architecture. But there are singular
advantages in telling the account in terms of an ancient cultural area now prostrate before the jejune confusion of Europe, Russia, and America. For this ancient cultural area has
been the seat of very modern and devastating wars. Such
countries as China and Japan may at times have seemed of
such scant interest to Westerners that discussion of them
appeared dull, recondite, even trivial. Their fate, hardly a
matter of passion some years past, now becomes a matter of
pressing concern. For the Far East is a microcosm in which
the world's longest-lived culture, forever juvenescent yet always decadent beyond the understanding of younger peoples,
conflicts with the brash efficient West and with materialist
and messianic Russia, which is neither East nor West. Furthermore, the Far East is far enough away in space to let men
look upon what they do not wish to see on their doorsteps.

For the account that follows deals almost altogether with
failure, the failure of well-intentioned men to reach any inward understanding of each other, the failure of men of good
will to move in any direction save toward breakup of community and conflict of war. It may even be that the failure is
beyond recall and that there are no longer any remedies except of the sort proposed two millennia ago by Horace, who,
looking upon the inward desolation of Rome, urged that men

desert their cities and courts and market places in a body and take themselves off to the hills by way of a cure for the corruption of their inward beings. For the failure of an entire historical epoch is contained in the failure of the East, in particular China and Japan, and the West, in particular Britain and the United States, to reach anything but an impasse in a conflict which is inward and cultural, which kept a quarter of the world smouldering for two centuries, made it burn during a third, and finally blew it up so violently in the space of ten short years that it set the West itself on fire, overwhelmed four-thousand-year-old China, and involved East, West, and Russia perhaps fatally with each other.

The decade began with international war in 1937 and ended with civil war and international commotions in 1947, a date which represented the point of no return from increasingly bitter cultural conflict in China, Korea, and Japan. Thereafter, events, impelled by what preceded them, wore the cast of inevitability. After 1947 the specific failure of East and West in their dealings with one another was widely recognized, even by the administrators, generals, diplomats, soldiers, journalists, technical experts, and assorted citizens who took part in them. The causes were argued, various men suggesting that adoption of this or that particular scheme would have staved off failure, but this multiplicity of opinion was but another indication of failure. Not only did Occidentals fail to find some basis of unity with Orientals; each group also found it futile to reach agreement within itself. A ten-year stretch of war, diplomacy, occupation, and civil strife, in which Americans acted as chief agents in one of the most important instances of intercultural contact in history, left East and West farther apart than before, and left each more perplexed about the nature of the other. It bred cultural confusion in Japan, prepared Korea for battlefield service, and set the stage for a political and military convulsion in China so vast that it is now impossible to speak of China as a continuing cultural fact.

For the time being, let a few facts suffice to recall the failure:

In China the United States went forth to set a disordered Oriental house aright, firmly believing that it could encourage the right people, effect the right coalitions, and establish a series of *quid pro quos* effective enough to settle peace on an upset continent. It dreamed of great hydroelectric dams, great reforms of cabinets and armies, great revolutions of customs. It even propagandized the artificial insemination of cattle and the construction of sewer systems. In particular, it sought to bring about a new and democratic order by insisting that a nationalist government unite with a communist revolution. The State Department appeared to think that China could be fixed up by combining a rather corrupt political machine with a group of high-minded agrarian reformers (as the Communists were for a time called) in a sort of Pendergast-Farmers Union arrangement. Secretary of State James Byrnes, in the course of a press conference in 1946, contributed with utter innocence and conviction an analysis of the psyches of China's Foreign Minister, T. V. Soong, and of her head of state, Chiang Kai-shek, in terms entirely provincial:

I think that some of our arrangements made with Soong (who is a very able fellow) have made for difficulties. I can just imagine Soong dropping in on Chiang after one of his trips to Washington and saying, "Well, I have just got another $500 million. . . ." And I can see Chiang saying, "The hell you say. . . ." and then calling in the Communists and telling them that there was no need to talk any further; that they would have to come to terms or else. There's a lot of human nature in the Chinese.

In Korea, the United States sought high-mindedly to liberate a people whom the Japanese had enslaved, but promptly

ran afoul of the doggedness of its co-occupier, Russia, and of
the complexity of native Korean political parties. The military government forces of General John Hodge could see
these two problems only as one problem, and set about classi-
fying the parties in terms of emotional and political distance
from Russia—extreme right, right, middle, left, extreme left
—and took to using the labels as a substitute for deeper political understanding. Anxious to encourage Korean hopes
for self-government and to stimulate democracy, the United
States forces held popular elections. When the Koreans voted
in forty-three "rightists" and only two "leftists," Americans
both in the State Department and in the field concluded that
the election must have been unrepresentative to produce such
an imbalance, and General Hodge was ordered to appoint
forty-five persons of varying views, most of them "leftist."
This appointment made Communism the big political question in South Korea, outraged Korean anti-Communists,
and bewildered such persons as could not understand how a
representative government could be appointed.

Meanwhile, the United States—in the person of General
Douglas MacArthur—was approaching Japan with the aim of
the reform of the whole country and of the destruction alike
of the means and the appetite for war. The Occupation ex-
tolled the virtue of representative government and the initiative of citizens over against controlled parliaments and
obedience to superiors. It generated so great an enthusiasm
for "democratization" that Japan prepared eagerly to go to
school to her late enemy. Political patterns, industrial habits, even ancient cultural forms were disrupted and cut up,
and the entire pre-defeat leadership of the country was
rooted out and purged from office, whether in government,
business, journalism, or cultural associations. Japan was consciously broken up in order that she might be remade by her
own people from the bottom up. But precisely at the time

that one General of the Army, George Marshall, was urging once-ally China to join forces with a native Russian Communist party that was an announced enemy of American democracy, another General of the Army, Douglas MacArthur was urging that once-enemy Japan become the bulwark of American democracy against Russian Communism. A bastion is of no use unless it is strong. To be strong, Japan needed sound industries and sound leadership and a stable government—and freedom from excessive popular movements and unwise labor agitation. Therefore one part of the Occupation took to putting together what another part was breaking up. American officials began to intervene more actively in the political decisions of a country which the same officials were trying to train in making decisions by herself.

It may perhaps be argued that encouragement of Communism in one country, compromise with it in another, and manipulation against it in a third contributed to a sound policy of dealing pragmatically and open-mindedly with Russia, the eye of the storm of international discord. But United States confusion in Asia did not center simply around Moscow. Disgust for ex-ally China and a conscious but seldom expressed unreadiness to trust her gave force to the strengthening of ex-enemy Japan, a people with whose habits of neatness and industry the United States had long been sympathetic. (The difference in Western reactions to China and Japan, based in part on superficial fondness for whoever adopts the surface forms of Western industry and government, has had for half a century a decisive part in the violent interplay of these two nations.) As for Korea, expediency became American policy only in the absence of any set of principles or any notion of principles with which to approach the people of a country with whose liberation the United States had charged itself. In not one of the three countries was there any wide Western awareness of the inner drives of the people who made them up, except so far as it was stated in terms of Western political activities; there was, indeed, little attempt to seek such awareness. The fact of Russia was the occasion for a confusion that would have occurred in any case. The fact was not in any sense the cause of the confusion, nor did it have bearing upon its nature. The cause, if any simple cause there be, was a failure to know what the Orient was, what China was, what Japan was, what Korea was, even a failure to know what the West was, a failure to know what was going on.

What is germane to failure in the Orient was not the increased precariousness of United States–Russian dealings but the collapse of American efforts to do for Chinese, Koreans, and Japanese what these various peoples were actually ready to have done: peace, a greater degree of freedom from government, and a lesser degree of poverty. In each country the United States set out to preach a doctrine of peace, freedom, and plenty; yet in each country it left a gospel of might, efficiency, organization, violence, and face. Its great lasting imprint on the minds of Orientals was its own prowess in war; the East is unlikely to imagine again that the good things of earth can belong to any but the mighty, the victorious, and the proud. American enslavement to face, for instance, went considerably beyond any Oriental preoccupation with it. The State Department long admitted in private the failure of its policies in China and Korea but repeatedly reneged on admitting the failure or attempting a new policy, on the grounds that the dignity of the United States must not be impaired.

In the face of evident Western good will and evident Western failure in Asia, it becomes essential to picture the failure and inquire into the inward facts of it. It is necessary that this picture and this inquiry be built in terms both of the near and of the distant past. For three hundred of the Ori-

ent's many years, East and West faced each other and refused
to meet. For a hundred of them China and Japan pondered
ways and means of setting new machines upon an old earth
and making some amalgam between old virtues and heady
new ideas. The critical ten years between 1937 and 1947 repeated in essence the years that went before. Two years after
the end of World War II, Asia confronted basic problems
that were much the same as those it confronted when Commodore Perry steamed into Tokyo Bay and when Britain first
wrested treaty ports from China; the West studied Asia with
much the same uncertainty and almost the same unconcern.
These problems, this uncertainty, and this unconcern were
in turn products of a time when East and West were not even
aware of each other's existence.

The all-important *now*, in short, can be understood only
in terms of an all-important *then*. But it can be understood
only through an attempt at an inward account of it, a new
account, an attempt to write neither facts nor history by
themselves but facts and history as they seemed to the minds
and emotions of the persons who experienced them. In such
an account the reports of scholars on the oracle bones of
China's Shang Dynasty (1766–1122 B.C., also called Yin) may
be as pertinent as the reports of journalists on the rise and
fall of government in Nanking or Peking.

Clearly, an attempt of this sort must be carefully limited.
It is too much to try to make a grand-tour history of the Orient, but it may be possible to suggest such of its inward reality as bears upon its dealings with the West. Thus, while
this book seeks to know the thoughts, the motivations, the
inner urges that make an Oriental or a Westerner seem one
moment clear, simple, and understandable and at the next
elusive, mysterious, and sometimes oddly threatening, it does
not seek to ferret out original primary causes for any inner
condition. No one will ever know finally what combinations
of happenstances, causes, determining factors—God, fate,

chance, the historical process, climate, class struggle, the soil
—ever produced what results. The encounter of East and
West can be known only in terms of the reactions of the human mind to what has passed through it. That mind, which
may not be the cause of anything that happens but is the avenue through which everything does happen, has left in the
Far East traces four-thousand-years long.

Let it be admitted that to discuss this mind is to try to
make clear what is not clear. The Far East stretches wide in
space and deep in time. It is not one Orient, but dozens of
them, each many faceted. It is the grave of all generalization,
and this book, being a book, is a series of generalizations.
One tries to write a series of exact truths, but, of course, the
best one can do, in terms of one's aim, is a series of partial
lies: a set of fuzzy half-truths, which if seen from a great
enough distance may fuse together like an impressionist
painting into some semblance of truth. For this book leaves
out much, and of what is in it no part can be strictly true.
Only as a unit can it attempt to approach truth; only as a unit
can it be read. It is an attempt to look into an inward reality
that is both too simple and too complex for full understanding.

For to look at the final clash of the minds of East and West
is to look at psychological causes, to examine cultural backgrounds, to ferret out the underlying emotional drives that
put the stamp of uniqueness upon Chinese, Japanese, Korean
and upon American, Briton, Russian. Needed in such a view
is knowledge of how people think they think; how they
work, love, suffer, eat, and amuse themselves; what they believe in; what they want, and how they get it. It is essential
to watch them fighting wars, organizing empires, running
governments. Only when it is possible to understand the
motivation of the Japanese who travels by streetcar to bow
before a torii (the gateway that is not a gateway but an
esthetic symbol, ancient, simple, and restrained) or of the

Chinese who studies physics but composes classical music for the ten-tone flute—only then is it possible to bridge the abyss that lies between two ways of life unlike—as are the lives even of persons within one family—in aims, methods, and motivations.

If the life of each country of Asia be seen in these psychological terms, there is one great reality uppermost in it, one that has been uppermost for almost a century. It is not political theory, or the revolt of peoples, or the grip of landlords, or the struggle for economic markets, or even nationalism or the urge to empire. It is the simple prime fact of mental collision, a reality of mind and emotion that covers every facet of Oriental life, even as it covers every facet of Western life, the only reality outside geographic propinquity that unites the world today, a reality that Western man will have to learn, at home or abroad, and resign himself to his fears of doom.

2

The Surface of the Conflict

THE COLLISION OF EAST AND WEST OCCURRED IN NO SINGLE intersection of space and time, but in a jumbled crosshatching of space-times: ancient towns and half-modern cities, traditional doctrine and new theory, old-fashioned farmers and up-to-date students just home from travel abroad. To the Westerner fresh from the parliaments and the bathtubs of his own country the Orient appeared unreasonably anachronistic. Over him swept a terrifying conviction of out-of-date poverty, darkness, and dirt. To the men who fought without knowing it the cultural war of 1937–47, the lot of most men and women in any country in Asia seemed almost subhuman in comparison with the advantages even of people crowded into the cities of the West. There were so many things they did not have, whether kitchen goods or hospitals, time pieces or efficient governments.

What is more, when Westerners showed them the splendid goals of more and better things, few Easterners confessed readily to the sin of poverty (so unspeakable to educated men in Europe or America) and promptly reformed. The Westerner learned that a whole system of ethics was breaking down, that the old ties of place and family were being shaken, that there was growing everywhere a numbing emptiness of spirit: in short, that the obstacles to a sudden change of manners were tottering. And yet there was no end to hunger and disease and superstition. The only solution seemed to be that something vast and important ought to be done, a whole list of somethings—health projects, farm reform, model government, legal codes, better officials, dams, factories, technical training—and before long the something that needed to be done stretched to include everything.

In those years the Westerner looked about him and he saw a thousand eyes probing him as he walked and ate and even as he awoke from sleep, eyes studying the cut of his garment, watching the way he took up food, observing the look of his car, guessing the weight of his shoes. He tried to look behind these eyes and he saw a vast continent in constant flux, a culture as confused as the surface of a lake disturbed all at once by a handful of rocks and a cartful of pebbles. Great movements for the reform of Buddhism or the spread of literacy or the framing of constitutions or the study of foreign literature coexisted with crazes for hair-bobbing, bridge-playing, Western-style dancing, and the wearing of American fountain pens.

There was the look of change everywhere, yet there seemed to be no change. Something was missing. In China, for instance, it was much more than a simple matter of a lack of factories. It was a lack of the condition of mind that produces factories, but it was even more than this. It was the presence of a whole series of ways of living antithetical to the entire course of modern Western logic, religion, literature, science, and, incidentally, industrialism. The closest China came to anything resembling an analytical process was during the recent Ching Dynasty (A.D. 1644–1911) when logical methods were worked out for the critical examination not of government or economics or anything so mundane as manufacturing, but of the Chinese classics.

Asia was a strange continent, and the Westerner woke at night to hear an ancient man howling rhythmically in the streets to drive devils away. The evening wind carried temple music of unfamiliar and therefore unearthly tone. The Westerner walked past a people who might be noisy or quiet, violent or restrained, but he was ignorant of what they said; and even if he understood their words, he was ignorant of what they thought. He could understand Europe far better; either he or his ancestors came from there; there was nothing queer in German poetry or Italian art, and even the motivations of a madman Hitler were to some degree measurable in his own terms. But the chicken-feet writing of the Chinese, the family habits of the Japanese, the political imbroglios of Koreans: for these he lacked background, even if he had been long resident in Asia, even if he spoke the language. In most cases, of course, the Westerner was always and forever unhearing and unspeaking, and even when this veil was pierced by interpretation, usually by Asiatics, he doubted whether the interpretation was right; and he could never know, even if it were right, the motivation for what was said, the idea in the mind, the plan, the scheme, perhaps the attack—yes, even physical assault—hidden behind the spoken word. This was more than bewilderment, more than not knowing where to turn and whom to trust; it was the fear of a man away from home who does not know. The fear was hidden; therefore the fear grew; and almost every Westerner in Asia during the critical decade knew it.

Plagued with this secret fear, the Westerner was confronted with an immensity of geographic space and an unfathomable depth of remembered history. And yet even current history was too complex to keep in mind. United States–Chinese relations, for example, did not consist simply of a few plans, a few discussions, a few decisions. It involved soldiers, civilians, administrators, journalists, cabinet officials, generals, war lords, special emissaries, heads of states, and, to mention only a few outward factors, three- and four-power meetings, strategy councils, world munition allotments, the man-power problem in the United States, British military aims in the Mediterranean, docking facilities at Cairo, the weather over northern Burma, student sentiment in Kunming, the price of rice, the press hostel in Chungking, the loess caves in Yenan, not to mention the heat of summer and the wet chill of winter. Alone in a strange country the outsider had to find his personal relationship to the people and the world around him, his friends, his solaces, his relationship to reality, to truth; and all the time the myriad details of what was going on passed through his mind, leaving him the knowledge of what he liked without the reasons for why he liked it. He was like a man playing a complicated hand of bridge, in which the cards were so many that it was possible to remember only a few of them, and in which it was inevitable to push out of mind each trick once it was played. There was no subconscious stock of experiences to which to relate it.

All the while, the Westerner talked with many Chinese and Japanese as well educated as himself or better—professors in modern universities, students returned from study abroad, officials, generals, journalists—all of them trying consciously or subconsciously to find themselves in relation to the culture of the West as desperately as the Westerner was trying to find himself in Asia. What went on in the minds of such educated Easterners was too complex and confusing for any sort of quick grasp. It was even too confusing to set down. So far as the Chinese were concerned, the sense of the conflict might be generalized in a series of entirely opposite statements:

China's great need is a new sense of nation, and it is right to insist that the state be above everything. . . . But patriots, as everyone has known for the last two thousand years, are not much better than bandits, and nationalism is somehow foolish and juvenile.

The people's conservatism is hard to budge. . . . But the people are the source of the intelligentsia, who come from the soil and return to it. Again, the people are the great national value. . . . But they are also just coolies. Still again, things must originate from the people, and they must start social change. . . . But the educated must be the messiahs of change and must read lectures in traditional fashion to the people.

Western culture is youthful and dynamic, and it has a great future. . . . But its dynamism has already produced slums, crime, and depressions; it may even break apart itself.

The United States is a wonder country and a great friend, and we must hope for United States understanding and aid. . . . But the United States has been a source of recent humiliation, and we must trust only in ourselves.

What China needs is an American chart of army command, American techniques of newspaper reporting, American standards of raising cattle, American ways of selecting governments, American types of political parties, American methods of running industries. . . . But in a pinch it is best to do things Chinese fashion.

Communism is Russian. . . . But the Communists are Chinese.

The fountain pen is a wonderful instrument. . . . But it ruins one's calligraphy.

There is a great social obligation in being a physician or a government official or an engineer, particularly since society bears some of the cost of one's training. . . . But of course it is essential first of all to look after one's family and friends.

It is important to be young and enthusiastic for reform. . . . But it is wise to grow up and relax.

How impressive it is to see the great numbers of men in

America skillfully organized into assembly-line plants. How moving it is to see multitudes enjoying the movies. . . . But there are great moments in the Chinese day. At morning the mist settles into the valleys and lies in folds at the foot of the hills. The air is clear; the clouds are sharp-edged; and the sun brings dew-drenched life to the fields. In the villages the tea shops take down their shutters; on the breakfast stalls dishes clatter; everything beneath heaven springs to life. At evening the shop lights cast patterns on the streets, and it is good to be alive, to be noisy, to stride the streets, to gesticulate with friends. Away from the city, it is good to hear at night the distant sound of temple music, a mellow nostalgic wail carried on a dying wind, peaceful with the knowledge of generations past and generations to come.

We must fight nature and harness it. . . . But we must be part of Nature and fit in with it.

The government must be rigidly centralized so that the country can be united. . . . But China is big sprawling China, rich in its diversity. There is the quiet greenness of Kwangtung and the loud barrenness of Kansu. In the lower Yangtze Valley the great plains lose themselves in distant horizons, and in Szechwan the mountains thrust up towards heaven. In my native place there is an old wall and a bamboo clump, and as I look across the brook to Purple Hill I can smell sesame biscuits steaming in the kitchen. My native place is forever China, but it is forever itself.

The West is to be admired. . . . But there is strength behind us.

This inner dialogue, never heard, was ever present. The Westerners talked with the Chinese, and suddenly the friendly man who was so entirely lucid and so very much like an American or a Britisher became perversely strange and incomprehensible and not a little odd. A great emotional distance intervened in the conversation, and the Westerner shrugged his shoulders, wished he were home, and said to himself that the people of China, whom he had not seen, must be more likable than the intelligentsia, whom he had seen.

At the same time in Japan two ways of thought clashed in equal degree although in very different manner. In 1947 a conversation between an American official of the occupation and a young and very progressive pro-American Japanese civil servant might have gone in somewhat the following manner:

The American might have alluded to the evils of militarism. The Japanese would warmheartedly have agreed. Of course it is clear that the militarists did great harm to Japan.

The American might have suggested that the Emperor was, after all, a human being, and the Japanese would have agreed again. And he would have reflected to himself on the wonderful condescension shown by the Emperor in His declaration that He is not divine.

The American might have insisted that Japanese workers be encouraged to join unions, and the civil servant would have said Yes. This is democratization, but certainly something as good as democratization clearly cannot mean something as bad as disorderliness on the part of the common people.

The American might have observed that governments exist for the health and happiness of the people, and the Japanese would have agreed once again. Is it not bad manners in Japan to say No to a direct statement? But he would have felt an instant of perplexity about Democracy's concern with petty material comforts.

The American might have insisted that the wartime heads of industries be removed from their positions, and the agreement would again be very careful and very polite. But after the conversation had touched on other subjects for some minutes, the Japanese might have suggested that too rapid a rate of dismissal would hurt Japanese industrial production and make harder the payment of reparations—a suggestion that covered his inner feeling of horror at the thought of breaking old ties of loyalty and of encouraging junior officers to compete for top jobs.

The American might have proposed that price controls be placed in the hands of one man. In such a case the Japanese might even have tried to upset the very plan that he himself worked out and endorsed, for he found it unthinkable that persons should become really important in politics as individuals, not just as representatives of a group.

He admired without reserve the American's energy; he was impressed by the fact that the American came from a race of god-like inventors. He was elated at being able to guide his own thoughts enthusiastically into the same channels as the American. But he was not thinking in the same terms. If he came to accept the idea of the happiness of the people, he transmuted it into the well being of a family-style nation. His very loyalty to the American was a traditional virtue, as were his orderliness, his courtesy, his agreement. He reacted as a Japanese, thought as a Japanese—and all in a state of great excitement and of some degree of confusion, of which he himself was not sharply aware. With overflowing warmth he told his American friend how democratic he was himself before the war; democratic above all else, so democratic that he wrote an essay on Japan's great mission, in which he said all the people must be absolutely united in order to bring democracy about everywhere. How wonderful it would have been, he exclaimed, if only the militarists had not upset things. Great flashes of intuitive truth flashed through his mind. He became positively intoxicated with the headiness of brilliant new Western ideas about government. He wanted to lecture to students about them, translate them. His face and gestures became highly animated. He cried out that he had never in his life had so meaningful and

moving an experience, that it was all wonderful and un-
believable. And in a burst of emotion he might very well
have proposed that his friend accompany him to a resort
town for a week end of recuperating from this tremendous
experience and of philosophizing in the Japanese way.

The Westerner was likely to follow such twists of idea and
such explosions of feeling with friendly interest, a slightly
wry sense of embarrassment, and a degree of well-meant condescension. It is pleasant to be enthusiastically agreed with.
It is enjoyable to touch off warm feelings. It is flattering to
be looked up to. And it is fun to go to resort towns and eat
sukiyaki dinners. But all the time the Westerner felt vaguely
uneasy. There was that going on which he did not know, and
what was it? What could it be? Some scheme? Some insincerity? After the sukiyaki he tried to piece together the puz-
zle, and he knew that he was not at home.

Between East and West there were never easy bridges. The
dissimilarities of two cultures separated both in time and
space were so great that whenever an Oriental managed to
Westernize his subconscious he became an enigma to his own
friends and his family, and whenever an Occidental managed
to think like an Easterner, he became another riddle that his
countrymen had to solve. There appeared to be nothing to
carry the Westerner over the confusion of a vast geographic
area, each country of which was crowded with a multitude
of unconnected or even actually contradictory facts. The
more he looked at the confusion and tried to make sense of
it, the more the confusion seemed to grow. And yet he had to
make enough sense of it to make decisions and get on with
his work.

He did not, after all, come to Asia simply to probe into
the Japanese or Chinese psyche. The urge to personal success stirred in him abroad at least as strongly as it did at

home. By and large, the businessman went abroad after money, the journalist after news, the diplomat after a good record, the missionary after the satisfaction, at least, of doing good. Money, news, good records, or good deeds are not achieved in a state of confusion. One had to make decisions, and to make them it was essential that there be some conclusion to what China or Japan or Korea added up to. It was too long to wait for certain hunches and a few convictions to come in the back door of one's feelings rather than in the front door of one's mind. The only way to speed up such conclusions was by adopting the formulas, the conclusions, the myths that compatriots earlier on the scene had built up.

Myth is essential, even to a man in his own country, because it gives a frame of reference for seeing only such facts as it is possible or tolerable to assimilate. It permits the discarding of whole series of otherwise persistent notions, facts, guesses, reports, and possibilities. To be sure, myths describe the people who believe them more than they do the facts they are supposed to describe. But myths have about them strong appearances of truth. Simple formulas are of insidious appeal to Western man's sense of logic and order; they are concepts that can be handled intellectually, not surmises that are entertained psychologically. Without myth Westerners could not have survived in the Orient.

The myths grew and changed, but they retained a very strong continuity. Thus the wartime vehemence of American distrust for China's Central Government was in considerable part a direct carry-over of the long prewar disbelief of Western diplomats and businessmen in the ability of the Chinese ever to govern themselves. The insistence of most Americans (and some Chinese) that the United States tell China how to run armies, cabinets, elections, banks, railroads, and farms was in considerable part a carry-over of an early missionary conviction that the Chinese must be told precisely what is good for them, a conviction that mission groups had been consciously trying to rid themselves of for many decades.

The myths were often dangerous. Japan not so long before the war seemed to be a doll-house country of miniature gardens and paper dwellings peopled by polite little men and women. They were deft and as delicate as the saucers of their own teacups, yet they catapulted themselves overnight into the twentieth century. They operated machines and purchased ships, and when they first took to cutting up territory in their war with Russia, the United States, particularly in the person of Theodore Roosevelt, was inclined to say Bravo! Even when this people began running other people out of considerable stretches of Asia, Westerners asked themselves only whether the Japanese were not acting too big for their size, and wondered whether their empire would not fall apart at the threat of really modern war. During the war, to be sure, the myth was broken in favor of generalizations about the grim morale of the soldiers, the raw barbarism of the civilization, and the mindless obedience of the people. But as soon as the Japanese gave their enthusiasm to the Allied Occupation, they started to become again polite and industrious little men and women.

Such myths were at the root of the inward collision of East and West. The very acceptance of them was, in a sense, the failure to resolve the conflict. They helped throw the ancient cultural bloc that once centered about China into uncertainty, confusion, and fretful and unproductive torments of inferiority. They helped buttress the youthful braggadocio of the West, which could not conceive of any valid social or psychological goals save its own. They helped make the troubles of other peoples seem at once irrational and also easy to solve, for they made it appear that other peoples suffered exactly to the degree that they did not have the things the West has: railroads, dams, technical knowledge, a scientific method, even realism or abstractionism in art and rationalism in philosophy. Myth made it difficult to realize that any people tend to choose the outward forms that best reinforce or restate their inward drives: that factories, radar, and atomic fission were choices of a culture seeking to know and conquer nature; that the sketchy improvisation in Japanese painting of trees and hills and mists fitted their very different sense of nature; that the Chinese choice of small footpaths resulted not from being unable to imagine broad highways but from being wise enough to know what they wanted. Myth made it impossible for West or East to do other than continue colliding with one another.

The essence of the myth-ridden decade, a short but decisive second of time, was a cultural collision so sharpened that it could not long hold an edge. Events took place during the war years that can be set down with greater or less accuracy, but the reality of those years can never be described, for it was composed of the impact of events on men's minds and was full of hope, paralyzing strangeness, goading fear, humiliation, superiority, shame, and the host of emotions that at once make a man and break him. It was not simply cultures that collided; it was people, and the collision meant now death, now anger between son and father, now growing perplexity, now enthusiasm, now determination, now despair. The conflict was all the suffering of mind and body of the unimaginably great numbers of living persons. The total immense bulk of the past, eternally inherent in the present, was concentrated on the passing second wherein nations or individuals made a guess, chose a policy, or simply did nothing.

Thus, behind the last terrible second of collision lay the eons: the generations of Asia from the time of unrecorded dynasties and the generations of Europe and America from the time of ancient soldier-kings. The collision of the two cultures was made up of everything, the best things and the worst things, that went before. To see Asia as it was, it is essential to see Asia as it had been before. It confronted the West with the solid weight of four thousand ever-current years.

3

Ritual and Music

Each country in Asia met the west at different an-
gles and recoiled from it in different directions, so different,
in fact, that the recoil often brought them into collision with
each other. The Chinese and Japanese, for instance, resembled one another in the fact of recoil, but not in the nature of
it: despite geographic closeness and certain cultural resem-
blances, there was no uniting measure of inward similarity of
mind. Both peoples must somehow be seen together, but
first they must be looked at separately. The Chinese, perhaps,
must be looked at first, for whatever urges or whatever notions the Orient shared came from an ancient cultural bloc
in which China was quietly and confidently the prime mover,
in which she was in fact the Center Country, in which even
the name of Japan, Rising Sun, described its geographic lo-
cation in reference to the country from which spread methods of ruling people and writing words, ways of putting ink
upon paper and of building wood into houses, not to mention such ways of thinking as Buddhism and Confucianism.

In 1947 much was happening in this country but nothing
happened: seen from the West, China appeared to suffer torments and turmoil beyond reckoning, yet she appeared to
change so little as to change not at all. The fact that pressed

most inescapably upon Westerners was the tenacious hold of
the past, relaxed enough to permit such alterations as a republican form of government, the building of highways, or
the use of steam locomotives, but yet clenched so tight that
none of the basic drives of modernism—from government efficiency to social awareness, from representative government
to mass production—were brought to pass. Whence this apparent lethargy? Why could not a country, particularly when
it had been shown the bright mechanical wares of the West,
and particularly when it had been put to school in the ways
of mind by which those wares were manufactured—why could
not that country free itself of strife, graft, and inefficiency
and embrace the things that the West believed it needed?

If the prime fact of the collision of East and West was a collision of minds, the chief factors in China's turmoil were not
feudalism (only traces of it survived) or landlordism (no
more prevalent relatively than in the United States) or illiteracy (never an obstacle to past accomplishments). The
chief antagonists were not even Nationalists or Communists,
nor yet the foreign offices of the United States and the USSR.
These forces set the stage but they dictated neither the words
nor the gestures of the actors; to the action itself they were
incidental.

What was not incidental was a starchy twenty-five-hun-
dred-year-old scholar, a tall man with a high, stately, and
somewhat bumpy forehead, meticulously ordered dress, a
love of knowledge, and a knowledge of ceremonies. What was
not incidental was a grinning old zany who went off to exile a
hundred generations earlier, sneering at the idea of progress
and seeking the simplicity of primordial nature. Confucius
(Kung-fu-tze) and Lao-tze, to be sure, were in no sense the
causes of China's twentieth-century noises and alarms. But
that China found change and adjustment difficult—and
finally gave in to the vast changes of Communism—resulted
in direct part from the fact that Confucius (551–479 B.C.), ac-

customed to thinking about society in static terms, neither made provision for change nor saw any desirability in it, and that Lao-tze, his early contemporary, wedded to the constant and unceasing changes of nature, saw nothing desirable in society.

These two men lived, wrote, and taught at the period in which root habits of mind and emotion were fixed, and it may seem strange that two such antithetical ways of thinking could appear at the same time. Indeed, it may be that in the sixth century B.C. they were not so dissimilar as they later seemed. The few aphorisms that can with some certainty be laid to Confucius, rather than to later Confucianists, state in much the same words and with somewhat the same feeling not a few of the ideas of Lao-tze, who left behind a few paradoxes, in which he used not only words but even methods of logic usually considered the monopoly of Confucius. However deep these similarities may have been—measurement of their depth awaits further and more probing study—they did not prevent the appearance of dissimilar schools of thought; indeed, the interaction of these dissimilars over more than two thousand years was one of the germinal inward facts of Chinese life and one of great bearing upon the collision of that life with Western ideas. The two men may have stated with great power and originality a single way of thought whose origins are lost in the origins of recorded life in Asia, but history makes them seem to state two distinct ways. It is therefore upon their separateness rather than their togetherness that an account of their impress on the Chinese mind must center.

The life of their times was not tranquil, for the Bronze Age into which Confucius and Lao-tze were born was as full of turmoil as a much later age of machines. The great feudal dynasty of Chou (1122–256 B.C.), dominant for six centuries, had begun to collapse. Dukes usurped the place of kings, barons warred against dukes, and adventurers plotted against barons. Violence was the substance of daily existence: a bit-

ter business of raiding, plundering, encroaching, taking cap-
tives, paying tribute, launching war. Between the rich and
the poor stretched a gulf as wide as an entire cultural era,
for those who lacked position lived not in the upper-class
age of bronze but in the old age of stone, to which their
artifacts and their dugout houses bore witness. The great
went into battle with sharp weapons, thick armor, and char-
iots. The small, grouped around the great, went almost
naked to death, for they were subjected to a ruling class that
could conceive of government only as it benefited themselves.

Bygone rulers had sought to carry with them the full
weight of the past. Government had in effect become ritual; its ministers were trained in the ceremonious slaughter
of cows, sheep, goats, and pigs to ancestor gods whose hand in
death was feared to be as heavy as their hand in life. Ritual
was exact and detailed; a misstep in handling the ceremonial vessels was believed to upset everything from the fer-
tility of fields to the welfare of states.

By the time Confucius was born, supposedly 551 B.C.,
there had long been a tradition of a great golden age under
ancient emperors, empty of class distinctions, of oppressive
rulers, of usurpers, of wars, of turmoil. Life was imagined to
have once been in balance, and all men were supposed to
have lived in a harmony so real that the natural disorders of
flood and famine were arrested. From this legend there sprang
a view of life which was in essence inward and religious. Lao-
tze expressed it by the question and answer, "How do I
know about the world? Inward Light!" [1] It turned toward
the workings of nature with feelings of mystery and awe,
advised men to let things happen of themselves and to adjust their inward beings to whatever happenings nature
brought about. "Do nothing," said Lao-tze, "and you will be
able to do everything." Harmony, in this view, had nothing
to do with customs, rituals, ranks, governments, traditions, or
even social righteousness. Simply let men follow Tao, the

timeless and the creative, and everything else will take care
of itself. Taoism inveighed against covetousness, preached
impartial kindness alike to the kind and the unkind, denounced man's ego as the source of evil, and saw reality as
a deep inward fact of man's spirit. From its observations
of the disordered life of the Chou Dynasty and from its actual
experience of nature itself, it attempted precepts very much
of the genre of Hinduism, Buddhism, and early Christianity.

This way of thought undoubtedly had effect on Confucius,
but he has long been associated with a different view, which
approached life from a more directly practical avenue. This
view saw man as a social animal and interested itself in practical virtues rather than in states of inner mind. The source
of evil rested in society, in family life, in community life, in
national life, and it was correctable by proper organization,
which in those times meant ritual. What was necessary was to
study the way the ideal past was organized and to recreate it
in the present through ritual, knowledge, and government—a
procedure not essentially different in pattern from that of
Western social research, but of a motivation altogether opposite.

Confucius himself was a research scholar—or so at least it
appears from the reports of the men who wrote about him
at various times after his death. He did not write about either his life or his wisdom; what exists, consequently, is a
blend of fact and fancy, report and interpretation, the more
important in that the residue left by followers of Confucius
has been far more real in Chinese history than the historical
Confucius himself.

Confucianism, the necessary but not necessarily correct
source of this account, makes the man a fussy scholar at that.
He was pernickety about dress, insisted upon matching a fox
coat with a yellow robe, refused red or purple pajamas in
favor of a nightshirt half again as long as his body, and was ex-

tremely nice about the way food was cooked, cut up, and
eaten. He had an almost Calvinist severity and sense of
duty, hated laxity of all sorts, and complained, "Few are too
strict." [2] Summoned to visit a queen with a reputation for
looseness, he later reported, "I did not intend to see her,
but during the interview we saw each other with perfect
decorum." In general, he took a low view of women. He tried
to avoid dogmatism but tended to fall into it. He and his
disciples spent much time talking about themselves, making comparisons and compliments. He was much displeased
when he was not treated with proper due; and he worried
about such things as the ceremonial bath. In his ceremonial
laws he was something of a Moses; in his love of ritual and
good form he was like a High-churchman; he preached virtue like an English schoolmaster; and he emphasized it like
an American Puritan. One is tempted to believe that he
would have found Queen Victoria highly congenial.[3]

This hardly inspiring person was at all times devoted to
order, and his great aim was to avoid trouble in society. At
a time when the feudal order was falling apart, he aimed specifically at the restoration of its ranks, insisting that barons
be barons, dukes dukes, emperors emperors, fathers fathers,
sons sons. Everyone must know his exact place and keep himself in it. The claims of obedience rested heavily on the Confucian mind: witness the four formal subjects he taught:
"Knowledge, conduct of affairs, loyalty, keeping promises."
He considered personal virtue not so much an end in itself
as a means of social order, for, unlike the more inward Lao-
tze, he put society before man, and when he was asked
whether evil should be repaid with kindness, he said: "Then
what are you going to repay kindness with? Repay kindness
with kindness, but repay evil with justice (or severity). . . .
When you repay kindness with kindness, then the people
are encouraged to do good. When you repay evil with evil,
then the people are warned from doing bad."

This concern for outward order inevitably made him into a traditionalist and turned his followers for twenty-five centuries into students of what to the Western mind seems on occasion the superfluous. Troubled that the forms of ritual and of music had degenerated, he set out to study and refurbish them, never doubting that they were the clue to harmonious living: "All that one needs to do is simply for the gentleman to fully understand ritual and music and then apply them to the government!" Confucius believed that ritual was important even though one be ignorant of what the ritual meant. His followers attributed to him the recording of specific ceremonies of bewildering complexity and wearisome length, replete with prescribed stances, expressions, attitudes, and positions. He was particularly addicted to funerals and their proper handling, an addiction that China has shared ever since.

The *Analects*, the simple record of his sayings, was not permitted to bristle with ceremoniousness but it was sufficiently punctuated with it to encourage later Confucianists to make it a preoccupation. In the *Li Chi*, read for generations by every Chinese schoolboy, the master was made to observe: "To gather in the same places where our fathers before us have gathered; to perform the same ceremonies which they before us have performed; to play the same music which they before us have played; to pay respect to those whom they honored; to love those who were dear to them —in fact, to serve those now dead as if they were living, and now departed as if they were still with us: this is the highest achievement of true filial piety." He wanted to restore something gone.

This ritualistic retrospection was not the whole of Confucius, whose character had many facets. He was preoccupied with genuine goodness, emphasized the idea of reciprocity (the golden rule turned backward: "Do not do unto others what you do not want others to do unto you"), and showed in himself not only a fairly constant integrity but even flashes of humility: "In the study of literature, I am probably as good as anyone, but in personally living the life of the superior man, I don't think I have succeeded." He discovered, emphasized, or popularized probably a greater number of specific and undeniable virtues than anybody else who ever lived. His wisdom was pithy: "A man who knows he has committed a mistake and doesn't correct it is committing another mistake." His sense of values was sharp: "The superior man understands what is right; the inferior man understands what will sell. . . . The superior man blames himself; the inferior man blames others."

His attitude toward the common people, in an age when they were little more than things of the rulers, was almost revolutionary: "To love what the people hate and to hate what the people love—that is to act contrary to human nature, and disaster will overtake such a person." He was strongly opposed to basing government on force and restraint: "Guide the people with governmental measures and control or regulate them by the threat of punishment, and the people will try to keep out of jail, but will have no sense of honor or shame. Guide the people by virtue and control or regulate them by *li* [propriety] and the people will have a sense of honor and respect." And he made it clear that government is the responsibility of rulers. He told the official Chi-kang-tze, "If you yourself don't love money, you can give the money to the thieves and they won't take it." A later Confucianist, Fan Chung-yen, who lived around A.D. 1000, wrote: "A scholar ought to begin to worry before anyone else begins to worry, and ought to enjoy life only after everyone else enjoys life." [4]

To ritual itself Confucius gave a new meaning, insisting that its efficiency lay not simply in its external performance, for he believed the real root of order was virtue. He came closer than any other social scientist in world history to grasping the all-importance of inward goodness. (Contrast Thomas Hobbes: Men are murderous and must give themselves over to tyrants for the sake of order; or Jeremy Bentham: Men respond only to pleasure and pain and must be confronted with fear of punishment; or Karl Marx: Men are moved only by economics; change economics and you change them.) Confucius, indeed, came so close to centering on personal goodness that he almost ceased to be a social scientist.

The important fact for China's adjustments to Westernism is that Confucius took a middle course between inward virtue and outward law. He did not cease to be a social scientist. He treated good behavior as valuable not so much for what it is as for what it leads to. Not particularly interested in the universe, he was not particularly interested in personal spiritual growth. Consequently, his precepts resemble a bundle of sticks; there are too many of them; there is no way to get hold of them except memorizing them by rote, in which case one loses them anyhow. It is possible to tell a man to love God and his neighbor and turn him loose in the world, but (to mention only cardinal precepts) it is impossible to have him respond to such a list as *jen* (true manhood), *li* (propriety), *shu* (reciprocity), *chih* (uprightness), *hsin* (sincerity), *i* (justice), *hsiao* (filial piety), *kung* (dignity), *ching* (respect), *kuan* (magnanimity), *min* (earnestness), and *hui* (kindness). It would be possible if the virtues were derived from a central idea of the universe that gave them a value whether or not they led to good social consequences. (Confucianism emphasized several times that this teaching had a center: unfortunately it was not always the same center.) Lacking such a center, the virtues lack drive—men, it would seem, do good for its own sake, not for the sake of society. The virtues can be affirmed, but in daily living it is hard even to remember them. It therefore becomes difficult to bring about change in society by the very means that Confucianists so wisely advocated—changes in individuals.

The Confucianists tried, somewhat naïvely it would seem, to overcome this limitation by linking their multifarious virtues together in ascending or descending orders of chain argument. One of the most famous of these reared a tottering edifice of sophistry on nothing more substantial than the right use of terms, long the first item on the agenda of any Chinese committee meeting. Confucius said: "If the terminology is not correct, then the whole style of one's speech falls out of form; if one's speech is not in form, then orders cannot be carried out; if orders are not carried out, then the proper forms of worship and social intercourse (in ritual and music) cannot be restored; if the proper forms of worship and social intercourse are not restored, then legal justice in the country will fail; when legal justice fails, then the people are at a loss to know what to do or what not to do." Another proposition went down, equally arbitrarily, from national life to family life to personal life to righteartedness to sincere wills to true knowledge to investigations of things, and then backtracked its way up—all much in the way of the nursery jingle of the woman who tried to get piggy over the stile. The connections between these virtues, philological rather than logical, are almost as tenuous as "Fire, fire, burn stick . . . stick, stick, beat dog . . ." and so on. Yet much of Confucian theory rested on these connections, for it believed in the possibility of starting out with certain orders of human nature and, by an ascent through abstract virtues, ending with government as it should be. In practice, the transfer from one virtue to the next was hard to make; hence Confucian ethical teaching tended to bog down at its starting points.

One such starting point was filial piety, the virtue of family already deeply rooted in the Chinese mind by Confucian times. The followers of Confucius spoke about it so often that it became the great virtue, the one to which Chinese automatically retreated in times of trouble. The difficulty in making connections between it and the general social good were so great that in practice the Chinese ethical horizon seldom stretched beyond its limits. Even in the 1930's and 1940's many of the medical students in modern China, for example, showed little interest in charity work or even in repaying society for the cost of their training; they wanted a private city practice, wherein they could make enough money from the well-off to treat their friends and family free. Confucius laid down five relations from that of son to father to that of subject to emperor. He did not, however, include any relationship with strangers, and, generally speaking, the Chinese ethical horizon did not include persons unknown. Ideas centering on a fellowship or a brotherhood of all men did not develop. Furthermore, family relationships were never a subject for direct and free discussion; the looseness of the Confucian ethic let them willy-nilly develop aspects of holiness: Chinese reformers in the twentieth century who tried to discuss them actually found themselves maneuvered into upholding the idea of patricide. The traditional, optimistic view was that if you only treat relatives and friends rightly, everything beneath Heaven will be all right.

Knowledge and ritual were similar root virtues: if you only know enough, everything will be all right. If you only behave according to your station in life, everything will be all right. Here again Confucius unwittingly abetted later un-Confucian amendments; by trying to make the word *li* include more than simple ceremony or even good form he ended in making it equivalent to the Will of Heaven. Heaven was certain to reward the good ruler as it rewarded the legendary emperors—and much as it rewarded the virtuous heroines of Samuel Richardson's sentimental novels of eighteenth-century England. Rites took on a horrendous aspect when later generations began propagating wholesale

ceremoniousness (everything from the five relationships and
governing the people to styles of dress and table manners:
"Do not roll rice into a ball, do not let your soup run out of
your mouth, do not pick your teeth," and so on[5]). Violated,
a rite upset the Will of Heaven and therefore produced natural disasters. Dress wrongly, and you produce an earthquake. Such application of ritual to *lex naturae* inevitably
discouraged any sensible discussion of it. In a stable, unchanging society, to be sure, ritual and family piety can reinforce social stability. In other times, they violently inhibit
even the proposal of reform.[6]

The problem of correcting social evil was made the more
acute by the absence in Confucianism of any sharp sense of
what evil is. Confucius' belief that there was widespread
goodness in the past and that it would take only a few true
gentlemen with knowledge of ritual to set the country right
once again, suggests that he saw no seriously entrenched obstacles of greed, covetousness, or ego, against which his Taoist contemporaries railed. In the fourth century B.C. his great
follower, Mencius (Meng-tze), made a positive principle out
of this oversight and declared that human nature is positively and inherently good, a wise and profound realization,
except that Mencius failed to suggest that it is at the same
time actively and inherently evil. This overemphasis, as great
as Western Protestantism's preoccupation with human de-
pravity, made it difficult to see sharply the problems of group
living. It even made it difficult to talk freely about individual
human character, a subject about which Confucius was in no
wise inhibited. Change was made the more difficult: nobody
could even start to go about it without upsetting some "good"
person. The reluctance to disturb anyone was still making
government and land reform difficult some two thousand
years later.

How then could Confucianism get anything done? Not,

certainly, through the actions of the common people. Confucius felt deeply their needs, which he accepted as weather vanes for the guidance of rulers. But he was always talking about, and to, gentlemen, and it did not occur to him that anyone else should have anything to do with government, beyond good behavior in his appointed station of life. He tended to distrust the common people he actually saw, and thought they could be made to follow, but not to understand. Mencius, to be sure, developed the idea of the right of revolution whenever the ruling power was corrupt, thus providing Confucianism with its one concrete method of social change. He wrote: "When a ruler treats his subjects like dirt, then it is the right of his subjects to treat him like a bandit and an enemy." This revolution, however, was to be a revolution of the gentlemen, not of the people. Mencius described the function of the gentleman as that of keeping the common people in order, the function of the common people as that of feeding the gentlemen. This dubious *quid pro quo* hardly encouraged popular political activity. There was no way for the people to express themselves, and only a catastrophic way for the better off.

The great political lever in Confucianism was leadership by example. "Raise the righteous men into power," said Confucius, "and let them serve as the measure for the unrighteous, and the unrighteous will return to righteousness." He insisted that there must be confidence of the people in the ruler and declared: "When one man is greedy or avaricious, then the whole country is plunged into disorder." Leadership thus became the start of a chain argument of descending and ascending virtues.

Example, unfortunately, does not always work, no matter how morally the ruler lives, no matter how warmly he exhorts the populace to follow the virtues. Besides, the people do not always listen. What then can be done? This question presented itself from time to time in Chinese history, and

the Confucianists never answered it. At certain times they
even had to fall back on the ideas of a rival school, the legalists, who insisted that the people were fundamentally bad
and that they must be played upon not by examples but by
rewards for obedience and punishments for disobedience.
Confucianists from time to time discovered that if they could
not get people to follow them, they had to chop off heads.
Legalism might be described as the wastebasket of Confucianism.[7]

Only infrequently were heads chopped off in China. One
of her great achievements was a steady avoidance of legal
punishment and a steady trust in Confucian virtues. But this
achievement rested on an almost conscious choice of a system
of static ethics and on an almost conscious rejection of a dynamic view of life, which could produce change but which
could also produce disorder. China passed through periods
of change to be sure, but her terrible, protracted, and recur-
rent birth pains were not eased by the inertness of static
doctrine.

Confucianism was taken over as state doctrine by the Han
Dynasty, founded two centuries before Christ (B.C. 206–
219 A.D.). In slightly modified form it so continued, even at
times when Buddhism or Taoism replaced it as the state religious cult, until the 1911 overthrow of the Ching Dynasty
and the establishment of the Chinese Republic. Various reasons are given for its phenomenal longevity, as for instance
its practical control of the educational and administrative
systems, in which the literati, somewhat like British public
schoolmen, were not only the schoolmasters but also the bureaucrats, the ministers, the research scholars, and to an
extent, the clergy. Even so, Confucianism could not have
survived without developing a highly acute sensitivity to the
mood of the people. Losing touch with the people was considered a clear indication of bad character. Not long after

Mencius propounded the gentlemen's right to revolt against evil rulers, it was assumed to be the right also of the people. Furthermore, the scholars came invariably from the people themselves. Confucianism established a bureaucracy, but it never even tried to establish a bureaucratic caste. The scholarly ranks were open to anyone, farmer's son or official's son, who could pass examinations. There developed few great families and no laws of primogeniture to keep the occasionally great family from splitting its wealth up among its sons and returning, usually in the course of three generations, to the soil from which it had sprung. There did not even develop imperial emperors. When Chin Shih Hwang Ti attempted to oust the scholars and establish a dictatorship in 213 B.C., the scholars so fulminated against his name and conspired against his rule that his dynasty came to a hasty end.

Confucianism, in effect, developed certain powers of adaptation. Over the core of its teaching it was able to wear without discomfort both Buddhist and Taoist garments. For example, Buddhism's negative view of human effort considerably reduced scholarly busybodyness, relaxed the severity of the application of notions of filial piety. Positively, it gave Confucianists a vague sense that some of the virtues might have validity apart from the goal of social orderliness they were supposed to induce: in particular, the ideas of the value of good works and of the sacredness of life. Confucianism may well have survived because it never became the sum total of the Chinese mind—a highly complex entity that is not simply or even predominantly Confucian. Minds highly conscious of Confucianism worked in patterns singularly, however subconsciously, Taoist, and at any given moment in China there were more than purely Confucian influences at work. Thus, in theory, Confucianism looked with favor on a controlled and managed economy, yet in practice it usually objected wherever there was overmuch management. The scholar Wang Mang, who made himself emperor between 8

and 23 A.D., undertook to establish state monopolies, to na-
tionalize the land, and to distribute it equally. The vehemence with which his fellow scholars denounced him then
and thereafter reflected in considerable part the Taoist feeling that things must be left to happen of themselves, and that
trying to grasp at something is a sure way of losing it. Of
similar origins was a large part of the strong opposition of
scholars to the reforms of Wang An-shih (Confucian official
who died A.D. 1086), which included price control, a state
trade monopoly, government farm loans, and general military service.

The achievement of Confucianism was its gift to China of
a deep and long-lasting cultural unity that civil wars and
changes of dynasties only scratched. In a sense, it was a gift
almost too good, for Confucianism remained a profound
force throughout the decade in which the final fate of China
was sealed. It was a force that inhibited changes that Westerners, and not a few Chinese, believed vital.

In the nineteenth- and twentieth-century phase of China's
struggle for new patterns of thought, Confucianism acted
usually as a brake. It was not, of course, in itself alarming that
the process of change in China went on by fits and starts or
that it took a long time, however alarming the human suffering involved in it was. Far more alarming was Japan's overnight "conversion" to the ways of the West, which brought
about the separate existence side by side of traditional folk-
ways and modern technology and armies; the two mixed no
more than oil and water, and fed the explosive tendencies of
the Japanese mentality. China's slowness, while it did not
preserve her from coming apart, at least prevented her from
suddenly blowing up.

The most potent force in the process of clash and amalgamation with the West came from Dr. Sun Yat-sen, who set
out to effect a palatable compromise between new ideas and

Confucianist views. This compromise was the more easy in that he was a man of two cultures; he had lived much abroad, but he never lost traditional Chinese overtones and under-tones. Even toward the end of his life he could write: "It is commonly alleged that the four hundred million people of China are like a heap of loose sand. Now wherein lies the way of molding the loose sand into an organic and unified state governed by law? The answer is that we must make a vow to rectify our hearts and purify our intentions. Only thus may we hope to succeed in cultivating our personal character, in regulating our families, in rightly governing the state and in introducing peace and harmony into the world." [8] Confucius would have put it little differently.

Dr. Sun said in effect: What we have won't do; neither will capitalism, which smacks of imperialism, nor Russian Communism. There must be a middle-ground rallying point for social revolution. We cannot have big-business capitalists, who are foreign to Chinese tradition in any case, but social-ization will not fit the anarchistic strain in Chinese life. Therefore we shall have socialism in heavy industry, and we shall guarantee free enterprise elsewhere. The country needs to be united around the principle of nationalism, but it will not unite—and probably should not—unless nationalism is admixed with cosmopolitanism. We need democracy accord-ing to the formula of Abraham Lincoln, but we must fit it to old patterns of centralization. We need guarantees of civil liberties, but they must be tempered by the need for unity.

Dr. Sun was careful not to carry his compromises to the place where he had to appeal to Confucianism for support. He did not need to. He had struck upon a practical compro-mise so instantly popular that Dr. Sun was before long can-onized. His successor Chiang Kai-shek, however, was unable to keep the past at an equally judicious distance, and pro-gressively fell back on Dr. Sun's work not only as a practical path of action but also as a bridge to the traditional virtues.

In his driving aim of unifying China, Chiang faced a different problem from that of Dr. Sun, who initiated the revolution. Chiang had to live with it, live with it despite the conflicting pressures of Japanese war lords and Communists. As his problems multiplied he therefore preached not only the reform of the country but the country's continuity, which the younger generations were often ready to overlook. Particularly he sought to tap the country's resources in its hidden ways of thought. Despite all China's modernism, despite the new position of women, despite the new interest in science and industry and government, Confucianism remained still a great, though not an obvious, citadel of the Chinese mind. And Chiang deduced that in a crisis China could be best held together by treating the people as Confucianists. This deduction was probably necessary and therefore wise. But the necessity was unfortunate. Emphasis on Confucianism loosened no mental bonds to traditionalism and very possibly impeded certain works of reform. Confucianism was not China's only obstacle to change; there were many concrete obstacles of wars, politics, and economics, many human obstacles of lethargy and greed. But the mental roots of Confucianism made it the one most difficult to budge. The world therefore saw the traditional image of Confucius, in the guise of Chiang Kai-shek, at the head of a revolution.

As a leader, Chiang Kai-shek was, of course, many things besides a Confucian. He was a Christian attached to Old Testament ideas of unity by way of fire and sword and to modern Methodist (though not un-Confucian) virtues of right conduct.[9] He was a political man devoted to various ideas of modernism. In many ways he did not fit the Confucian ideal of the worthy person. He was no scholar, but instead a soldier, and thus on the lowest level of the traditional hierarchy of social worth. Like Dr. Sun, he was strongly attached to nationalism—"the state comes first, the nation comes first"—an idea more Western than Confucian. But it is remarkable how far Chiang cast his thought in Confucian patterns. In 1934 he founded the New Life Movement with the aims of reforming the nation and encouraging widespread social action. These aims were hardly Confucian, but to achieve them he pleaded for the old virtues, *li i lien chih*—propriety, justice, integrity, and conscientiousness. The New Life Movement undertook to propagandize propriety in dress, cleanliness of streets, unwaved hair, honesty in business and government. It insisted, in good Confucian style, on disciplined social behavior. It inveighed against laxity of all sorts, took the six arts of Chou times as patterns for recreation, and argued that only such amusements as music, athletic exercise, and the study of arts and sciences were proper.

The problem was not that Confucianism made China's National Government antagonistic to change, but that it robbed it of any concrete methodology of change. Chiang fell back on old-style exhortations packed with lists of Confucian virtues: loyalty, filial devotion, harmony, propriety, and many others. He inveighed against bad habits: "Insincerity now characterizes the conduct of most men, and procrastination has become a general habit. Everywhere we find frivolity, deceit, irresponsibility, and indolence. The people in general lack seriousness, decision, faith, and determination." [10] Elsewhere he remarked, ". . . propriety, righteousness, integrity, and honor . . . are manifestations of our four cardinal principles and eight virtues, loyalty and filial devotion being the basis of all." Some of his public speeches took on the aspect of addresses on history; in them he lectured the people on the historic lessons of the collapse of the Ming (A.D. 1368–1644) and Sung (A.D. 960–1279) dynasties, and he sought in the classics support for such current ideas as political tutelage.

Besides this Confucian indoctrination through history, which was particularly marked in the schools, the government made valiant attempts at rulership by example. It attempted to set up model county and village governments, model farms and dairies, so that the people could come, see, and imitate. Unfortunately imitation rarely stirs initiative. Confucius said: "The character of the ruler is like wind, and the character of the common people is like grass, and the grass bends in the direction of the wind." Chiang said: "So long as we have a few men who will set an example, the people in a village, in a district, or in the whole country will unconsciously act likewise. As the grass is bent by the wind, so the social tone is influenced by the example of such men." And Chiang himself tried to set a severe and strict example of the virtues.

But once China was thinking in terms of the virtues, it found itself boxed in the closed cabinet of Confucianism, which made pointed discussion of personal failings unproductive. The doctrine was a poor backdrop to the work of reform. It not only served as a refuge for rascals, but inhibited even men of good will. The more one pleaded for order, discipline, and obedience, the more difficult it became to insist that land reform or tax reform or local-government reform or even currency reform—which are bound to upset people and create unseemly disorder—be pushed through; and in the absence of these reforms China's Central Government lacked weapons that could have been used with success against the Communists. Instead of reform, there was a feeling that the dignity of the state was being threatened by any measure of opposition to the government. During the Sian kidnapping of 1936, Chiang's behavior was one of high dignity. He refused to parley with his captors, insisted on denouncing them for their own rebellious perfidy, and in general sought to comport himself with the bearing proper to his high office. His personal objections to General Joseph Stilwell as his wartime chief of staff can be summed up in the word *insubordination*. It appeared to him that the great trouble with China was dissension, and therefore personal wickedness on the part of those who caused it: whence his bitterness to his opponents. Virtues remained social. Bad conduct was still held to produce bad political ideas, selfishness, bad economic individualism, a bad life—everything from dishonesty in office to nonsupport of the government. One could only plead for the virtues. One could only urge everyone to be loyal to the Kuomintang. If these exhortations failed to work, there was nothing to do but to fall back on the ideas of the legalist philosophers and cut off heads.

Yet even the latter-day Confucianists who practiced legal restraint were reluctant to own up to it in theory. Chen Li-fu, a man who believed that, except as regards science, all Chinese ideas (including Chinese medicine) were superior to those of the West, served as head for a crusade against Communists, first as director of an underground police group ferreting out and arresting suspects in the years following the Kuomintang revolution and later when, as Minister of Education, he tried, with only slight success, to institute thought control under the form of a tutorial system. He preferred to make the mistake of arresting genuine liberals to that of overlooking even a few Communists. While he was Minister of Education, numerous students disappeared from university campuses into camplike reindoctrination centers. He believed that the intolerance of Communism had to be fought with intolerance, and it may well be that he created more Communists than he cured.

Chen's means, in short, were the means advocated by the ancient legalists, but his tone was always that of high and sincere morality. He was strictly honest and his diversions included nothing less austere than early morning practice of Chinese shadow boxing, wherein motion is carried out not in straight lines but in curves. He had a keen mind, a good sense of logic. He made some concessions to the West, even to the extent of admixing some Bergson with a lot of Confu-

cius in a theory of education. What came out of this mixture
was highly traditional: harmony, Chen said flatly, is the highest social good, and too much public discussion weakens it;
the common people and those out of office should not discuss
politics. He approved of democracy, and defined it as the
running of a nation for the people but not by the people:
direction is the task of scholars and the best people, into
which group anyone of ability is welcome.

Chiang, too, liked to look back to a time when there were
order and tranquility. In *China's Destiny* he tried to avoid
the fact that Confucianism had broken down as an effective
doctrine of life, by blaming external factors: the foreign concessions, the unequal treaties, the soft and wicked life of the
big port cities. Yet the removal of these external factors effected no change. China's dissension was not cured by an
appeal to Confucianist habits; it was only made worse. Confucianism did not fit very well mass literacy movements, machine production, the break-up of close family living, and
the new political theories of the West. The strength of Confucianism lay in part in the absence in it of that sort of
dynamic which provokes sudden and sharp social or cultural
changes, such, for instance, as were provoked in Reformation
and Counter-Reformation Europe. When a time arrived when
change became imperative, Confucianism made change difficult.

Confucian habits tended to hide what was actually happening in China. The absence of a sense of social responsibility, which Chiang so condemned, sprang not from a life
opposed to Confucian virtue, but from a life derived from it,
particularly from that great starting point of Confucian chain
argument: family loyalty. Hence arose the nepotism and
graft practiced particularly when salaries were low and economic life out of joint. Loyalty to friends and family cannot
be purified by imagining that one can build up from it to love
of society or to love of reform. It was not enough to say, "It is

high time for us to wake up and reform ourselves thoroughly." If a way of thought is static, there can be no reform, personal or social.

During the final twenty years of National Government in China, years of civil and foreign wars, years of rebellion, years during which the country's energies had to be centered not on the necessities of reform but on the grimmer necessities of sheer survival, it was inevitable that China should clutch at her past. It is significant that almost all attempts during that period to woo the Chinese people politically were couched in terms that either came from Confucianism or were not repugnant to it. During the war, the shrewd Japanese (whose own Confucianism, more rabid even than that of China, is discussed later) put most of their propaganda effort and money ($500,000 a month) into an organization called the Hsinminhui, dedicated to sniping at democracy, communism, and China's Central Government from behind the façade of orthodox Confucianism. They tried to give currency to the notion that the Will of Heaven, always correct, favored Japanese conquest. Meanwhile the Communists, who once looked like *enfants terribles* playing hob with sacred notions, minimized their differences with tradition. They emphasized the order and harmony and obedience they claimed to exist in their ranks, looked down their noses at the disorder they saw in Nanking. They exhorted their followers as fervently and as abstractly as Chiang did his. This approach was effective not only because many Chinese of traditional mind misunderstood the harmony of communism but because not a few Americans mistook Chinese communism for Chinese democracy. Actually it was closer to an ideological oligarchy that employed in its fight for power both the dissatisfaction of farmers and the thought concepts of ancient aristocrats. It used the tactics not only of the Russian Empire but of the Chou Empire.

At no time, of course, was change impossible in China—

very little more so than in Western countries, hidden from
their own cultural crises by their relative wealth. But this
change would have involved a change in the way of thinking;
it could not have been artificially speeded up. At the time
when Communism put an end to Confucianism as an effective cultural fact, though not as a dormant inward drive, it
was being modified by other elements of the Chinese mind:
Buddhism, Taoism, and the new element of Christianity. In
the past it had undergone many renaissances; the slow process of reinterpretation and addition had modified it sub-
stantially, and it was again being altered by contemporary
thinkers.[11] This alteration by its very nature had to be slow.
An important fact of the decade of disastrous contact of East
and West was that the Westerners insisted that the alteration
—or at least the outward consequences of it—be quick. Probably there was nothing more Confucian than the Western
insistence that China's turmoil be quickly and unnaturally
over.

4

Empty Hearts and Full Bellies

WHILE CONFUCIUS WAS STRIDING IN THE FRONT DOOR OF the Chinese mind, Lao-tze was sneaking in at the rear. If the tradition of Confucius gave conscious direction to Chinese life, the tradition of Lao-tze gave it deep inward urges. Out of this tradition sprang China's fundamental recognition of Deity, Tao, the true but camouflaged reality that for several thousands of years was the more powerful in that it was the less openly recognized. The outward religion to which Tao-ism gave its name very early became debased. Tao itself was never very much talked of and certainly never directly prayed to. It could not be named, defined, described. Yet whenever voices cried from the simplicity of the wilderness against the complexity of civilization, whenever plans failed or old age crept nearer, whenever a railroad had to be built, whenever suffering had to be faced, whenever life had to be lived, then prime ministers, scholars, farmers, poets, house-wives, the poor and the landless, the rich and the respectable became its witnesses.

> The Great Tao is universal like a flood,
> Which cannot be turned to the right or to the left.
>
> All creatures live upon It,
> And It denies nothing to anyone.

> It does Its work,
> But It makes no claims for Itself. . . .
>
> It is just because It does not wish to be great
> That Its Greatness is fully realized.[1]

Whatever this Tao may be, it is sharply antithetical to notions of wealth and greatness and to schemes of knowledge, industry, and empire. If it was in opposition to Confucianism, it was in even greater opposition to Westernism; perhaps nothing except early Christianity is more utterly inconsistent with attempts of science to control nature and attempts of states to control people; nothing more set against courts, exchanges, and law offices, government bureaus and advertising agencies, universities and laboratories, movies and radios. It was from the point of view of Tao that the mass of the Chinese people looked at Westernization and wondered whether it was good.

Chwang-tze, great Taoist prose writer of the fourth century B.C., tells the story of a man called Tze-kung, who once watched a gardener watering vegetables by hand:

"If you had a machine there, you could irrigate in a day a hundred times your present area. The labor required is trifling compared with the work done. Would you not like to have one?"

"What is it?" asked the gardener, looking up at him.

"It is a contrivance made of wood, heavy behind and light in front. It draws water up smoothly in a continuous flow, which bubbles forth like boiling soup. It is called a well sweep."

Thereupon the gardener flushed up and said with a laugh, "I have heard from my teacher that those who have cunning implements are cunning in their dealings, and those who are cunning in their dealings have cunning in their hearts, and those who have cunning in their hearts cannot be pure and incorrupt, and those who are not pure and incorrupt in their hearts are restless in spirit. Those who are restless in spirit are not fit vehicles for Tao.

It is not that I do not know of these things. I should be ashamed
to use them. . . ." [2]

Such notions were hardly encouraging to moderns who
wanted to build factories.

Chwang-tze writes also: "When Prince Wen Wang was on
a tour of inspection in Tsang, he saw an old man fishing. But
his fishing was not real fishing, for he did not fish in order to
catch fish, but to amuse himself. So Wen Wang wished to
employ him in the administration of government, but feared
lest his own ministers, uncles, and brothers might object. On
the other hand, if he let the old man go, he could not bear to
think of the people being deprived of such an influence."

These notions were hardly encouraging to moderns who
wanted to go fishing. Farmers who watched city walls being
torn down and said with magnificent stupidity, "If it goes
down, it goes down" (or, more magnificently, said nothing
at all); workers who pounded stones, carried dirt, dug cul-
verts for new roads, and shrugged their shoulders; men and
women who faced hunger, sickness, famine, poverty, war, and
death, and yet found joy in loving, laughing, gossiping, working, talking—all these very human obstacles to the bright
proposals of visiting Westerners were Taoist.

Until Communism won the say, Confucius, the pet of
princes, had pretty much the say about what should be done
in China; Lao-tze was the way in which it was done. Confucius drew the confining circle of relationships of friends, family, and government; Lao-tze taught men how to live within
the circle. For Taoism is no bundle of ethical sticks; it is,
rather, a central truth about life itself, and to that truth all
its specific ideas are tightly yoked. From the vantage point
of that center, Lao-tze belabored filial piety, snorted at rank,
ritual, and ceremony, dismissed governments and kings,

spoke ill of the rich, and sympathized with the poor. He cried
for inward truth not for outward order. Confucius, thinking
of society, said that unkindness should be repaid with justice; otherwise how could kindness be repaid? Lao-tze, thinking of a truth beyond society, said, "The Sage . . . is kind to
the kind; he is kind also to the unkind; for virtue is kind."
Confucianism was always out in the open, in the family, in
the court, in the works of worthy men. It spoke the sober
language of sense and scholarship, while Taoism used the
sharp weapon of paradox, the piercing flash of inward truth
provoked by the shocking realization of the togetherness of
opposites; for paradox cuts through the accumulated debris
of the mind to provoke awareness of things already dimly
believed: "He who speaks does not know; he who knows does
not speak." Taoism was always hidden; it preached camouflage; it was always camouflaged itself; and thus, while Confucianism dripped down from above, alike from the upper
levels of the mind and the upper classes of social rank, Taoism percolated up from below.

Lao-tze shared the same experience of life as Confucius:
the disorder of the declining days of Chou and the tradition
of the golden days when there was harmony.[3] By the time of
his birth, the ancient tribal unity of China had been shattered by a dim but vastly increased sense on the part of individual men of themselves as separate men. Group oneness
had broken; men acted no longer as vegetative bits of a single
plantlike tribe, but as men unto themselves, men who could
wrangle, battle, and usurp on their own account. Seeing
these facts, but not sensing fully the force behind them, Confucianism in effect demanded that the facts be denied and that
men return to the remembered tribal harmony of the golden
age. Seeing the same experienced present and the same imagined past, Lao-tze saw something very different. He made
for China the overwhelming discovery of the inward source
alike of outward disorder and outward peace: the egos of

individual men. He said in effect that so long as egos clashed with other egos no outward measure could bring outward harmony. The trouble was inward, and its cure was inward. Lao-tze denounced ego as an obstacle to harmony, but he did not for that reason argue a return to vegetative bliss. When he imagined the golden age, he imagined something far deeper than the tribal and the undifferentiated, something as deep as the springs of life itself, and he sought a common ground which could bring separate men together with separate men, a ground wherein they were themselves and yet part of one another.

The common ground was Tao. Lao-tze plowed it with astonishing thoroughness. From its vantage point, he put before men a way, a whole series of separate ways that were essentially one way, to lose themselves and to find themselves:

> One on tiptoe cannot stand.
> One astride cannot walk.
> One who displays himself does not shine.
>
> One who justifies himself has no glory.
> One who boasts of his own ability has no merit.
> One who parades his success will not endure.
>
> Therefore, the Sage wants to remain behind.
> But finds himself at the head of others;
> Reckons himself out,
> But finds himself safe and secure.
> Is it not because he is selfless
> That his self is realized?

To such sharp slicing through of ego, Lao-tze coupled blasting denunciation of anything that increased ego: wars, brawlings, possessions, jades and stone chimes, patriotism, bright swords, outrageous discords, and wealth, not to mention rituals, ceremonies, and possessive family relationships.

He would not have anything to do with names (his own name is not a name but a nickname meaning variously old philosopher or old child or old fellow), and he let so little of his personal life be disclosed that he is known to history only as the author of a short book of some five thousand characters, now called the *Tao Teh Ching*.[4] He even dared to see that knowledge of the sort men use to conquer the world and capture nature is part of the ego's urge to self-destruction: "When intelligence and wit arose, there appeared great hypocrites. . . . Have done with learning and you will have no more vexation."

In support of the same idea, Chwang-tze wrote:

When Knowledge traveled north, across the Black Water and over the Deep Steep Mountain, he met Do-nothing Say-nothing, and asked him about Tao, and Do-nothing Say-nothing did not reply.

He turned back and went to the south of the White Water, up the Fox Hill and asked All-in-extremes about Tao. "Ha! I know. I will tell you——" But just as he was about to speak, he seemed to forget what he was going to say, and Knowledge also received no reply.

Then he came back to the royal palace and asked the Yellow Emperor concerning Tao. And the latter [told him all about it] . . .

"Then you and I know Tao, and they don't," said Knowledge.

"Do-nothing Say-nothing was right," replied the Yellow Emperor. "All-in-extremes was quite near it. But you and I are still far from Tao. He who knows does not speak, and he who speaks does not know."

"I asked Do-nothing Say-nothing about Tao," said Knowledge, "but he did not answer me. Not that he would not, but he could not. So I asked All-in-extremes. He was just going to tell me, but he did not tell me. Not that he would not, but just as he was going to do so, he forgot what he wanted to say. Now I ask you and you are able to tell me. Why do you say, therefore, that you are far from Tao?"

"Of the two," replied the Yellow Emperor, "the former was genuinely right, because he really did not know. The latter was quite near it, because he had forgotten. You and I are still far from Tao, because we know."

When All-in-extremes heard this remark, he praised the Yellow Emperor for knowing what he was talking about.

This extraordinary and profound story cannot be labeled an exaggeration and lightly dismissed. It cannot by any formal analysis be dismissed at all, without summarily dismissing all of Taoism with it. It is possible to take Taoism or leave it, but it is impossible to reason about it or define it or break it up and look at the parts of it: it is a unity of perception concerning the relationship of self and Tao. What it dislikes —ritual, relationships, fussiness, knowledge—it dislikes because it interferes with something more important. Tao is wholeness, a reason for awe not for explanation; it should be experienced, not analyzed. Western critiques of it or explanations of it invariably come apart, and the authors of them fall back on name-calling as a substitute for understanding, putting down Lao-tze variously as a cynic, a mystic, a quietist, an anarchist, a negativist, a holy man, or what not, depending on whether they like him or not. The reader is warned that everything that is said about him in this book at very least strains truth. Criticism is impossible except out of fuller experience of the inward ground, Tao itself.

It is thus almost impossible to talk about Taoism, and yet the attempt to talk must be made. At the very time that Confucianism was formalizing the emotional horizons of the Chinese, Taoism was blasting them into the far reaches of the eternal, giving to China a timeless point of reference to assess—and dismiss—all attempts at fussy material betterment. Taoism deals with the ways that are dark. The clear ways of social manipulators—from American experts to Chinese Communists, to whom Taoism is anathema—are foreign to it.

Therefore there is no help for it: attempt at understanding must be made. But it will have to be made by trying to talk about Tao indirectly in terms of something else: that is, in Taoist terms, in terms of stories, witticisms, paradoxes, and particularly in terms of what was still as late as 1947 China's great and unbroken popular culture. Every Westerner in China in some measure confronted that culture and often was repelled by it. Yet even after that culture was broken in outward form, it retained inward drive.[5]

One great affirmation of popular Chinese culture—so long as there was chance to embrace it—was the quiet life, the life of simple rural pleasures, the lessons of wind, rain, and earth. To most Chinese, city life was not a little immoral. Few city residents, indeed, admitted that the city was really their home; rather home was the nostalgically remembered country spot from which they distantly sprang although their ancestors might have left it three centuries before. The city was considered parasitic, a place of empty wealth and empty show. A man would never go there for an outing; he would go away from it. Traditionally, it was not even a place to learn something. Most of the Confucian scholars themselves grew up in villages. Lao-tze said:

> Without going out of your door,
> You can know the ways of the world.
> Without peeping through your window,
> You can see the Way of Heaven.
> The farther you go,
> The less you know.
> Therefore, the Sage knows without traveling,
> Sees without looking,
> And does without fussing.

The place from which Chinese found it unnecessary to travel was the country. It was simple, quiet, and—despite the immensity of the Chinese earth—small.

Big things were done in China—old canals, a Great Wall, or huge stone sculptures of elephants, for instance—but the typical Chinese achievement was not large to the degree of being grandiose. Chinese architecture grew to be a perfection of harmony, of low-lying uptilted roofs, of graceful beams, brackets, and lintels. The Temple of Heaven in Peking is highly moving to look at, but it is not the pyramids, not Versailles, not Chartres, not a castle, a skyscraper, or a stockyard. Chinese poetry did not become heroic, art not flamboyant; no Chinese could ever have conceived of painting the superhuman figures of the Sistine Chapel that scowl forbiddingly upon the petty life below. Calligraphers could dip brush to ink and trace characters that are strong, frequently robust; but calligraphy from its very nature is not immense. The great inventions of the Chinese were small, as for instance the compass or printing. The box bellows, the most efficient preindustrial device for making iron, was like most Chinese tools, a brilliantly simple small device. Traditional China could not have imagined anything as stupendous as a Bessemer converter.

The Chinese never, of course, went to a completely antimechanical extreme. They used box bellows; they used well sweeps. But they took due care not to overreach themselves. "Go too far," said Lao-tze, "and you will be lost. . . . Only he who knows what is enough will always have enough." Even personal life on a grand scale was considered unwise. Opulence and display, too much entertaining, too many possessions, were dismissed as immoral. A rich man might wear fur in winter, but he wore it as the hidden lining of a simple blue gown. In China, even agriculture came to settle for the sound and simple rather than the luxurious. Cattle, which consume the energy in grain without giving equal energy in meat, were developed almost altogether for draft purposes; the great Chinese crops—the ones that made it possible to sustain the lives of almost half a billion people—came to be vegetables and cereals, meat being supplied by pigs and poultry, scavengers who can live on what otherwise would go to waste.

There were also big events in China: great changes and great cataclysms of history, numerous dynasties, hundreds of wars, thousands of revolts. But the Chinese, however saturated with history, considered history, so far as it was a matter of noise and alarms, a curse. The ideal life was one of tranquil contentment centered around people, babies, work, food, soil, nature; it was in no sense a vigorous participation in the course of history. Chinese bestirred themselves to clean up after history, but very few of them wanted to make history. Their knowledge of the past was extensive —a single twelve-line poem of Su Tung-po, for instance, will allude fleetingly to more than a dozen famous events—and their sense of the immense past fanning out to become the immense present was acute; but history in this sense meant to them eternally-unfolding life, always changing and always changeless. History was to them what moving mountains was to the old man in the story of Lieh-tze:

[Old Man Fool, it seems, was annoyed at having to walk up and down mountains every time he left home, so he summoned children, grandchildren, and the orphan son of a neighboring widow, and started digging the mountains down. The wise man of the area] laughed at the old man and tried to stop him, saying, "What a fool you are! With all the strength and years left to you, you can't even scratch the surface of this mountain. What can you do about the rocks and soil?"

Old Man Fool . . . drew a deep sigh and said, "It's only your mind that is not made up; when it is made up, nothing can stop it. You are of less use than the widow's son. When I die, there will be my children (to carry on the work), and the children will have grandchildren, and the grandchildren will again have children, and the children will again have grandchildren. So my children and grandchildren are endless, while the mountain cannot grow any bigger in size. Why shouldn't it be leveled some day? . . ." [6]

In place of the big things and the big history, there were the simple things. There were the simple amusements of conversation, going to plays, and listening to story tellers. There was the simple enjoyment of food—look, taste, aroma, feel—upon which was built perhaps the greatest cuisine in the world. There was the simple pleasure of walking around to no purpose, looking at trees, hills, rocks, and fields. There was the simple joy of working; of hand-tending the soil, of trotting under loads from village to village, of making garments, tools, boxes, baskets, iron pots, and plows. There was the exhilaration of working together: of chanting in unison while carrying a coffin up the side of a mountain or pulling a boat up stream through rapids. There was the pride of work well done: of the stone crusher, for instance, swinging his heavy flexible-handled iron mallet high over his head, and flinging it dramatically upon an iron chisel, shouting all the time the tempo of his action. There was the ideal relaxation of sitting easily upon a bench and doing nothing, looking at nothing, and thinking of nothing. And always there were the simple and lasting joys of sunrise at morning, sunset at evening, lighted lamps in the houses, talk in the tea shops, racket in the streets, quiet at home; sky and cloud, sun and rain, hot and cold, children, wives, friends.

It is not always a simple thing, of course, to enjoy simplicity. China always had the horrors of sickness, famine, and flood; she underwent recurrently the horrors of history, and she suffered them almost continually for the century before her collapse as a cultural entity. There were destruction of cities, villages, and farms; confusions of voices; inflation, poverty, hunger, migration, suffering, death—events viewed by no means with indifference. Yet China continued to hang on to the greatest wonder of life, its everyday normality. Chwang-tze wrote:

Death and life, preservation and destruction, ill and good fortune, poverty and wealth, worth and degeneracy, criticism and fame, hunger and thirst, cold and heat—these are chance events and the operation of destiny. Day and night they succeed one another, but knowledge cannot espy their origin. Hence they are not worthy of being allowed to disturb one's harmony. . . . One should make his mind harmonious, contented, and comprehending, so that it will not lose its cheerfulness.

In China's attachment to such inward peace in the face of such outward trouble, she much resembled the old poet Liu Ling, who rode about in a rough cart, carrying a pitcher of wine and calling out to a man carrying a spade behind him, "If I should die, bury me immediately as I am." [7] The smile so often on the faces of Chinese, even in the presence of twentieth-century ruin and destruction, was the smile of the Taoist old fellows. The frown on the face of Chinese in the presence of the bright schemes and the bright machines of the West was the smile of the same old fellows.

Pursuit of the quiet life does not in practice mean unawareness of trouble. Under emperors, war lords, and nationalists, Chinese farmers showed a strong sense of things being out of joint. They had a firm distaste for officials, civil or military, and were as much given to grumbling as a Vermont farmer. They grew indignant at not being left alone. Lao-tze himself was indignant:

> The more taboos and inhibitions there are in the world,
>   The poorer the people become.
> The more sharp weapons the people possess,
>   The greater confusion reigns in the realm.

> The more clever and crafty the men,
>   The oftener strange things happen.
> The more articulate the laws and ordinances,
>   The more robbers and thieves arise.

Closely yoked to the ideal of the quiet life was the ideal of the free life. This ideal resembled the Western ideal of democracy only in so far as it involved freedom from government. It was based, in part, on a strong attachment to the free union of the individual person with Tao and on a dislike for law, moral or civil. Lao-tze thought the chief end of man was to be moved by the spirit of Tao (like St. Augustine: "Love God, and do as you please"), not to obey a series of commands or injunctions. Tao *is* the inexplicably mysterious universe; it is not a moral or even physical government *of* the universe; it does not, like courts or temples, offer rewards and punishments. It is a truth which the world should take as its pattern, social wickedness arising from the fact that it is not taken. The chief duty, therefore, of human government is not-governing. "Ruling a big kingdom," Lao-tze said, "is like cooking a small fish"—fussing with it destroys it. The Sage rules his people, he said, by "emptying their hearts of desires and filling their bellies with food."

This urge to what Westerners might call anarchism expressed itself first of all in a traditional opposition of the people to all officials and in a particular opposition to bad ones. Chinese history is full of instances of the burning of houses of unjust magistrates, an action for which both public and government opinion blamed the magistrate and not the people. There were, further, various and devious means of expressing indignation, from howling in the streets in front of the magistrate's court to participating in rice riots, staged regularly in some sections of China, Fukien for instance, whenever the price exceeded a certain figure. Furthermore, there was the weapon of the strike, often used with high indirection. Early in the war a magistrate in Chungking decided that pork was too high-priced and put the blame on the retail butchers. The butchers immediately began observing a series of Buddhist holidays. The official countered with an edict that butcher shops should not observe Buddhist holidays in times of emergency. The shops reopened, promptly closed, and the butchers solemnly announced they could not operate because of the high cost of rent, a matter that had nothing to do with the point at issue, actually the high wholesale price of pork. At this point the magistrate gave in; typically, he did not go to the extreme of forbidding strikes altogether; he made the only possible choice between the alternatives of giving in quickly or carrying on the game of indirection so long that the strike would succeed anyhow.[8]

Lao-tze wrote:

> Why are the people starving?
> Because those above them are taxing them too heavily.
> That is why they are starving.
>
> Why are the people hard to manage?
> Because those above them are fussy and have private ends to serve.
> That is why they are hard to manage.
> The people have simply nothing to live upon!
> They know better than to value such a life!

The traditional Chinese way to handle rich and venal officials was to have nothing to do with officials. In matters of government most Chinese—excepting in particular the Communists and those who wished the efficiency of a modern centralized state—desired no authority but custom and themselves. The extent to which the Chinese people, who had no guarantees of freedom of press, assembly, or person, were free from government often shocked Westerners, strong devotees of what Rousseau called elected oligarchy. Until the arrival of Communist law and order, the Chinese people did not suffer oppressive government in silence; they talked, argued, denounced. Poetry even served as a form of public protest; a light lyric of highly decorous appearance could be made, by way of fleeting historical allusion and *double entendre,* to carry pointed criticism. Li Po was a literary rebel. The great eleventh-century poet Su Tung-po was twice exiled because he belabored governments with harmless looking weapons but with wide popular effect.[9] Governments at times attempted to control the thought and speech of the intelligentsia; they did not, however, for more than two thousand years dare attempt to control the thought and speech of the people. One might as well have tried to stop a river by means of a bucket. China, in fact, was never policed, except in times of great trouble, and then never effectively. As late as 1947 the government had the say about the currency; it had some say in Western industry, communications, and banks; otherwise it had no say whatsoever about the vast Chinese economy.

It had little to do, even, with civil and criminal law. The courts of its magistrates and judges, by sober estimate, handled 90 per cent fewer cases than do courts in the United States. Litigation was settled publicly, more often than not in the streets, with passers-by the judge and jury. Difficult cases found their way into the tea shops, a village elder acting as referee in noisier cases. Litigation, consequently, ended usually in compromise, all sides being anxious to avoid courts, judges, or lawyers. Divorce was usually handled by means of mutual denouncement in public. Theft was, by custom, an offense punishable—if the thief was caught—by showing the thief in his wickedness to the neighbors, by giving him a beating, or by turning him over to his clan.

Theft, of course, does not involve the use or possession of weapons. Robbery does; it fell therefore into the same class of crime as murder and banditry, and as such inevitably

went straight to the magistrate and his soldiers. (A thief or
an embezzler or a man who does not pay his debts takes no
unfair advantage: it is wits against wits—an equality which
does not prevail when a man is armed.) But except in disordered times when banditry existed, robbery and murder
were rare in China. The people remarked, "Heaven is high
and the Emperor far away," and went about their own business. They arranged co-operative systems for repairing and
digging out irrigation canals (one such system worked un-
interruptedly in Szechwan for two thousand years without government help), built bridges, maintained dikes, ran
market places. Their co-operative loan system was the main
method of financing funerals, marriages, land purchases, even
education until the distress of the twentieth century began
to deliver people into the hands of loan sharks.

This practice of freedom without a theory of freedom was
Taoist in a great many ways, but here Taoism only insisted
more pointedly upon that which orthodox Confucianism
already accepted. In the prehistoric reign of Shun (about
2000 B.C.) a minister was declaring: "Heaven sees through
(the eyes and ears of) our people. Heaven expresses its disapproval through the expressed disapproval of the people." [10] Before the times of Confucius, the *Book of History*
was talking about the mandate the emperor held from the
people. The feudal system was abolished in the Chou Dynasty, which ended in the third century B.C.; by the end of the
fourth century B.C. farmers owned their land; primogeniture
was outlawed about the time of the birth of Christ. No fixed
system of classes, of the order of Japanese and European hier-
archies was ever built up; anyone could be an official or a
prime minister, the examinations being open to all. Furthermore, the whole government, including the emperor, was
subject to independent criticism by special censors.[11]

In such a situation dictators did not easily survive. The
only one of any consequence in the last two thousand years,

Chin Shih Hwang, lasted just fourteen years. When an emperor is wicked, Mencius pointed out, he is no better than a thief. When a dynasty was oppressive, fussy, fumbling, decadent, or simply unlucky, everyone agreed that it was a matter of duty to get rid of it. There were about thirty-six of these more-than-democratic changes of régime during Chinese history. Despite all modern preachments about the state, the great mass of the Chinese people shrugged their shoulders at it. They disliked centralization—why should all parts of the country be alike in habits and speech if all parts have the same fundamental culture?—and they believed no rule the best rule. They believed in short that things should happen by themselves. Lao-tze wrote:

> Does anyone want to take the world and do what he
>   wants with it?
> I do not see how he can succeed.
>
> The world is a sacred vessel, which must not be tampered
>   with or grabbed at.
> To tamper with it is to spoil it, and to grab at it is to
>   lose it.
>
> For every creature has a time for going ahead, and a
>   time for going behind;
> A time for slow breathing and a time for fast breathing;
> A time to grow in strength and a time to decay;
> A time to be up and a time to be down.

Such teaching hardly offered fertile ground for developing the customs of law, manufacture, and consumption on which modern industry and government rest. It did not even encourage the physical unity of the country, for it was indifferent to systems of transportation and hostile to systems of police. It was talking about something altogether different from what the West talked about in China.

The third Taoist affirmation—if that which includes all else

can be so called—was Tao itself, that reality of harmony with
nature that formed Chinese architecture, Chinese poetry, and
even the Chinese landscape, sculptured over three millennia
into fields and paths whose contours fit intimately the slope
and curve of hills and valleys: a human reproduction of
the countless geometric shapes of nature, an immense work
of profound subconscious co-operation. That spirit put its
stamp upon centuries of history on the one hand and on the
other upon the coolie sitting on a bench and gazing vacantly
into the hills. Its hallmark was the sense of awe, the feeling of
wonder, joy, and mystery at seeing people, animals, birds,
trees, grass, earth, stones. Its method was inner awareness.

Taoism not only modified Confucianism but also nour-
ished Buddhism, which, indeed, apart from its effect on individuals, contributed comparatively little to China's basic
inward drives that was not already there. Taoism was skeptical of fussy activity; Buddhism for its part was skeptical of
human effort. Taoism pleaded for the simple life; Buddhism
pleaded against human desires. Taoism had its life in the
individual's inner awareness; Buddhism, the Chan sect in
particular, took up its residence there. Buddhism gave to
China metaphysical systems theretofore lacking. It contributed a wonderful variety of sects—from the True Word
school, which went in for rituals and images, and the Lotus
school, which made reverent repetition of the name *Omitofu*
the only essential to salvation, to Chan, which required inner
enlightenment, and Fa-hsiang, which called for reflection
and logic—a variety amazingly well adapted to the variations
of human interest and capacity.[12] But all the time the spirit of
Tao worked the more profoundly for its deep subconscious
lodgement. It remained sharply opposed to all efforts at conquest over nature, whether by knowledge or by machines.

It was not only the Taoist yea-saying that got in the way of
the West in China; it was also the sharp nay-saying, an inte-

gral part of the great affirmations themselves. It may be doubted whether Western systems of life, education, government, and production could survive did not individuals who participate in them have some secret but overweaning desire to prove themselves, to justify themselves to themselves by chasing outward success. Before a man can direct a large enterprise, work in a large government, run a large amusement, build a large building, or write a large book, he may well have to become highly involved with his own ego.

Taoism says a simple *no* to ego. This *no* was spoken quietly, almost secretly, instead of loudly and insistently, and there did not develop in China any deep-grained torment over the problem of ego. This fact is unexplained and very possibly inexplicable. It arises, clearly, not out of the conscious following of ancient maxims but out of the entire fabric of Chinese living. To try to trace the exact causes that made Chinese culture unique is to launch upon highly tentative and highly conventional oversimplification. Facts, in such cases, are lost in the labyrinth of formal analysis, particularly when the device of analysis, as for instance Freudianism, is based on the mental predilections of the West and is yet used to explain the mental predilections of the East. It is enough to try to see psychological facts and drives; it is dangerous to try to isolate their final causes.

Thus it is simply, but supremely, a fact that the pattern of Western neurosis did not develop among Chinese. From time beyond counting some of them were grasping and selfish; some of them were ambitious for wealth and possessions and rich foods; some of them sought power; some of them were cruel to the point of sadism. But in China, except for emperors who simply assumed they were heaven's representatives, even the bad man did not consider himself as the center of the universe; he could not bring himself to the belief that the world revolved around him, and that everything that happened, from war to the weather, had to be related to him

personally. Few Chinese were driven by a relentless urge for
recognition or fame. Few felt that there was merit in getting
the better of one's fellows:

> [The Sage] does not make a show of himself,
>   Hence he shines;
> Does not justify himself,
>   Hence he is glorified;
> Does not boast his ability,
>   Hence he gets the credit;
> Does not brandish his success,
>   Hence he endures;
> Does not compete with anyone,
>   Hence no one can compete with him.

The state of Taoist perfection was never, of course,
reached, but the counsel of it was followed, followed to an
extent that most Chinese even in times of crisis had other
urges more compulsive than the supposedly primary urge
of self-preservation. The Chinese ethic operated, to be sure,
within the relatively narrow horizons of Confucianism—it
was limited to relatives, friends, employers, employees—but
within these limits each man took liability for the other man.
On one occasion in the province of Szechwan, a Western family, returning by way of sedan chair from a summer vaca-
tion in the mountains, had to cross a stream swollen into a
torrent by heavy rains. A long plank bridged the stream; onto
it ventured the first carriers, supporting a double chair in
which sat the two children of the family. The first carrier
stamped on one end of the plank, judged it safe; but when
the two men reached the center, it began to sink into the
rushing water. The Westerners on the shore saw that the
chair was inevitably lost, and that the carriers must drop it
and grab at the plank to save themselves. But the men did
not let go. When the bodies of the carriers and the children
were found several miles downstream, the men's fingers had

to be pried loose from the carrying pole. This was no isolated act. Life itself, it was agreed, should be given up in preference to deserting family or friends or even the employer for whom a man assumed responsibility. Even such evils as graft and nepotism were to some degree practiced in behalf of others.

But such self-forgetfulness was hardly to be recommended as the best way for a bright young man to get on.

The great negation of Lao-tze is *do nothing*. Literally the phrase means non-action; it is represented in Chinese characters by a negative symbol and by an ideograph whose exact derivation is in dispute: it represents either a female monkey or a man's hand on an elephant's nose. It has the sense of "don't be a female monkey or don't try to pull an elephant by the nose," in short, don't fuss. Thus if you are bringing up children, don't try to bring them up, but let them bring themselves up. Don't hedge them with rules, coddling them when they keep the rules and frowning at them when they do not. Let children do what they want to, and let them grow without thinking of living as a cock-fight competition with playfellows or as a series of trials of ability and virtue. If you avoid these actions, the children will naturally, early, and easily take grown-up responsibility. For the consequence of *do nothing* is that everything shall get done.[13]

On one occasion the United States Embassy was adding to its buildings in Peking a structure that called for five immense monolithic pillars. They were quarried, cut, and laboriously rolled to the site, whereupon the American engineer in charge became worried over the lack of machinery to hoist them into place, the nearest suitable crane being on the West Coast of the United States. The Chinese contractor begged the engineer not to worry and assured him that he would accept all responsibility and guarantee that no workmen would get hurt. The engineer let the contractor go

ahead, but, edgy over the whole affair, went off on a hunting
trip to avoid the strain of watching the job bungled. Worry
got the better of him, however, and after a week's absence
he returned to Peking. Four of the pillars were exactly in
place; no one had been hurt. The final one was being raised
by a typical do-nothing do-everything Chinese contrivance—
a tall structure of bamboo poles, wider at the base than at
the top, the whole affair held together only by plaited bamboo rope. Atop the framework was a large wooden cylinder,
a set of wooden gears, and half a dozen levers projecting on
each side. Over the cylinder passed bamboo ropes attached to
the monolith; from the levers several hundred other ropes
led to the ground. The workmen came forth, put hand to the
ropes, gradually hoisted the pillar into the air, carefully let it
slip into place. Afterward the engineer examined the device
and exclaimed, "But it can't be done!"

Such skills, of course, are those of many preindustrial
people. The way in which they were exercised, however,
was peculiarly Chinese: no complicated set of administrators, foremen, timekeepers, supply bosses, and what not, but
rather a group of workmen disagreeing, arguing, and then
agreeing upon what shall be done and when and how it shall
be done; no orderly procedure, but a great falling-to in
which every man had his own say about his own work; a
hopeless tangle of men, ropes, and equipment; and finally a
tranquil concerted effort that miraculously got the job done.
Things must be let happen by themselves, big things and little things. Tao can be illustrated even from butchering. In
the fourth century B.C., Chwang-tze wrote:

Prince Hui's cook was cutting up a bullock. Every blow of his
knife, every heave of his shoulders, every tread of his foot, every
whssh of rent flesh, every *chhk* of the chopper, was in perfect
harmony. . . .

"Well done!" cried the Prince. "Yours is skill indeed."

"Sire," replied the cook, "I have always devoted myself to Tao.

It is better than skill. When I first began to cut up bullocks, I saw before me simply whole bullocks. After three years' practice I saw no more whole animals. And now I work with my mind and not with my eye. When my senses bid me stop but my mind urges me on, I fall back upon eternal principles. I follow such openings or cavities as there may be, according to the natural constitution of the animal. I do not attempt to cut through joints, still less through large bones.

"A good cook changes his chopper once a year—because he cuts. An ordinary cook, once a month—because he hacks. But I have had this chopper nineteen years, and though I have cut up many thousands of bullocks its edge is as if fresh from the whetstone. For at the joints there are always interstices, and the edge of a chopper being without thickness, it remains only to insert what is without thickness into such an interstice. By these means the interstice will be enlarged, and the blade will find plenty of room. It is thus that I have kept my chopper for nineteen years, as though fresh from the whetstone.

"Nevertheless, when I come upon a hard part, where the blade meets with a difficulty, I am all caution. I stay my hand, and gently apply the blade, until with a *hwah* the part yields like earth crumbling to the ground. Then I withdraw the blade and stand up and look around; and at last I wipe my chopper and put it carefully away."

"Bravo!" cried the Prince. "From the words of this cook I have learnt how to take care of my life."

Whatever this way of life may have been, it was not dynamic; and action for its own sake was never its goal. Chinese culture never approved of sloth; streets always rang with work and business, pursued hard and enjoyed well. Nor did Chinese thought applaud fatalism: if something could be done without fussing over it, it was done; if it could not be done, what was the value of fretting? If nothing could be done in the face of disaster, farmers, merchants, and artisans would give way to it—they would have to anyway—and not worry about making a final defiant stand against it. Means

of avoiding famine were present in the great plain of Szechwan: never-failing rivers channelling water to every field
over a vast area. They were first put to use about the time of
the birth of Christ. No such means existed in the province of
Shensi. Faced with famine, farmers did not cry out, "We must
have a water system, we must fight for a water system." Nor
were there adequate means for sending grain to Shensi from
areas of relative plenty. Farmers, consequently, did not form
protest groups to insist that food be sent.

This is not the Western fashion. George Meredith put
into the mouth of his character Mrs. Berry the remark, "In a
dilemmer, it is al'ays best to pray God and walk straight forward." Contrast the Chinese version of the story: "There
are thirty-six ways of meeting a dilemma, and the best of
them is to run away," a policy adopted whether a man is in
trouble with the police or in trouble with a famine.[14]

This was not simply a policy of giving into things instead
of standing up to them; it was a policy of standing up to
things by giving into them; and it was thus that the Chinese
stood up under the heavy bombing attacks in the earlier
phase of the war with Japan. While bombs were falling, fear
was evident on their faces; their voices were tense; their gestures uneasy. Between raids, fear was absent. Everything had
been done that could be done—shelters where the subsoil
was not too watery, a series of caves at Chungking, dug into
rock within a few months with the help only of ordinary
iron chisels and firecracker powder, and an almost infalli-
ble spotter and alarm system. Nothing more could be done;
therefore why fuss? Day after day, the Chinese plodded out
through city gates at the sound of the alarm for refuge in
the countryside; day after day they trudged back. They lost
friends, relatives, houses, and household goods secured by
great exertion: chairs, garments, cooking utensils, tables,
beds. At these losses they were sad, sad as they would have
been had cholera instead of bombs killed a friend; sad as they

would have been had accidental fire, not purposeful bombs, destroyed their houses. They did not cry defiance—very sensibly, to their mind—for they had nothing to defy with. They simply went on living—talking, laughing, loving, gossiping—whether there were ruins around them or not. And despite the sack of cities, the loss of industries, the destruction of communications, the wreck of their economy, despite one of the longest periods of continuous war in history, they did not stop living. The shutters came off the shops; the tea shops opened; carriers trotted unconcernedly around ruins; business was argued, silk was woven, boxes made, linens embroidered, food cooked, arguments concluded, settlements made, conversations enjoyed, and babies conceived. This lack of thought for the morrow resulted essentially from the old advice, Do nothing.

Do nothing, in practice of this sort, means indeed to do everything—everything that keeps a person whole, complete, natural, simple. Chwang-tze tells of the man who was not interested in achieving the greatest results with the least labor. "Coming into life, he lives among the people, not knowing whither he is bound, infinitely complete in himself. Success, utility, and the knowledge of skills would certainly make a man lose the human heart. But this man goes nowhere against his will and does nothing contrary to his heart, master of himself, above the praise and blame of the world. . . ."

Such fitting-in with the natural order of things was assumed to produce good. On the other hand, any attempt to interfere with the natural order was thought to produce evil—as evil as the interference with natural simplicity described in Chwang-tze's story about Chaos:

The divinity of the Southern Sea was Sudden Change, the divinity of the Northern Sea was Destruction, and the divinity of the Center was Chaos. Sudden Change and Destruction often met in the territory of Chaos. Chaos treated them well, so that Sudden

Change and Destruction planned to repay Chaos for his kindness. They said: "All men have seven orifices for seeing, hearing, eating, and breathing. Chaos alone has none. Let us try to bore some for him." So each day they bored one orifice. On the seventh day, Chaos died.

This single story sums up a century of well-meaning Western attempts to reform China. *Chaos did die.*

5

The Way of the Gods

THE FATAL INTERPLAY OF CHINA, JAPAN, AND THE WEST arose out of the fact that while China changed herself by slow and infrequent fits and starts, Japan erected the surface look of modernity. She developed factories, dynamos, and double-entry bookkeeping. During the war she had radar of a sort and even a cyclotron. After the war she had enough adaptability to survive as a nation, even while China, a victor, was breaking up. Whence this adaptability? Whence these evidences of change? What the state of mind out of which they sprang? Were there changes in the state of mind itself? Is it possible that the men who ran the machines were only acting as Westerners but reacting as Japanese? In short, what inward facts did the West confront in Japan? Such questions can be approached only by a close look at the surface life of the country during the decade of war and occupation and by a long look at the life that has moved for tens of generations underneath.

Even at the very beginning of the decade, it was a country in which men did not stride the streets exuberantly. Talk did not rise boisterously in shouts and laughter above the clacking of wooden slippers. Friends meeting in the street bowed, and refrained from gesture. The houses along the

streets were severely plain, so sensitive in taste that they were
delicate, almost fragile. There was no glitter, no false ornament, but instead a harmony of line, of delicately curved
roof, of supporting brackets, and of overhanging eaves. Inside were simple surfaces of wood and matting broken only
by single dramatically rectangular chests and by single scrolls
of painting or calligraphy: no ornament, no excess, no gaud-
iness of taste, no display. These were houses in which one
flower was worth a garden, in which one tiny tea jar was
appreciated more than a cabinet of curios, in which life was
simple, frugal, and quiet. The people in the houses were
friendly and likable; they had a keen sense of courtesy, and
they talked with other people only after highly mannerly
introductions.

Yet it was men from these houses who, in times of victory
in war, twisted bayonets in the breasts and bowels of women;
who roped old men and young children together, drenched
them with kerosene, and set them on fire; who lunged at
live civilians in bayonet practice; who slashed, bedaubed,
and set fire to dwellings in which they had been quartered.

Behavior of such grossness was not unique; the armies of
many peoples have practiced excess. What was uniquely Japanese was the sharp contrast of occasional excessive behavior
and the constant quiet decorum of everyday life: a contrast
of fundamental bearing upon Japanese attempts at Western-
izing themselves. In many ways, of course, the Japanese were
at all times like any other people; they ate and slept, kept
well and fell sick, rejoiced in their friends, loved their children, and forgot social differences when engaged in common
tasks. But there was also much that set them apart, and nothing reveals the differences more than the fundamental paradoxes of Japanese life. On the one hand, the Japanese kept
to extremes of restraint; on the other, they exploded in extremes of excess.

The Japanese, for instance, appeared to Western visitors

to be an obedient people. When they were told to bow, they bowed. When they were told to obey, they obeyed. When they were told to die, they died. When they were told to Westernize themselves, they studied promiscuously everything from Kant, Hegel, and Herbert Spencer to Samuel Smiles, and they learned how to operate machines. When they were told to hate the West, they studied the way of the gods and built an army. When they were told to welcome the occupying Americans, they welcomed them with enthusiasm.

But these people, however docile in appearance, were not docile in nature. During the war they required the services of an immense body of thought-control agents. Thousands of them went into political prisons; other thousands bore the scars of police beatings. They all seemed to follow orders unquestioningly, but one of their rigidly controlled newspapers in 1941 bluntly announced, "The Japanese people cannot go on following the government blindly"; and in the spring of 1944, when the government closed some of the larger theaters, another paper complained openly that "the people cannot live on patriotic speeches and moral sermons alone." [1] They appeared to be subservient to the government and to the emperor, but the emperor himself was the center around which brawling cliques struggled for power.

Nowhere else in the world is there record of such ingrained long-enduring self-restraint. In few other countries is there evidence of comparable sudden excesses. Loyalty to overlords had for centuries in Japan the strength of a fetish, but Japan's history drips with the blood of lords slaughtered by men whom they raised up, men who in turn were cut down by underlings. Placid acceptance of oppression and unthinking obedience to superiors are the essence of the history of a country that never had a popular revolution, but small groups of people many times rose up blindly and assaulted their officials. The very simplicity and severity of

Japanese life seem to be the forces that produced such powerful explosions of pent-up emotion. The same men who
carried themselves with high decorum when sober went mad
when drunk.

Sometimes the intoxication that released their emotions
was war, sometimes it was vaulting ambition, sometimes it
was disgust with oppression. Sometimes it was drink itself. A
third-century Chinese traveler among the Japanese set down
the remark, "They are much given to strong drink." A little
liquor often produces the drunkenness of a repressed mind
suddenly set free. The consequences were sometimes funny.
General Kawabe, who later became commander of Japanese
forces in Burma, was once moved to walk out of a formal
cocktail party on his hands. Amusing incidents of this sort
have no apparent connection with the violence of Japanese
soldiers in the Philippines and in China, or of the sixteenth-
century soldiers who cut off the ears and noses of thirty thousand Koreans and Chinese. But the behavior pattern is the
same: long and steady repression provokes outbursts.

The objects of these outbursts were by no means exclusively or even predominantly foreign. The lives of many
Japanese were punctuated by spasmodic outbursts of murderous passion against their fellow citizens. Soga no Umako,
for instance, was one of the first Japanese overlords to en-
dorse Buddhism, a religion that considers life so sacrosanct
that it forbids the killing even of animals. This religious
worthy murdered many of his enemies, including two imperial princes and finally the Emperor himself. What is more,
whole groups rose up at various times against each other;
there were, for instance, many cases of quarreling and brawling between monasteries. Even the country itself punctuated
its life of quiet self-repression with periods of violent bloodletting, feudal wars, succession quarrels, and dynastic intrigues.

Japanese life was not, of course, a matter of continual wildness and conflagration. Violence was never the pattern of life; rather it was a break in the established pattern of quiet and restraint. It was an outburst quickly come, quickly spent. The emotions that other peoples discharged in occasional anger, grumbling, and brawling, the Japanese stored up and discharged all at once. Without reference to the frame of life in which they occur, these outbursts would seem unusual only in their infrequency and in their intensity.

But the frame of life was the most important factor. There was very little in traditional Japanese life that permitted the harmless diffusion of emotion. There was everything that locked it in, repressed it, choked it. Traditionally, it was bad taste to disagree with someone else's ideas, good taste to agree and to keep your thoughts to yourself. It was only proper to observe precise ceremonies toward friends, family, strangers, fellow workers, superiors, inferiors, and a host of persons of all conceivable stations. It was unthinkable to treat those in superior positions without befitting and ceremonious deference. The Japanese language, imbued with the upper and lower notions of the Japanese mind, became essentially several languages, the choice of which depended upon the rank and sex of the person addressed. A Chinese traveler wrote as early as the third century: "When men of the lower class meet a man of rank, they leave the road and retire to the grass. When they address him, they either squat or kneel with both hands on the ground." [2] They kept on squatting. The social structure of the Japanese became as orderly as their houses, and even their amusements became highly disciplined.

High spirits could not find an outlet in art. The art grew up severe, simple, disciplined. Japanese taste veered away from the strong and the powerful; when it welcomed the artistic methods of China, it rejected, even in matters of calligraphy, the robustness of line and imagination the Chinese had put in them. A Chinese could put his hand to the brush and trace characters that sometimes had great strength, sometimes great imagination. Sometimes the characters were somber, sometimes even grim. A Japanese, working with the same brush and writing the same characters, usually produced a delicate almost airy pattern of line, full of nuances of expression.

A Japanese could attend the traditional drama. On the stage there was so careful an avoidance of anything even resembling overstatement, so minute a preoccupation with taste, so determined a desire to suggest and not to describe, that the smallest movements of fingers at times carried the burden of the acting. The actors themselves had been trained since childhood to both precision and preciousness; the discipline was rigorous; and the men who played women's parts dressed and lived as women so that on the stage they would make no false gesture.

A Japanese could also quote poetry. He could read characters that when spoken mean literally, "Old pond, frog, leaping into water, noise." It would be an offense against taste had this epigram said all it meant. A spade could not be called a spade. The ideographs of the poem were intended to mean little but to evoke much, to suggest a fleeting emotion of the evanescence of life, which the West could approximate only by the use of many carefully defined words. Dr. Karl Löwith translates it thus: "Life is like the sound caused by the leap of a frog, foolish, pathetic, and transient; it causes a little noise that is soon over, and then perfect silence once again settles over the old pond." [3]

The tea ceremony was even more severely simple. This ritual took place in a quiet room graced by a single painting or tea jar or spray of flowers. A few friends gathered, drank tea according to a carefully prescribed ritual, and discussed the merits of the single *objet d'art*. A single object. Nothing could be worse than overdisplay. A Japanese living in the sixteenth century became famous throughout the land because he owned three objects—a tray, a picture, and a small tea jar—each of which he always exhibited alone.

This good taste and restraint did not by themselves raise any psychological walls between Japan and the West, but they were inseparably tied up with inward drives that begot barriers of great height and weight. Restraint, for instance, was inseparable from the old feudal notion of loyalty, considered in Japan the chief end of man. Confucianism, introduced in the seventh century, was one of the early means of stressing this virtue, and by the end of the eighth century filial piety was taught in all the schools. Later the samurai tradition re-emphasized it. The samurai were a class of warriors, products of the feudal wars, who followed a special code of behavior and a special morality that emphasized bravery, obedience, and loyalty for their own sake—a code still later put together under the name *Bushido,* the way of the warrior. It put no emphasis on protection of the weak, no emphasis on right doing or high thinking; duty to the overlord was the point, right or wrong.

The formalizing of these notions powerfully reinforced the cement that held Japanese society together. It is noteworthy that practically without exception all Japanese thinkers supported the existing state. The great moral decisions of the Japanese hinged not on the battle of good and evil of the individual's inner consciousness, but on the opposition between various sets of social duties and between social duties and personal inclinations. Duties clashed with duties with a more than Miltonic severity; their conflicts were the basis of classical Japanese tragedy.

The argument of one of these, *The Forty-seven Ronin,* runs somewhat as follows: The Lord Asano, insulted in the shogun's palace, attacks one Kira with his sword. Unsheathing a weapon in the palace is a capital offense, and Asano is forced to commit suicide. His property is confiscated. Forty-

seven of his followers, or *ronin* as leaderless samurai were
called, bound to their dead master by loyalty, undertake to
avenge his death. To accomplish this end, they try to give the
appearance of not wanting to, of being lost to loyalty and
honor. To make the deception the more effective, they pur-
posely fall into bouts of drunkenness, suffer insult, and let
themselves be spit upon. One kills his father; another sells his
wife to a brothel; still another sends his sister to serve as spy-
concubine in the palace of the enemy, a position of certain
death. After a long period of waiting, the forty-seven men
corner Kira, kill him—he basely refuses to kill himself—and
display his head over Asano's grave. Everyone now rushes
forward to congratulate the *ronin* on their morality. But a
great ethical perplexity arises. Their crime is not murder
but a more serious offense—murder committed on the do-
main of the shogun without the shogun's express permission
—yet this offense is committed for the sake of the high moral
virtue of loyalty. After extensive differences of opinion occur,
the law of the shogun is adjudged sacrosanct, and the forty-
seven men are forced to commit suicide. This ending makes
them more heroic than ever.

Given the Japanese social code, the events of this apparently unlikely little moral lesson had to be as they were. At
every turn Asano and his followers acted the part of thoroughly *good* men. Asano had to attempt to kill Kira; his face,
or honor, had been struck, and only a weak or insincere person would fail to strike back. It was only proper, furthermore, that Asano be forced to kill himself. However worthy
was Asano's duty to himself, it was more worthy to fulfill
duty to the shogun. The Japanese moral code was in essence
a chart of the relationships of fealty. There were conceived
to be various sets of these arising out of a graded series of
obligations laid by superiors upon inferiors. In the times of
the shoguns the greatest obligation was placed by the shogun
himself, a somewhat lesser one by the feudal lord or daimyo,

one still lesser by parents, and so on down to trivial obligations conferred by persons unknown.

These obligations had to be repaid, whether they clashed or not. When they did clash, a superior obligation did not cancel a lesser one. The individual felt the full force of all of them at once. Asano, for instance, had to fulfill his obligation to himself by trying to kill Kira; he had then to fulfill his greater obligation to the shogun by killing himself. His *ronin* were honor bound to fulfill their ties of loyal obligation to Asano by way of revenge upon Kira, who had tarnished Asano's honor, and it was only proper to sacrifice two women and even a father to the plot. (The honor of these persons was posthumously brightened by their participation in it.) But the *ronin* had their obligation to the shogun too; in fact, they knew all along that they must die to repay it. When there was a conflict within the system of duties, death was an act that straightened everything out: witness the Japanese moral injunction, "Live as if you were already dead."

Like the Chinese, the Japanese put other urges before that of self-preservation. Unlike the Chinese, they came to think of death as a means of repaying debt to the liege lord, to the family, or to honor. The Chinese, relatively speaking, was a free and unobligated person; his greatest debt was to the great and almost impersonal past. The Japanese found themselves in pawn to a very great many persons in the present, and death—made easier for them by the conviction that they would become gods so long as they treated honor as everything and life as nothingness—became a proper manner of settling with the broker.

This set system of obligations, debts, and honor did not vanish with the end of shoguns and daimyos and the appearance of parliaments and machines. It continued to operate in a somewhat simplified form, but in undiminished force. There remained the class of greater obligations, long-term debts impossible of complete repayment: the debt to the

emperor, fountainhead of the system of loyalty, the debt to
parents, and then the debts to master and teacher. There
remained also the class of lesser obligations: the debt to more
distant members of the family and the debt to unrelated persons who might do a favor or give a gift, even if it were no
more than a cigarette. Into this class fell also the obligation
of honor.

The function of the individual in this rule-bound scheme
of loyalty had nothing to do with principles or even decisions
about how principles were to be carried out. His sole duty
was to act as became his place in the hierarchy and to discharge his obligations according to his place, an activity not
a little frustrating. In their individual lives, the Japanese
were given little opportunity for self-expression of any sort,
simply because they could hardly conceive of themselves as
individuals at all. They existed as a unit of a family, as an
object of the state, as a step in a complex system of rank. In
the brothels of the nineteenth century there was a rigid hierarchy of whores. The entire Japanese social fabric existed on
the Confucian proposition that younger sons should obey
older sons, the sons should obey fathers, fathers their fathers,
and that in exactly the same way should all men unquestionably obey and, all important, repay—those above them. It
was Confucianism with a vengeance. It was not a middle way
but an extreme way. It explains why the Allied Occupation
was fitted into the Japanese scheme of life within a very few
days after the surrender of Japan in World War II. The Occupation, clearly, was something to be obeyed.

Obedience to overlords was never a matter left simply to the
loyalty and honor of the underlings. The masters evidently
knew well that human nature could never entirely adapt
itself to detailed codes of behavior and clashing sets of obligations. Therefore they thought not only of encouraging
compliance but of punishing infraction. They took particu-

lar care to know everything that went on; as early as the eighth century there were complete registries of the inhabitants of places with information down to scars, moles, and warts. They took equal care to see that nothing happened without their consent, and that anything that did led to immediate and usually horrible punishment. Oppression maintained a steady high in the so-called feudal period (roughly from A.D. 1000 to 1867).[4]

So also did the supervision of minutiae. The lords dictated journeys, marriages, the floor plan of houses, the employment of servants, and even the presents for children. The high daimyo insisted on a system of hostages, whereby their retainers left their families in pawn whenever they went on a journey. The daimyo themselves had to leave their families with the shogun, and they had to spend half of their time at his castle so as not to get into mischief. Barriers were erected around castles and cities; anyone moving about without permission was disposed of. Classes were rigidly fixed, and it was more difficult to travel socially than it was to travel geographically. The economy itself was planned by the overlords, and none too well, for time and again they taxed agriculture practically out of existence by forcing it to support their own idle numbers, which increased polygamously until there were too many idle for the farmers to feed. They were completely confused by the spread of metal money in the fifteenth and sixteenth centuries and stood by helpless as debts mounted and prices fluctuated madly. Furthermore, the upper classes attempted to suppress all new habits, and they looked upon internal dissension of even the mildest degree as a sign of dangerous weakness. In 1445 a proclamation announced: "All quarrels and disputes are strictly forbidden. If this is disobeyed, both sides will be put to death, without inquiry into right or wrong."

The full force of this system of repression fell most heavily, of course, on the peasants. As early as A.D. 700 there were forced labor and conscription. Even in those times poverty was taxed while wealth went free. Offenses were punished on the basis of social status, and actions for which samurai could be pardoned meant death for a farmer. The samurai could cut down commoners if they fancied any rudeness in speech or behavior. (They were finally used in the early nineteenth century to put down starvation riots.) As Sir George Sansom points out, the peasant was simply a machine for producing rice.

Within the limits of the hierarchical system, a small degree of redress was occasionally given to peasants. If they were being taxed, for instance, far beyond the approved limits, already extreme, they would march to the daimyo or even to the shogun with petitions; the leaders would be punished for this crossing of hierarchical lines by such deaths as boiling in oil, but the petition would be read, and in the Tokugawa Shogunate (A.D. 1603–1867) about half the petitions were judged in favor of the peasants. There were also a number of wider and more violent revolts, none measurably effective, although a few of them led to a general cancellation of debts. They followed the familiar pattern of Japanese emotion. The peasant suffered quietly and obediently. In rich years he had only enough to live on. In lean years he starved. He was kicked about, prodded to produce more. He went on suffering quietly and obediently. But suddenly he had had more than he could stand. With all the force of a bull and not much more calculation, he rushed angrily against local authorities. There was a series of such uprisings during the unsettled times of the fifteenth century, and another series during the decline of the shoguns in the eighteenth and nineteenth centuries. One of these uprisings involved one of the few Japanese scholars ever to desert the overlords—Oshio, a philosopher who under the influence of the Chinese writer Wang Yang-ming sold his books to feed the hungry and led them in an attack on the city of Osaka. This revolt, like all the rest, was as evanescent as the petals of the cherry blossom.[5]

It was not until the last three decades of the nineteenth century that the emperor figured as the keystone of this edifice of duty, oppression, and self-restraint. Before 1867, the emperor was an almost forgotten man living in the shadows of the great shoguns. By the time the idea of imperial supremacy was first stated in the sixth century, the various clans already had more power than the imperial throne. In the centuries that followed, the power, the dignity, and finally the persons of the emperors were constantly under threat. There were bloody succession quarrels, intrigues, and abdications—five abdicated emperors were once alive at the same time. By the eleventh century there was no power and very little prestige, although the imperial throne survived as the theoretical source of power and fountain of formal honors. To have done away with it would have been to upset the order of things—even the calendar, based on imperial reigns. The country, furthermore, never wanted for rulers. Actual power in Japan was exercised by a succession of powerful families and individual dictators. The Soga and Fujiwara families gave way to the Tairas, who were soon displaced by the Minamotos, who in turn gave way to the Hojos and the Ashikagas, who were followed by the adventurer Nobunaga, the megalomaniac Hideyoshi, and finally Ieyasu, founder of the Tokugawa family that ruled until the restoration of the emperor in 1867.

The aristocrats changed, but the principle of aristocracy did not change at all. Even in times of disturbance when no one knew just who the aristocracy was, the principle itself was never questioned. Japanese society at all times operated from the top down: religions, for instance, did not grow up from the common people, they spread from the aristocracy downward; and the early religious teachers went into the courts and not into the fields and market places. In the ninth century, the great teacher Kobo Daishi introduced tea, bridge building, path making, and even the kana syllabary, the first method of writing that did not involve a hopeless mix-up between Japanese phonetic polysyllables and Chinese ideographic monosyllables. His achievements were many—painting, calligraphy, invention, and exploration— but his chief interest was Buddhism. *Therefore,* he frequented the palace. For a long time Confucianism was the concern only of the upper classes. It was upon such a foundation of. entrenched aristocratic ideas that Japan later attempted to fit an industrial superstructure.

The strain of living under such an extreme dispensation of aristocracy and obligation mounted slowly but inexorably. This increase occurred particularly at the time that the Japanese were attempting to enlarge the dimensions of what might be called their morally off-limits area, a section of life in which the individual could find some outlet for high spirits. In the eighteenth and nineteenth centuries, during the rise of the *chonin,* the business class, there was a frank indulgence in the less fine-drawn pleasures. The brothels were popular; the theater became at times a little extravagant; there were wrestling matches and carnivals. These activities met with disapproval from the more conservative. They nonetheless survived, and to them were later added Westernized movie houses and barrooms. These too met with disapproval. One of the first steps of the Japanese government after the invasion of China in 1937 was to prohibit Western dancing, although it had been prohibited some years before. The Army always approved an extreme of Spartan restraint at home, bewailed modern frivolities, and advocated a return to the frugality of the past. But even during the war dancing did not altogether stop. It was essential that there be a sphere of relaxation.

This off-limits sphere was that of "human feelings." By

itself there was nothing wrong with it in Japanese terms; disloyalty, the only real sin in Japan, having nothing to do with the patronization of fleshpots—so long as it did not interfere with a man's ability to discharge his social debts. But the more the sphere of personal inclination enlarged, the more chance there was for a new set of conflicts with the old and honored obligations. Paradoxically, the more room there was for amusement, the more opportunity there was for frustration. "Human feelings" had no status at all; they had to be promptly extirpated at the call of duty. The man who gave in to personal inclination by seeking a marriage of his own liking or by refusing to pay debts of loyalty to the bitter end or by declining to commit suicide when honor called for it was a bad man. Feelings had always to some extent been in conflict with duty. As soon as feelings were given more room, conflict increased. It even found its way into the drama. Sir George Sansom writes thus of one of the new tragedies:

A handsome young tradesman, though his marriage is arranged, falls in love with a fascinating Yoshiwara girl [a prostitute] whom a rich merchant protects. To pay for his pleasures, or to buy her out of servitude, he embezzles his employer's money, fears discovery, and then decides that he cannot reconcile *ninjo,* human feelings, with *giri,* moral duty. The lovers therefore agree to die together. He "takes up his dagger and stabs her, crying Namu Amida Butsu. She falls back with a groan, and he twists the weapon until her limbs squirm. Another thrust and the agony is upon her. Again he twists and twists the dagger. Her eyes grow dim, and she draws her last earthly sigh, and enters the Dark Road!" . . . The unhappy young man, having dispatched his sweetheart takes up the dagger to wipe it before plunging it into his own body. Then he remembers that this blade was given to him by his parents as a keepsake. To use it on himself would be a crowning offense against filial piety, and he therefore takes the girl's girdle and hangs himself.[6]

It was a people of this conflict of emotion who undertook to hold parliaments, create cities, operate factories, and establish colonies.

There was more to the Japanese mind, however, than the way it operated in public. Its root concepts stretched back to a period that antedates its written history, and these concepts gave to Japanese thought, Japanese art, and Japanese behavior an impress that set Japan off from any other country in the world. In the beginning they centered around a simple nature worship, different from other animisms in that it was genuinely simple. Nature was appreciated, not feared. There were gods of useful things, of the cooking pot, for instance. There were gods of beautiful things, of mountains and of lakes. Yet, in a land shaken continually by the settling earth there was no earthquake god; and even the storm god was chiefly benign. The early religion, perhaps as a consequence, never proceeded beyond a rather mild and pleasant appreciation of natural objects. There was no attempt, as in Chinese Taoism, to take moral lessons from nature.

The result, of course, was a system of perception that was not deeply perceptive. Simple appreciation and intuition are not basis enough for any sort of a world view. The early religion of Japan for a long time remained so nebulous that it could not conceive of a soul or make any differentiation between live bodies and dead spirits. It made no distinction at all between ethical right and wrong—if one sees no distinction between these categories in nature, it is difficult to conceive of them, as it were, in a vacuum. The early taboo system emphasized not wickedness but uncleanliness—simple physical uncleanliness along with the discharges of birth, the menses, sexual acts, wounds, and sickness, without regard to causes or circumstances. There was no distinction between the person who caused a wound and the one who suffered it.

Both were guilty. Washing was the chief religious exercise. Generally, there was none of the gnawing anxiety of doubt, nor of the curiosity that in other countries led either to a deeper appreciation of the quiet timelessness of nature or to a determined escape into an active and scientific life. Instead of developing a religious center of life, as did the Taoists, or an ethical teaching, as did the Confucianists, the Japanese developed a highly intricate social code that covered all the possible relationships of life. This code rested inevitably upon an edifice of loyalty to superiors and repression of self, not upon convictions of the individual person.

While the Japanese did not exist as persons, they certainly suffered the torments of the egotistic damned. A man who is eternally in moral debt, who must repay one set of obligations instantly and use a lifetime trying to repay another set, is not a man easy in mind, particularly when repayment is a matter of honor emphasized by family, social, and religious morality. In such case, the individual is forced to take his cue not from what he considers right and wrong but from what other people would say of him—honor is, after all, how you look to others—whence the Japanese sensitivity to public and even world opinion. Perpetually alert to shame, they found themselves perpetually alive to criticism and insult. Ridicule either crushed them or maddened them. No wonder. The sense of social indebtedness of most peoples never became sharp; the Japanese sense of it never became dull: social debts here and now were a staggering burden that made it difficult to accept a minor favor and almost improper to offer one. Upon the man who had been entertained at dinner, given a present, or helped in business rested a weight unbearable until the obligation was repaid; furthermore, the weight of the never completely repayable obligations to emperor, family, and master could never be shifted. At the end of World War II the whole Japanese people was still thinking about its obligation to the Emperor Meiji, was still overcome by its debt to Hirohito, and, at that time, had to begin worrying about repaying General MacArthur. Many times the Japanese tried to narrow the area in which they were subject to debt, and therefore shame; they became fussy over etiquette, ready to agree with any direct statement. They eschewed cursing, even succeeding in keeping profanity out of their language; and they said thank you with such obligation-shifting phrases as "Oh, this difficult thing" (i.e., the acceptance of a favor), "Oh, this doesn't end" (i.e., the feeling of obligation), or "I am grateful and insulted" (i.e., at thus being put in debt).

But there was no real help from these devices. The complex system of rank, debts, loyalties, and obligations ran about in a man's mind all at once, one thing conflicting with another, many of them conflicting with personal inclinations, and all of them tied up with honor. Within Japanese life there was no escape. The child, as Ruth Benedict makes clear in her acute and probing study of the Japanese character, *The Chrysanthemum and the Sword,* lived for a time an idyllic life, not much different from the childhood of Chinese, interrupted occasionally by parental admonitions of what-will-people-think and by threats of giving the child away. The child was also trained in the gestures of courtesy. Until the age of eight or nine years he was largely free of the terrible burden of obligation. Then it descended on him all at once. Inexorable expectations of perfection were put upon him, and it was made clear that he must either live up to them or suffer the loss, already threatened, of the respect of the family and, what is more, the respect of the outside world. Indeed if the outside world did not give respect, the family would not. The child, understandably enough, was overwhelmed; he had to conform punctiliously to a vast code of morality, or he would not be accepted. He had to devote his life to self-respect. He had to be caught up in the whole

meshwork of honor. The early events of his life, school haz-
ing and examinations, involved him in great conflicts, great
shame, great feelings of inadequacy, great urges for violence
and revenge. Meanwhile his life was becoming minutely ordered. Ruth Benedict points to the experience of a young
Japanese woman learning the Chinese classics from a Confucian scholar:

Throughout my two-hour lesson he never moved the slightest
fraction of an inch except for his hands and his lips. And I sat
before him on the matting in an equally correct and unchanging
position. Once I moved. It was in the midst of a lesson. For some
reason I was restless and swayed my body slightly, allowing my
folded knee to slip a trifle from the proper angle. The faintest
shade of surprise crossed my instructor's face; then very quietly
he closed his book, saying gently but with a stern air: "Little
Miss, it is evident that your mental attitude today is not suited
for study. You should retire to your room and meditate." My
little heart was almost killed with shame. . . . I slowly went to
my father to report as I always did, at the close of my lesson.
Father was surprised, as the time was not yet up, and his unconscious remark, "How quickly you have done your work!" was like
a death knell. The memory of that moment hurts like a bruise
to this very day.[7]

The only possible consequence of a régime of this sort, it
would seem, is a state of tension hard for any human being
to live under, no matter how acclimatized to it. The Japanese
had to seek always to strengthen himself to carry his honor
burdens. He had to temper himself into a bright sword
blade. He had at every minute to keep himself in a high
degree of fitness—and edginess—for whatever conflict, debt,
insult might come upon him. And in the twentieth century
he had to do all these things while living under the strain of
two dissimilar cultures, one Western, one immemorially Japanese.

Under such circumstances, what could put an end to the
frustrating restraint, whether self or officially imposed, that
engirdled Japan and her people? There could be only a moment of glorious but evanescent outburst, an instant in which
a goaded man, a class, or a nation achieved a pinnacle of egotistic honor and shattered temporarily the world that encased
him. There was no chance of emotional follow-up; after the
single shout, the single blow, the single mad rush, the rebellion was entrapped, encircled. The poet Basho writes:

> The summer grasses!
> All that is left of a warrior's dream!

The glory of the moment fades into the eternal greatness of
the nation, which is as great as the greatest victory and far
greater than any defeat, but which is full of profound bore-
dom, depression, and repression for the individual.

The theme of momentary fleeting glory runs as a re-echo-
ing theme throughout the whole of Japanese culture. In his
study of the Japanese mind, Karl Löwith points out: "Momentariness is characteristic of their outlook on life. Each
moment and experience is absolutely alive and significant.
Hence the typical topics of poetry: the frog leaps, the cricket
sings, the dewdrop glistens, a breeze passes. The Japanese
mind is trained in the imaginative elaboration of these eternal instants." [8] Sir George Sansom says of their language, "It
is the very thing for rambling romances, little love songs, and
elegant praise of flowers."

Confucian and Buddhist garments were draped upon the
Japanese spirit. That spirit, however, changed little. Japan
went to school under the Chinese, but she refused to hear
any ideas she did not like. She took over the Confucian classics, but she did not hear the Confucian emphasis on virtue
as the prerequisite and only excuse for rule. She took over

for a time the Chinese civil administrative system, but she did not hear the Chinese insistence that the administration should be open to anyone of learning and wisdom. She never conceived of the emperor holding a mandate from the people, never thought of the right of revolution; the Confucian virtue of *jen* (gentlemanliness, righteousness), she did not refer to. And Japan did not take over at all the teaching of the rebel Lao-tze who inveighed against courts and armies and who preached humility and lowliness as the right attributes of rulers. Time and again she appropriated Chinese forms—language, dress, art, land systems, architecture—but the only one of the principles underlying them that she took over was a warm sense of wonder and pleasure at the appearance of nature. Generally she fitted the imported forms to her own state of mind to the end that her culture was in no sense a copy of China's.

This uniqueness particularly characterized Japanese Buddhism. It took over intact the idea that repetition of the name of Buddha will ensure salvation; it provided colorful images and temples, places to pray for favors and to hope for living after death. But in many ways it was a new Buddhism. The futility of human effort or the extinction of desire had small place in Japan; meditation and reflection as avenues to truth, while practiced, were not emphasized. The highly important Zen sect became, to a large degree, an instrument for dealing with the special tensions of the Japanese ego. The Chinese counterpart of Zen, the Chan sect, taught inward enlightenment and the sudden realization of truth. The Japanese used this discipline partly as a device whereby warriors and rulers could get more self-assurance into their duty-ridden minds. The goal of Zen is self-reliance, sincerity, making the desire to do the great and right thing inseparable from the doing of it. If the mind is freer of worry about shame and emptier of conflict, it is clearly possible to grapple somewhat more successfully with the content of Japanese life. Zen tries

to preach these goals by means of shouts, blows, kicks—jolts
that may let the learner break through his self-entanglement
into the positive state of mind that understands nothingness.
The whole purpose of this exercise is suggested by the story
of the cowherd who lost his cow (that is, his soul), and went
out to find it. First he came upon traces of the cow; then he
seemed to see its tail, finally its body and head. After a struggle he caught hold of it, got on top of it, and rode home playing the flute, mindless of himself. This self-mindlessness, in
which it is possible to be less frustrated and more efficient,
would seem to be a high—and seldom reached—goal of Japanese life. But it was not something that could be got once
and for all. Japanese aristocrats had to go back again and
again to the Zen monasteries to get their conflicts somewhat
straightened out. Zen itself emphasized with approval the
fundamental Japanese paradox—the fragile cherry blossom
and the sharp sword, the austere life of the home and the
gore of the battlefield, the butterfly and the heavy temple
bell, symbols of a frustration out of which the only final escape was mindless violence, in which an instant of glory is
followed by an eternity of death.

Like Zen, all new ideas in Japan ceased quickly to be new.
The filter through which all ideas passed in Japan was the
aristocracy, whose chief aim was either to maintain the *status
quo* in which they themselves were maintained or else to
control changes to their own profit. Learning was at first a
simple matter of adornment, and who but the aristocracy
should wear fine clothes? In Japan there was little basic
change; there was effective thought control, so deeply a part
of the cultural structure that much of it was unconscious.

It was this country that industrialized itself faster than any
country in the world.

6

Japan Meets the West

"THE BLACK SHIPS" OF THE AMERICAN COMMODORE MAT-
thew Calbraith Perry sailed into Yedo harbor in 1853. After
complex political skirmishing, ending in a rising up of
the clans against the ruling Tokugawa Shogunate, the Emperor Meiji was restored in 1867. Moved perhaps by a fondness for a novelty always denied her, Japan thereafter
appeared to open herself almost spontaneously to Westernism. Nothing in Japanese history, not even the reception of
Chinese culture more than a thousand years earlier, can be
compared with the sudden preoccupation of Japan with
things Western. During the previous two hundred years of
exclusion of foreigners, Western ideas had seeped into Japan
and whetted her appetite for more. Now her psychic isolation was suddenly shattered. With astonishing speed and
driving energy an Oriental nation undertook to catch up
overnight with the West and succeeded so well that in fifty
years the country gave the surface appearance of a progressive modern industrial nation.

During this period a thousand new ideas assaulted Japan
all at once and ancient Japanese customs seemed to slip into
limbo. Thousands of Japanese traveled freely abroad. Shinto,
the classic faith of reverence for the emperor, was established

as the state religion. Religious freedom was guaranteed the Japanese "within limits . . . not antagonistic to their duties as subjects." Torture was formally abolished and telegraphy introduced. There was a mushroom growth of public schools; English and physics became popular items of the curriculum. Vaccination was practiced, railways were built, and a system of government-regulated banks was set in operation. By court order all government officials put on Western clothes. Universities were founded, legal codes translated, and a cultural embassy was sent around the world. The samurai were pensioned off and the wearing of samurai swords was prohibited; military service was prescribed for all adult males. Education was made compulsory. The Emperor Meiji had declared that knowledge should be sought all over the world, and his subjects managed at one and the same time to be enthusiastically Western in interests and aggressively Japanese in patriotism.

There was a daily newspaper in 1871, a railroad in 1872. The first baseball game was played in 1876. A stock exchange was founded in 1877, a marine insurance company in 1878, a streetcar company and a clearinghouse in 1880. In 1882 a powerful government banking system was formed around the Bank of Japan, and in 1885 various shipping companies amalgamated to form the NYK line, which even then had fifty-eight ships. In 1887 came electric lights and an income tax; in 1894 bicycles; in 1897 the first Japanese investment in China. In 1900 there were seven thousand factories. In 1904 an envoy went abroad to raise fifty million dollars' credit and raised four hundred ten million dollars. Motion pictures appeared in 1908.

Instead of the old shoguns there was the Emperor Meiji, and the Emperor seemed to Westerners to resemble less an Oriental despot than a constitutional king. He esteemed his counselor, Prince Ito, who as a young man had disobeyed the law against foreign travel to run off to England, where he became an ardent convert to things Western. He cherished his wife, moved freely throughout the country, took a profound interest in mines, industries, and constitutions, visited dying statesmen, took up residence at army headquarters during wars, and even suggested that the public continue about its business when he passed through the streets of Tokyo. The people held him in great affection, and it was for him that they first broke the ancient rule of silence in the presence of the emperor by shouting "Banzai!" ("May you live ten thousand years!") Japan, it seemed, was launched upon an entirely new way of life.

Westerners watched and were amazed. From the very beginning of the change in Japan, myth was in the making: the little men and women were very polite and very affable and astonishingly able. Furthermore, they were copyists of the West, a fact at once flattering and reassuring, for certainly there can be no hostility from a people who treats you as an example to be followed. It was not necessary, of course, to have these people at one's dinner table or to take them into one's own country, but it was only right and charitable to help them, applaud them, and encourage them in their playing with their toylike Western way of life.

Translated into policy, this myth led directly to warm Western partisanship for Japan in the clash of Japanese and Russian imperialism on the continent of Asia in 1904. Theodore Roosevelt was chiefly responsible for the drawing up of the Treaty of Portsmouth, favorable to the Japanese, who, however, did not think so, despite the award of independent Korea to Japan as a protectorate, a form of Western relationship that Japan considered synonymous with colonialism. When Japan in fact made a colony of Korea, Western powers did not object. When she made the Twenty-one Demands of China in 1915, demands that would have reduced China to a slave state, Woodrow Wilson showed no interest in blocking Japanese expansion. And in 1931 the West was still too much impressed by the little Oriental country become big Western empire to protest more than verbally the seizure of Manchuria.

What went on in the Japanese mind was very different from what Westerners saw happening on the surface. The arrival of the West provided for Japan only an additional measure of incentive for change, the need for which had been felt for many decades. The economic order had long been in confusion, partly because of the recurring problem of too many idle retainers living off the too-limited grain of the farmers, partly because of the consequences of introducing metal money two centuries earlier and thereby creating rich merchants. In earlier times, whenever a feudal dictatorship fell into hard times, feuds, battles, cancellations of debts, and general bloodletting managed to get a new dictatorship off to a fresh start. But when the Tokugawa Shogunate began to decline, there was a means of exchange; and there was a group that had established an almost complete monopoly over it. Barring the prohibition of money and the throwing of it into the sea—a step that could hardly have occurred to a people grown used to copper and silver—there was no means of getting a new aristocracy off to a fresh start. Merchants and aristocrats alike were thus sharply aware of Japan's internal weakness. They were sharply aware also of her exposed position before the outspreading West.

At this juncture, four ships of the fleet of Commodore Perry rounded Cape Idsu and dropped anchor in what is now Tokyo Bay. Perry, himself, was modest and punctilious ashore, but at sea—cloaked in the majesty of Navy—he became dramatic and pompous. He was half explorer, half research scientist; half sensitive, half blustering, half modest, half vain. He had studied minutely all available literature on the Orient; he had interviewed people, hired translators, garnered every known bit of information on Japan. He had thereupon become convinced that nothing could match Oriental intrigue and palaver except American intrigue and palaver. He conceived for his own person the role, which he undertook with enthusiasm but without humor, of "Lord of the Forbidden Interior." He became almost as mysterious and unapproachable as the Shogun himself and refused to move without escorts, panoplies, elaborately wrought sedan chairs, bands, and multi-gun salutes. In negotiation for the treaty that was to open Japan to trade, he was as devious as the Japanese High Commissioners, matched his own polite excuses against theirs, wrangled over minor details and split hairs as endlessly as they, and made ready to wear out Japanese patience before they wore out his. In entertainment he was lavish. Bargaining in the morning passed into drinking in the afternoon and feasting at night; the Japanese guests departed happy and buoyant, High Commissioner Matsusaki once falling into the arms of the Commodore, who was himself abstemious, and exclaiming, "Nippon and America, all the same heart." When the Commodore put to sea on April 4, 1854, he carried with him his treaty.

Perry was sharply conscious of the fact that all negotiations had been carried on in the presence of United States warships, but he was inclined to credit his success not so much to this show of might as to his method of negotiation.[1] Such Americans as were interested in Japan agreed with him. But the Japanese did not. What Perry had impressed them with was might not negotiation. Even so, Japan was not immediately thrown open. The treaty had to be buttressed by further negotiation in the presence of warships, and on several occasions Western navies bombarded Japanese cities. For thirteen years after Perry's arrival, the Shogun still ruled Japan from the power center of Yedo, and the Emperor continued to live meanly in retirement at the old spiritual center of Kyoto. During this time Japan squirmed but did not change.

During this time, however, plots against the Shogun multiplied. The Satsuma, Choshu, and certain other clans wanted to overthrow him and take power themselves, but they had not the money for it; they had in effect to accept the merchants as allies. This alliance, envious of the strength of Western powers, conscious of Japan's weakness, and covetous of new sources of wealth, at length concluded that the country should become strong enough to prevent its becoming a colony of some Western power, and that it should make use of Western learning. The consequence of the threat of Perry's warships was the refurbishing of old Shinto legends (set down around A.D. 600 to justify the position of one of the then many Japanese ruling groups) and the bringing forth of them to support a doctrine that equated the emperor with the nation.

This doctrine, new only in appearance, simply transferred to the throne—and thus to the nation—all the obligations formerly due the shogun and the daimyo. When the clans finally rose up against the shogunate, they forced the shogun to transfer power to the emperor, moved the person of the emperor to Yedo, which they renamed Tokyo, and gave modernized Shinto their strong support. They saw to it that the emperor was not only the source but the center of power; at the same time, by acting as his "advisers," they held practical control themselves as the genro, the elder statesmen. Immediately Japan sought to make herself strong and mighty; immediately Japan began to Westernize herself.

The initial step of the new régime was to abolish the remnants of the feudal system and to preserve the feudal code. The abolition, of course, was more dramatic than the preservation; it looked to Westerners as if Japan had spontaneously changed her spots. Despite measurable opposition, the daimyo and samurai were pensioned off, some of the daimyo receiving enough to set themselves up as new-style businessmen. As their prestige collapsed, the prestige of the emperor took its place. But prestige itself did not pass away. The clansmen were not opposed to change, but they were determined that change should proceed in the proper manner. Men like Prince Yamagata were willing for the antiquated samurai system to pass, but they were not willing for the samurai spirit to fail. They had no idea of doing away with the power of aristocracy itself. They buttressed it, and the buttressing meant holding onto the whole luggage of the traditional code of behavior. At the very time that Japan was reaching out most eagerly for Western things she was clutching most firmly at traditional ideas.

Thus there was a constitution, framed on suitably Bismarckian lines, in which there was created in appearance a constitutional monarchy and, in fact, something that resembled an oligarchy. The clans and the merchants had upset the feudal system for themselves, not for the people. In their minds the emperor was the keystone of an edifice of duty, loyalty, and subservience, and not the dispenser of a people's government. The new ways of industry and communications and government that stirred Japan so violently were handled in the same way as the new ideas of time past—they were let down from above through the filter of the aristocracy. Japan was Westernized by edict.

To wield national power, the new aristocrats not only had to make the Emperor their captive, but also to give his name as much weight as the unanimous will of the people would have in a democratic country. They were extraordinarily successful not only in keeping him a captive but also in making it appear that he was not one. Before long they believed in their own creation as deeply as anyone else—for they too had need of someone to feel obligation to. Thus the emperor became a spiritual institution in which centered the energy, the loyalty, and even the morality of the Japanese; he was the divine source of temporal power and the fountain of honor;

he was the reason for existing and also the reason for dying. Everyone was called to serve him and to "set his mind at rest."

This august position was reinforced by legends artfully assembled and cleverly merchandised. The emperor was the offspring by unbroken descent of the Emperor Jimmu, founder in 660 B.C. of Japan and great-great-grandson of the sun goddess. Japanese were taught to consider the name of the emperor too awful to utter and certainly too sacred to print, and they therefore referred to him as *Aramikami, Akitsukami, Kamigoichinin,* and *Otenshisama*—Incarnate God, Manifest Deity, Upper Exalted Foremost Being, and, most common, Honorable Son of Heaven. The people were told the story of the Yokohama father who inadvertently gave the not-to-be-named name to his son and atoned by killing the boy and himself as soon as he learned of his sacrilege. The people were instructed also in the protocol of avoiding less obvious acts of *lèse majesté*. No one could look down on the emperor; no one could ride a white horse, no one could picture the sacred sixteen-petaled chrysanthemum, and so on. Heroic tales were circulated of teachers and students who were burned to death trying to save the imperial picture and the imperial rescript on education from school buildings. (Both objects were required in all schools, and schools frequently caught fire.)

It was not of the slightest importance who the emperor was. The father of Emperor Hirohito, son of the Emperor Meiji and of a lady of the court honored for her services to the throne, was insane for some years before his death in 1926 without in the least upsetting imperial procedure or lowering the prestige of the imperial position. It was always the name and not the man that carried weight. The name approved plans, and made decisions theoretically immutable. The name under an imperial rescript—whether the emperor wrote it or not—gave to a declaration of war or to a statement on the duties of soldiers the awesome attribute of divine law. The famous Meiji Rescript to Soldiers and Sailors contained the sentence, "Bear in mind that duty is weightier than a mountain, while death is lighter than a feather." The imperial name turned this figure of speech into a categorical imperative. Any Japanese who disobeyed it automatically became a traitor to his emperor and thus to his country, his religion, and his family.[2]

The emperor was completely and conveniently sovereign. He had all the trappings of legend, but he also had all the weakness of legend. He had no say. The people had no say: they were exhorted but not consulted. At times when the government appeared to be influenced by political parties, it was in fact influenced by party leaders who expressed the will of their backers and not the will of their followers. For a time, the clansmen who deposed the shogun had the say, but their influence was passed on to no single group. It was passed on instead to the new aristocracy of generals and capitalists.

These new aristocrats no longer occupied the exact and unchanging positions of their predecessors; they were not an entirely homogeneous body. For one thing, the old opposition between the lords and the merchants was perpetuated, but the merchants had become lords themselves, thereby gaining more voice. The businessmen fell particular heir to one of the two legacies of the reign of Emperor Meiji—moving the country toward greater perfection in Western industrial techniques; the second legacy fell to the military, who emphasized the overlord system and the transcendence of national over individual concerns. The fortunes of each group fluctuated according to the status of the argument—which they had to settle for themselves in the absence of any *de facto* authority—over which group should control the voice of the emperor.

This argument was the easier to control in that the two

groups were small. There were not only relatively few top generals (important less as individuals than as representatives of cliques) but relatively few big capitalists. By skipping directly from a kind of feudalism to monopolistic capitalism, Japan put the bulk of her economic power in the hands of a very few families. But the argument nonetheless brought division—enough division to keep Japan from establishing a static system of rule. During a period of increasing militarism, for instance, big business and the army and navy were bound to differ on certain points. The industrialists wanted to control their own monopolies. The militarists wanted to control the entire economy, although not necessarily to direct it. The industrialists believed in steady profits as the basis for Japan's increase in power; the militarists believed in quick seizures of territory. The industrialists favored gradual changes; the militarists wanted direct action.

The argument was always friendly in essence. No businessman complained over the wars with China in 1894 and with Russia in 1904, or with the taking over of Korea. None objected to Japan's acquiring a mandate over many of the islands of the Pacific after World War I. Nor did any military man object to Japan's industrialization. Each group recognized the legitimacy of the other's aims. But they continued to differ on matters of emphasis. After World War I, for instance, businessmen reached positions of great weight in the government; even a system of political parties appeared. Western customs of dress, sports, and recreation became more pronounced. But in 1930 the military began to assert their power. They expressed it by assassinations of political rivals and by striking and capturing Manchuria. They expressed it also by demands that the country eschew surface Western customs and cling to those of the past. The army re-emphasized the old traits of loyalty and subservience, the old virtues of restraint and of simplicity, even though these traits had scarcely been weakened. It inveighed against everything from permanent waves to the music of Beethoven. It tightened its control on the economy. Thought control blossomed. The emperor was in his divinity proof that the world needed the moral guidance of Japan, and the army, in time-honored fashion, exhorted the people with the moralistic slogans of restraint, frugality, work, and piety.

Essentially, the balance of power between big business and the military depended at any given time on their relative value to the nationalist, expansionist aims to which both groups adhered and to which the equation of nation and emperor lent emphasis. To describe it negatively, the balance of power tipped in favor of the group that could cause the most difficulty by declining to co-operate. Big business could embarrass an army government by saying in effect: you run the factories. And the army, with the support of the navy, could embarrass a business government by saying: build your economic empire without the aid of military force.

But the degree of difference was not wide. The two groups disagreed on matters of method and of timing. They did not disagree on fundamentals. Expansion meant wealth for the one group and for the other glory. When Admiral Sekine, in discussing the development of East Asia, wrote, "If the great Central China, rich in agricultural and mineral products, and inhabited by two hundred million obedient masses, is industrialized, the mere imagination of it would give a sudden solvent effect on all residues we have in our stomachs," he was expressing an appetite for huge enterprise common both to the military and to big business. Controversy hinged basically on the question of whether, regardless of profits, the whole economic structure should be put directly to war uses, or whether profits should be protected during the period of military action. Yet the military by no means wanted to strip big business of all power; they looked to the monopolists to keep Japan rich just as much as the monopolists looked to them to keep Japan safe.[3]

Thus the military at times ran the country in co-operation with businessmen, while at times the businessmen ran it in co-operation with the military. Both groups were at one on the preservation of the entire onerous system of aristocratically dispensed feudal duties. With this as a point of meeting and the emperor as the point of obligation, the new rulers exercised as complete a control of Japan as had the old shoguns. Westerners looked at Japan and saw parliaments and panoplies; Japanese looked and saw traditional duties.

The expression of overlordship in economic life was as great as it was in the army and navy. A single family would control far-reaching interests in trading, coal mining, banking, shipping, textile manufacturing, and other fields, partly through direct ownership, partly through security and director deals, partly by sales, patent, and credit contracts. In 1937 fifteen family companies controlled more than two-thirds of all Japanese business; six of them controlled one-third; Mitsui, the biggest, controlled one-tenth. Very little business was done in Japan without big-family permission: little business, for instance, had to borrow from banks owned by big business. The economy was not directed by a free-market system or by the acumen of individuals. It was a working out of the prejudices of the Japanese mind, in which there was little place for anything so anarchic as competition and much place for direction from above. Individuals, indeed, did not run the economy at all; groups did. They made up business rules as they went along and changed them whenever they saw fit. Since the big combines had their own banks, for instance, they borrowed in effect from themselves, and found no need for the various procedures and safeguards of Western finance. At any time the banks would have been considered bankrupt by Western standards. Account keeping was hit or miss.

But business was extraordinarily profitable. The Japanese discovered that the very anachronism of their culture was their profit. The people still lived by the slogans of restraint, frugality, work, and piety. The new machinery of the West produced goods, not for their consumption, but for foreign sale. The economic costs were fixed on the basis of a two-thousand-year tradition, but prices were fixed in the world market. Textiles were the first big opportunity for this old-new squeeze. Silk was an obvious opportunity, but so too was cotton. Japan bought cotton abroad at low rates, transported it to her own mills, turned it into cloth, and then sold it at high international prices. Her profit lay in the fact that her people did not ask what they certainly were not given—any measurable share of their own production.

Once import and export became an important base of the country's economic life, the Japanese directed their interests into shipping; by handling their own transportation they could further reduce costs, further increase profits, and thereby gain further capital to put back into industrial expansion. After World War I this expansion continued into various fields of cheap consumer goods, hardware, toys, gewgaws, and what not. Textile manufacturing, however, remained the base. As late as 1930 one worker in every three was so engaged.

In that year, the great transformation of Japanese industry began; the profits from consumer goods were put into the creation of a heavy industry economy. This date coincides with the rise to power of the military, and the coincidence symbolizes the closeness that existed between the two sets of overlords. It was not until 1930 that the Japanese could have put hands on sufficient capital for the metals, machines, and factories necessary for big-scale war. The new power of the military was more than advantage-taking of the success of the businessmen; it was a deliberate policy of widening the sphere of Japanese economic activity by force of arms—an enterprise, if successful, of signal advantage both to men interested in the glory of battle and to men interested in the rate of profits. It was at the same time a gamble of certain profits from light manufacturing for tremendous profits from continental overlordship. It was a gamble taken perhaps from industrial weakness rather than from industrial strength. By 1937 Japan's entire steel production was only slightly more than the four million-ton production of the Carnegie Steel Company in 1900; she had an automobile industry of sorts, but its 1936 production was less than ten thousand cars. She had a moderate shipbuilding capacity. She had a small machine-tool business, a small chemical business. She did not yet have an aircraft industry. She had, in short, a small economy, measured in Western terms. But she had a great economy measured in Asiatic terms. In terms of the Japan of just seventy years before, she was an industrial giant.

All this Westernism was simply added to the top of a structure immemorially Japanese. Nothing mixed. There resulted a knowledge of industry without a flare for it. Science could make final sense only in relation to a typical Japanese goal, the well-being of one's liege. The urge to understand nature and dominate it was antithetical to the Japanese conviction that nature be felt and appreciated. The men called upon to make radar equipment had the ideas of Western science but they had the deeper Japanese convictions of intuition and sensitivity as the only conceivable approaches to life. In the middle of the war, when the Japanese became acutely aware of their deficiencies in technical ability, the government took to the radio to plead with the people to be inventive, and saw nothing strange in the idea that scientific discovery could result from exhortation. The new samurai who were trying to run an instrument that produced for the masses as if it were an instrument that produced only for a feudal daimyo never quite sensed that it was an infernal machine that sneered at nature and intuition and momentary emotion and demanded instead an allegiance of logic. By modernizing herself overnight, Japan kept a great part of her cultural conflict with the West hidden in her subconscious. As a group and as individuals, the Japanese were unaware of the highly dangerous anachronism of attempting to preserve ancient thought ways intact beside modern machines. Japan recurrently swallowed more than she could hope to assimilate, and she was bound sooner or later to suffer wracking bouts of mental indigestion.

For during the brief historical hours during which Japan was trying to modernize her outside, her inside underwent very little alteration. The life of the family did not change; the position of women did not change, even though women went to work. Even the styles of dress and hairdo imported from China's Tang Dynasty, which ended A.D. 906, did not change. There grew up huge steel and concrete factories, a network of railways, tall and modernistic office buildings. Huge chimneys floated the dirt of industrialism into the air. But around all these evidences of change clustered the evidences of no change: the austere little wood and paper houses with the upturned roof edges, the same houses with the same straw floors, the same alcove for the display of single bits of decoration, the same food, the same way of cooking, the same order of precedence, the same ideas of obedience, the same feeling for nature, the same belief that life is a matter of relative indifference and an honorable death something to be welcomed. In the factories there was the racket of machinery, of steel hitting against steel. Outside on the streets there was quiet—no unseemly laughing or shouts—and restrained bows to friends. In the offices, businessmen wore sack coats and trousers and sat on mahogany and imitation leather chairs, but as soon as they got home they changed into kimonos and sat on the floor. The very wealthy built houses which had the façades of Western-style mansions, but inside was another house of wood and paper. Students studied enthusiastically abroad, diplomats enthusiastically served their country, but few Japanese enjoyed travel: in the international hotels of Europe and America almost every nationality of man made himself luxuriously and often expansively at home except the Japanese.

Meanwhile the Japanese worker lived on in a sea of tiny set-together houses of severe line and graceful roof, above which stretched from pole to pole the wires of modern electricity. His life revolved around the mats on the floor, the clay brazier for cooking, a few pots and dishes, a few quilts on which the whole family slept, and the family treasure—a vase or picture. He went to the public baths, saw a movie if he could afford it, hoped someday to have a meal at a restaurant. What happened in his government or his factory or his trade union was all very well, and not a matter for him to take thought about. His role, he conceived, was to practice frugality, savor simple pleasures, and do as he was told. If there were savagely conflicting ideas within him, he did not think of them. If he was to fight, he fought; if he was to vote, he voted. Like the farmer, more insulated among his little neatly kept plots of paddy fields, he felt himself a part of a nation to be blown by the wind as a single leaf.

Yet all the while something cataclysmic was going on. Tension and pressure increased. They did not increase because of any outward pressure of the West, which continued to look at Japan as warmly and as paternally as it had looked during the decades that preceded. The pressure for the Westernization of Japan came largely from Japanese. The West did not push into Japan in the way it pushed into China. Such pressure as the West did put upon Japan was the pressure of humiliation working upon highly sensitive minds. The mere existence of powerful countries spurred Japan's surface Westernization; the existence of Oriental Exclusion Acts and the superior bearing of Westerners drove her into agonies of shame. It was not to be borne that other countries were su-

perior in anything; it was not to be borne that they were
unfriendly to Japanese immigrants; nor was it to be borne
that they were condescendingly friendly to Japanese efforts
to become a big power. It was maddening, in particular, that
neither near-by Russia nor distant America nor faraway Britain recognized Japan's spiritual superiority.

Of this conviction of superiority, Japan made much. It
rested, to be sure, on nothing more than an ancient code
under which she was attempting to live a twentieth-century
existence. To the Japanese the world looked uncouth—ma-
terialistic Russians, anarchistic Americans, overbearing Eng-
lishmen—and yet the opinion of these peoples who did not
understand orderliness and rank and ceremony penetrated
deep into the minds of a people ridden with ideas of honor
and shame. The Japanese felt the more humiliated in that
their new power was founded upon Western discoveries.
Even the form of their imperialism was new; they had taken
it over along with the machines and the constitutions and the
cost-accounting systems they had studied in New York, Ber-
lin, and London. Only the motivation was Japanese.

The motivation was all important. Japan was still suffering
all the restraints and frustrations of her peculiar way of
living and thinking. She was also suffering from increasing
attacks of cultural indigestion. The relationships of feudal
lords have little bearing on the organization of industries.
Women working in factories put a strain on the old belief
in the subordination of women. It is not easy to maintain
traditional habits while tending textile shuttles, oiling dynamos, running trains, fabricating steel, or erecting bridges.
It is hard to pursue the home habits of a retainer and to go
to work in a streetcar. It is hard to insist on a Confucian
family ethic when the family splits up to live in cities. It is
even hard to be single-mindedly Japanese when two sets of
overlords fall into disagreement about exactly what it means
to be Japanese—an important fact in a country where minor

differences of opinion are considered disorderly. Japanese industry and Japanese thought patterns mixed not at all; the emulsion that resulted from their side-by-side existence served as fuel for the explosion that was building up in the Japanese mind.

The time had come for a frustrated nation to break out of its restraint and run amok. The army called the moment; the whole nation broke forth. To the rulers of Japan, the outburst appeared promising; there was the promise of great moments of glory on immense battlefields; there was the hope of great gains of territory and profits. There was little fear, even if hopes should be dashed, that Japanese power, spent in a moment of great glory would collapse. The Japanese spirit had often before expressed itself in such moments, but the moments had faded, not into military and social weakness, but into the retrenched strength of a nation that had for centuries planned wars, economics, and social customs in meticulous detail. Meanwhile, inside Japan's gates, sat the machine—the instrument that produced for the masses, the Mammon that sneered at nature and intuition and momentary emotion, the Moloch that demanded an allegiance of logic and science. The real issue was whether the machine might not prove more powerful than the new samurai who were trying to run it.

7

China Meets the West

W‌HILE JAPAN WAS SUFFERING CULTURAL INDIGESTION FROM her eagerness to bolt the techniques of the West, China was chewing endlessly, tasting much, swallowing little, and suffering vast confusion. Instead of two groups of overlords who pursued a common aim with a rather simple enthusiasm, there was a great clashing of a hundred voices that talked at cross purposes about everything from the nature of shoes to the nature of society. Confronted with the need for Westernization, China was highly unwilling; confronted with the fact of it, China was highly disorderly. Change in China was so slow that it seemed not to be change at all.

This reluctance was inevitable. The Chinese, farmers and scholars alike, were highly conscious of their own ideas, their own traditions, their own art, literature, family habits, their own ways of making and selling things, and their own system of government or lack of it. Each of these was valued for itself, not because it fitted into a code of obligation. It would have been impossible for any scholar, viceroy, or emperor to prod the country into embracing the new and startling ideas of the West. The country would not have been inclined to listen: it did not like prodding; it did not have the habit of obeying; it distrusted plans of all sorts; it paid little attention to officials. Had it listened, it would not have been impressed. Many Chinese may not at once have understood the precise nature of Western ideas, but they understood enough to sense very shrewdly that those ideas were considerably out of harmony with their own, which they understood very well. They saw the simple fact that their ideas were clashing with outside ideas, and they liked the ones they already had. Change in China was consequently bound to involve a slow process of cultural accretion and to avoid any quick attempt at cultural revolution.

Thus there was avoided the cultural indigestion of a nation of 450,000,000 people. China took only what she was ready to chew and not much at that. In Japan it was possible quickly to introduce factories; while the Japanese, as a group, have no more mechanical dexterity than the Chinese, they are accustomed to the idea of supervision, which is highly important in maintaining the standard quality of a product and the least expensive method of making it. In China, however, the idea of supervision was unpleasant; it implied an improper relationship of persons; it was not to be borne. In Japan it was possible to give, if not a Western legal definition, at least an orderly definition of corporations and business practices and to extend to business the protections of government. In China there was not for many decades even the possibility of such definition. Essentially there was no law. Chinese custom, as John Earl Baker points out, endorsed the idea of equity; it did not support the idea of contract. If conditions changed after an agreement had been reached, the agreement was modified, a state of things impossible for corporations of Western or even Japanese pattern. Chinese industries had difficulty even in protecting themselves against theft. Mr. Baker reports:

In the middle twenties a certain ironworks near Hankow was brought to bankruptcy, according to the owner, largely because of the pilferings of small castings that the workmen carried away and sold on the junk market. When a thief was detected and brought to trial, the judge reverted to the instinctive role of "peace talker" trying to settle a dispute between two people on the streets. Consequently he took the attitude, "Here is a rich man making a big fuss over a few cents' worth of iron. This poor man needs the money much more than does the rich man. Rich man, you ought to be ashamed of yourself." And when the prosecutor insisted upon the law and the culprit was sent to prison for a minimum sentence, the judge stipulated that the complainant pay for the prisoner's food.[1]

The Chinese language itself was inhospitable to Western ideas. For a long time there was simply no way to write many of them down. The Japanese language includes, in addition to Chinese characters, widely used phonetic symbols in which new names can be written. The Chinese language, on the other hand, is not well served by phonetic symbols. It is based on ideographs, or characters, and these have only a tangential connection with the way words are pronounced. Had new characters suddenly been made up or old characters suddenly brought out of disuse and redefined, few persons would have had means of knowing what they meant. The Chinese vocabulary is immense, but the growth of it involved slow and subconscious stylization of pictures. Since the language lacked any of the scientific and technical presuppositions of Westernism, it was difficult to combine existing ideographs into new ones. Consequently it was advisable for anyone who wanted to understand foreign technical disciplines to learn a foreign terminology first; it was difficult for one Chinese who already understood such disciplines to teach another in the Chinese language. During the last war, truck mechanics had to be taught enough English to read and to pronounce such words as *carburetor, differential,* and *piston.*[2]

In the early nineteenth century, when the West was knocking insistently at China's gates, the Chinese were not aware of the many precise obstacles to the West's effective entrance. They did know that they did not want the West inside, and they declined to open of their own will. The West thereupon undertook entry by force. Unlike the Westernization of Japan, the Westernization of China was from the beginning a matter of foreign pressures and foreign wars.

China, to be sure, had long had contact with Westerners who were never forbidden the country as they were in Japan and Korea. Christian missionaries were present before the ninth century; Nestorians raised a monument in 781; there were Jesuits as early as the sixteenth, from whom, however, China picked up little more than astronomical calculation and gun-making. In the eighteenth century she had much more influence on the Western world than it had upon her. She then enjoyed probably the highest known standard of living and had more wealth and more people than any other country.[3] Her philosophical traditions made a deep impression on the Age of Reason. But by the end of the first quarter of the nineteenth century a fever of commercial and imperial activity came upon Europe in the wake of the new age of industry; Westerners became convinced that they had missions of trade and enlightenment to the rest of the world.

Precisely at this time, after a rule of more than two hundred prosperous years, the Manchu Dynasty (A.D. 1644–1911) began to decay in strength and inspiration. Corruption increased, bandits appeared, emperors began to vacillate, court favorites began to influence government; there was, in short, a beginning of all the portents that usually mark the end of dynasties in China. Had it been left to its own course, the dynasty would have been changed in the same way dynasties before had been changed: by revolt and by the establishment as emperor of a man strong enough to take power.

The dynasty was not to be left to its own course. Westerners seeking trade were troubled by hindrances put upon them in the form of port dues, taxes, regulations, and even special places of residence and business. For a long time they were cooped up in a narrow area along the Pearl River in Canton. They were appalled by the legal system, or absence of it. They were enraged by the easy and negligent manner in which Chinese officials dismissed them as barbarians. In part, these difficulties rose out of a Chinese belief that foreigners were fair game for squeeze; in part it arose from a simple will to sabotage objectionable enterprise, but in greater part it arose from China's comfortable self-containment and assurance. China was what her name implied, the Center Country, and to most of her neighbors she was in the older-brother younger-brother relationship of suzerainty. Whoever sought her out was a younger-brother or a barbarian. Commercial and diplomatic representatives of the West fell into the class of barbarians, and when presented in court were instructed to behave according to the protocol governing the behavior of representatives of nomads and tribespeople. This classification was bad for Western self-respect; furthermore, it was damaging to trade.

In 1839 the West first undertook to force the Chinese gates by war.[4] There was war again between 1856 and 1860, and shortly thereafter Westerners helped put down the anti-Manchu Taiping Rebellion, which had developed strong antiforeign sentiments.[5] In 1894 Japan went to war with China. In 1900, Western powers put down the Boxer uprising, encouraged by the shrewd but ill-informed and violently antiforeign empress, Tzu Hsi, in the hope of slaughtering all Westerners.

The dynasty was critically weakened. Already the foreigners had been granted extraterritoriality, whereby they lived and worked according to the laws of their own coun-

tries; already they had treaty ports. And the British long had
owned Hong Kong. Now every major power except the
United States flung itself upon China in a scramble for whatever it could get. Frontiers were redrawn at China's expense;
ports and other territory were taken on ninety-nine year
leases; there were mining and railway concessions. The Germans got large areas in the province of Shantung, and the
Russians got Dairen, Port Arthur, and the Chinese Eastern
Railway, from which they attempted to fan their power out
over all Manchuria. The dismemberment of China was
blocked, it seems likely, only by the Open Door policy of the
United States, which stood for free commercial access to
China and stood against foreign domination of China's half-
a-continent.

By the fall of 1911 the dynasty had arrived at an impasse.
There were a few feeble attempts at reform, but political
confusion, corruption, and banditry increased throughout
the country. There were symptoms of cultural confusion, and
cries that China must learn from the West. At length the
country rose up, and after remarkably little violence, the
Manchus were out.

The revolution did not, however, bring peace and order.
Revolutionist Sun Yat-sen was the first president but he held
the position only a few days, retiring to placate leaders more
personally ambitious.[6] For many years no stable government
could be formed; for many years there was no central government at all. War lords and local generals sprang up. In the
midst of this confusion, the foreign powers kept extracting
loot from the country on the old terms, and Japan in particular took pains to make the terms better.

The chief cultural consequence of the protracted period
of foreign pressure upon China was the existence of two
physically separated spheres of ideas, technics, and habits. In
Japan, these same two spheres, however much they refused

to come together, had their dwelling in the same place, the Japanese psyche. This was not the case in China. The Chinese lived by their ancient counsels and their ancient habits. The Westerners lived in a little microcosm of their own; indeed they were not even living *in* China but *at* China. They did not so much introduce Westernization to China as they exhibited it. Consequently, the Chinese psyche suffered none of the hidden tensions that beset the Japanese, but the spread of Western ideas was artificially dammed, and for a long time the Chinese mind received little stimulus from new ideas while the economy enjoyed little benefit from new techniques.

Separateness between individual Chinese and Westerners was marked. The Chinese for their part looked without enthusiasm on the peoples who made off with not a little of their territory and a good deal of their wealth, and who, by treaty dictate, managed such lucrative enterprises as the salt gabelle and the customs service. The only Chinese who had experience of foreigners were those who acted as personal or business servants, and these persons drew their life not from their masters but from their compatriots. The Westerners for their part sought out the Chinese no more than the Chinese sought them out. They lived in tight little social spheres, talked to one another at business, at tiffin, at tea, and at dinner; and when they wished to discuss China there was no one to talk to but themselves. The favorite teatime sport of asking one another what the Chinese were thinking flourished without any real contact with China; the Westerners could only imagine that the Chinese were thinking what they themselves would be thinking if they were what they thought the Chinese were. When they read translations of Chinese pronunciamentos about business or government, they saw nothing but flowery words, for they were unable to catch the innuendo and hidden meaning characteristic of Chinese public statements. Consequently, what contact Westerners had

with the reality of China depended largely on the behavior
of servants, talking miserably in English or pidgin instead of
impressively in Chinese; or on the business habits of com-
paradores, wheedling their way into more squeeze from
their vantage point as commercial middlemen between the
two spheres; or on fleeting glimpses of Chinese in the streets
or in the countryside. These glimpses revealed little more
than a lower-than-European standard of living. There grew
up what came to be known, variously, as the Hong Kong
mind or the Shanghai mind, and this mind—it was all the
same—gave birth full grown to the China myth: Chinese are
corrupt; they cannot govern themselves; they are cunning,
but otherwise not very alert; they are noisy, fractious, ab-
surdly full of notions of face; they do things backwards; they
eat horrible food; they deform women's feet, kill off their
girl children, show no respect for human life, live in a big
collective mass, and have little knowledge of what is really
going on.

This myth supposed Chinese philosophy abstruse and the
Chinese people illiterate and therefore ignorant. It supposed
that the farmers, the artisans, the water carriers—those, in
short, who did the labor of the country without enjoying due
share of the fruits of it—were persons so long bent down as
to know nothing but the dull routine of the soil or the empty
grind of physical labor; it supposed that they had little information, few interests, no ideas, and many superstitions
—in short, that they did not think. The myth overlooked
altogether the part the people of China—rural people and
the little people of the towns—had played in their own culture, which, for two thousand years at least, had not been let
down from above. Unlike the Japanese, whose ideas move
irreversibly from rich to poor, unlike even Westerners themselves, whose culture is highly nonpopular, the Chinese people were the source of their culture. All literary forms, for
instance, were of popular origin, not only the novel and the

drama but even the forms of high poetry. The scholar or landowner was only a step from having been a farmer and from becoming one again, and the transition within a lifetime from a country fellow to a man of culture was effected smoothly by many Chinese. The Westerners who were creating the myth overlooked the tablets that stood in front of many farm houses commemorating ancestors who were distinguished officials.

More important, the Westerners overlooked the daily living of the Chinese people themselves, who could by no means be dismissed as persons who do not know any better. Unlettered, they were by no means untutored. Most of the men had had a year or two exposure to letters, if only by way of the old-fashioned rooster schools, so-called for the crowing out of the classics; and while so short a time is inadequate for mastery of written Chinese, it is ample for early absorption of the ideas of the classics and of the cadences of high Chinese style. The speech of almost all Chinese farmers, even when shot through with localisms, is still measurably more reflective, considerably more terse, more colorful, and more fluent than that of most educated Westerners. The Chinese farmer had long had the word-of-mouth education of the family, of the theater—strongly didactic—and of street preachers and storytellers. As if in compensation for illiteracy, he had accumulated other resources, not only fluency of speech, but sharpness of memory. An unlettered servant or shop assistant could make twenty purchases of a morning, none of which he could write down, remember the goods bought, the prices paid, compute his ten per cent commission, render an exact account to his employer, and hand back the proper change.

But whenever these people were quizzed by someone foreign to them, they at once stared blankly, and only the more courageous of them went so far as to shake their heads. They carefully practiced Taoist camouflage. Did they know anything? Certainly not. He who speaks does not know; he who knows does not speak.

The effect of the myth, naturally enough, was to widen the gulf between the two ways of life. That China learned anything about the West and the West anything about China depended on persons daring enough to try to bridge the gulf. Some did. A number of the missionaries, some of the consular officials, and a few businessmen with latent enthusiasms for scholarship undertook to learn the language, study the customs, and translate the classics, and in so doing achieved for themselves a feeling for China more comparable to that of the eighteenth-century Age of Reason than to that of the nineteenth-century age of trade and respectability. To these individuals, the West, which had forgotten the eighteenth-century writings on China, owed most of what it learned. But a handful of Western scholars could hardly hope to explain their own culture to a sprawling populous country. The building of a bridge from West to East was undertaken by missionaries and by Chinese returned from study abroad.

It can be argued that this bridge was not built as effectively as it should have been. The earlier missionaries thought their own ideas of religion, education, and government so sacrosanct that they considered any dilution of them with Chinese ideas sacrilege. The peculiar notions of nineteenth-century Protestantism—complete with prohibitions against tobacco and alcohol and card playing—were transferred to China intact. Worship took place whenever possible in an imitation Gothic church; the doxology and the hymns were sung to the familiar Western tunes; there were the same prayers, the same responsive readings, the same benedictions, the same sacraments. The language was Chinese, but even in language there were difficulties. The missionaries had particular difficulty deciding on the proper name of God, passing over *Tien* (heaven) as too Confucian, pushing aside the conceivably adequate term *Tao* as too impersonal, deciding against *Shen* (spirit), and finally settling on *Shang Ti* as being closest to their idea of personal Deity. Literally translated, this name means *supreme god,* but the word *Ti* has imperial connotations; it came, indeed, to mean *emperor,* a title perhaps not entirely in keeping with the spirit of the New Testament. Few missionaries remarked the similarities between Lao-tze and Jesus; the Taoist writings might have made an effective Chinese Old Testament. For persons who believed in the verbal inspiration of the Bible, such supplementation was impossible. Taoism, besides, shocked many missionaries, more impressed by the bundle of virtues of Confucianism.

There was, thus, no altering the alterations Western Protestantism made in Christian thinking. These alterations had, however, a remarkable cultural effect. Roman Catholicism, less rigid—for a time in the seventeenth century, Jesuits refused to disown Christians who carried on native practices on the side—made more converts but had less cultural effect. The Protestants had an effect entirely out of proportion to the number of their converts. The Protestant congregation is a literate congregation; it is expected to understand dogma and theology. Schools became, therefore, as necessary as churches, and the missionaries threw themselves into the building of an entire system of Western education, from kindergarten to medical school. Furthermore, nineteenth-century Protestantism was much preoccupied with social behavior; in China it inveighed against plural marriage, ancestor worship, and the binding of feet; and it was upset by the idea of family responsibility and family justice. All-important, missionaries introduced the study of English, essential for understanding Western ideas, and encouraged Chinese to study abroad.

The effect on China of the returned students was profound. During the first quarter of the twentieth century they

almost completely displaced old scholars as the men of learning. They not only went into the missionary universities to
teach; they overflowed into new national universities, into
various provincial and national governments, and into translating and publishing firms. They came home with new
ideas of family life, city life, marriage, local government,
national government, methods of farming, art, literature,
philology; they had studied everything from engineering to
logic. They constituted an entirely new group living within
still traditional China; they fervently argued China's modernization.

They built, in a sense, bridges between East and West, but
the bridges never touched; there was always the hard-to-jump
gap in the middle. The student comes home ready to sweep
traditionalism out of his country. He comes home ready to
get rid of dirt, poverty, and superstition. But after a time he
looks at the dirt, and asks what dirt is. He remembers that
his countrymen spend more time washing themselves and
their clothes in their wooden tubs than do the farmers of
Iowa or the white-collar men of New York in their tap water
baths. He asks himself what poverty is, and he suddenly
understands that it is a state of mind as well as a state of
body, that his countrymen have only their own experience of
poverty and their own ideas of opulence and that they cannot picture the enormity of their condition. He asks himself
what anyone wants with radios, movies, and better mouse-
traps anyway. He remembers the little superstitions of the
West—from popular beliefs about unlucky numbers to ha-
bitual patterns of putting on clothes or locking up houses—
and concludes that they are not much smaller than the little
superstitions of the East, and that at all events the latter are
less alarming than the West's neuroses. In other words, he
suddenly understands the necessary existence of a cultural
conflict that formerly seemed to him unnecessary—very suddenly and simply; he realizes how much a part of the conflict

he is himself. He still abhors poverty, still disapproves venal
governments, but he knows the power of tradition because he
sees it working upon himself. He comes to understand that
there is no chance for panaceas, that there is hope only for
confused groping.

He comes home, for example, to teach in a university, and
he insists out of his experience in the West that faculty committee meetings proceed step-by-step in the most regular
procedure of Robert's Rules of Order. But he finds that he
himself prefers a meeting in which there are no agenda, in
which everyone talks at once and it is hard to decide who, of
the numerous men sitting up front, is the chairman. In such
meetings nobody mentions quorums, motions, or recogni-
tions. The meeting even breaks up into smaller groups, all
arguing vociferously. Ten minutes before the end of the
meeting, there appears not the smallest possibility of agreement or even of an orderly statement of disagreement. Then
almost miraculously, objections begin to lop off from one side
and the other and suddenly there is revealed a solid core of
decision that everyone had somehow been working on ever
since the meeting began. To this, a great majority agree, and
no one feels surprised at the way the agreement was reached.

Thus, the cultural gap between the West and China refused
to close. A desire for change had been born, but a method of
it had not been discovered, let alone any political forms for
carrying it out. After the 1911 revolution the political confusion was great; the new national government in Peking
gradually lost control over the rest of the country; and before long war lords became the *de facto* rulers of the country
and even of the capital. The ambitions of these men were
largely traditional. They saw the revolution of 1911 as dy-
nasty-changing of the old pattern; they saw the inevitable
struggle for power, success in which would mean the establishment of the next dynasty. More often than not the strug-

gle was not particularly bloody: battles were usually fought
according to rules; the hours of hostilities were often publicly
announced; battles involved negotiation more often than
shooting; the shooting itself was noisy but few soldiers were
hit; usually one side or the other withdrew before hostilities
became warm. But the struggle was debilitating. Fields were
ruined, towns looted, the people in some areas taxed decades
ahead, and opium grown in others for additional revenue;
the economic energy of the country was dissipated in military establishments. And the struggle itself came to nothing;
there was no quick rise to power of a single man, no quick
restoration of order; none of the signs, in short, that always
had ushered in new ruling houses. The days of dynasties
were over. Any government that came into existence had
to cope with the problems of Westerners and the West, and
simple attempts at controlling China by the sword were no
cure for them. Yet the fighting went on.

So did the ferment within China. By the end of the first
quarter of the twentieth century, women were less fettered
by custom and feet were no longer bound. A school system
of Western type had come into operation. Publishing houses
were putting out translations of thousands of Western
books. In East China the appearance of cities had begun to
change: roads were widened, new cottage industries established, even native factories built, and banks established.
There were 7,683 miles of railroad; in 1894 there had been
just 195. These outward changes were symptoms of a deeper
turmoil. It was not so much as if the Chinese had found something new; it was as if they had started to relinquish things
that were very old. The returned students with their stories
of the less trammeled life of the West had kindled warm interest in personal emancipation. Young people of education
toyed with rebellion against family, against paternal orders,
against arranged marriages. They turned their backs on the

classics and began devouring the major works of the Western literary and philosophic tradition.

The force that set this ferment working was no imported
idea. It was the very human, very universal emotion to which
Chinese life and Chinese morality had always paid careful
court: face. Chinese, to be sure, were free of the particularly
intense variety of it that meant personal honor in Japan.
Face, self-respect, self-confidence was something that Chinese had always had, not something they had always been on
the verge of being without. All at once they found that their
strength, compared to the strength of the West was a source
of shame and inferiority at one moment and at the next of
pride and self-respect. At the root of much of the desire of
Chinese intellectuals to study the philosophy of Montes-
quieu, to follow the preachments of Communism, or to keep
up with every change in the fashion of Western ideas, from
neohumanism to existentialism, was the potent urge to learn
somehow the knowledge that keeps one's country from being
humiliated by others. The Chinese, as individuals and as a
people, have contrived to live in the presence of floods, fam-
ines, and wars; they have survived bandits, war lords and
emperors both Chinese and foreign; dictatorships, socialist
states, systems of thought control, and almost every sort of
scheme and calamity known to man; and at the same time
they have found a very real warmth and joy of living even at
the very moment they were confronted with what troubled
them most. But humiliation upsets them. Indirection in their
habits of conduct saved them from it personally, and nation-
ally they were saved—until the nineteenth century—by China's position in Asia, so obviously central that there was no
reason to brag about it or to become patriotic. But for many
decades they had a strong and increasing dose of humiliation.
They were not personally shamed; they felt themselves na-
tionally shamed. Reformers felt humiliated even when they

inveighed against humiliation. It was no help to reflect that
all peoples feel face when they lose it. China had been bet-
tered by outsiders only too obviously in residence. Until she
was again united, proud, and strong, humiliation would remain. The country even observed special "humiliation" days.

There were many Chinese who, in their anxiety to remove
this humiliation, were attracted to the devices of the West
only because they had read the lesson of Western might:
China, they thought, must become outwardly strong without
any profound inward changes. The strength of Japan and the
solicitude shown her by Western powers, in such marked
contrast to the plundering practiced upon China, made a
deep impress upon the minds of many Chinese, and they
wished to adopt only such modernisms as would contribute
to political and military power.

Yet the conflict with the West involved more than a desire
to learn whatever was necessary to restore self-respect. It involved a search for something not known, not seen, and only
dimly sensed, something that was somehow felt to be necessary without its necessity being understood—a desire to grow,
a strong urge to expand mental and emotional horizons,
which had recurrently gripped Chinese culture in the past.

The more extreme of this mind at first advocated the embracing of Westernism *in toto,* even though they were not
sure just what all of Westernism was.[7] Later on, the more
thoughtful, the great majority of the reform group, began
ransacking the experience and the ideas of China's past at
the same time that they began ransacking the writings of
the West. Their hope was to find some bridge between tradition and modernity, some catalytic idea that could precipi-
tate a genuine amalgam of ideas, or some age-honored idea
that could illuminate new paths. This group for a time
pushed Confucius bodily aside, at least in his orthodox form:
he had been so closely identified with the sort of government
that had turned out to be weak that he seemed to be almost

personally responsible for China's humiliation. Very little interest, at the same time, was shown in Lao-tze, aside from a few unlikely literary arguments. The Old Fellow was too anarchistic; and an excess of freedom seemed to be partly the trouble with China: the country was a diversity of units as formless as sand without cement.

Lesser known and less influential thinkers aroused great interest. One of these, Mo-tze (also called Mo Ti), who founded in the fifth century B.C. a school of thought that died out about the time of the birth of Christ, excited young Chinese scholars because his ideas were somewhat similar to certain ideas of the West and yet entirely Chinese in origin. Mo-tze, like Confucius, was seeking the good society, but he did not believe that ceremony was an avenue to it. Like Lao-tze, he believed Deity to be the center of life, but he felt that the will of God could be fathomed and followed not by inner light but by reason and logic. He condemned offensive war, reasoning that since God loves men, men should love one another.

This doctrine did not treat of evil as energetically as some of the young scholars, exposed to the corruption and venality that had survived the fall of the Manchus, believed it should. These men fell with enthusiasm upon the teachings of Han Fei and the legalists. What was needed, they concluded, was the repression of bad men by means of an all-powerful state and a rigid set of laws. The legalists offered justification, on the one hand, for shooting rascals, and on the other, they went far beyond the Confucianists in proposing the exercise of state power in matters of the country's livelihood.

This line of inquiry centered attention also on Confucianists long roundly condemned by history for straying off into heretical paths, as for instance, Wang Mang, the regent who tried to make himself emperor A.D. 8. Wang called for agrarian reform and the nationalization of the land; he set up imperial monopolies over salt, iron, and money—reforms

that produced dissension, revolts, and his own overthrow.°
Even more interesting was Wang An-shih, who established
towards the end of the eleventh century what a Westerner
would call state socialism. He sought more taxes to help
carry on wars against the encroaching barbarians, and to that
end proposed that the government run business and take the
profits of it. His reforms had, however, produced as much
hostility—even among the farmers whom they ostensibly favored—as had the reforms of Wang Mang a thousand years
earlier.

Before long the young scholars had unearthed out of
their cultural past enough ways of thinking to put together
almost any Western system of thought, except those based on
mathematics, with extra systems to spare. The program of
Wang An-shih, for instance, could have served as a blueprint
for modern collectivism. Add in a bit of Confucianism, a
touch of Taoism, and a fillip of Moism, and something startling was bound to result. But eclecticism of this sort never
succeeded. There was no easy way out, no panacea. What
had to be altered and modernized in China was the Chinese
way of thinking, in which Confucius and Lao-tze figured so
prominently, not because they had lived twenty-five hundred
years before, but because they were still alive. The same
forces that had made Wang Mang and Wang An-shih fail
would make them fail once again. China could only go on
colliding repeatedly with the West in the hope that someday
an amalgam would come out of the collision.[8]

Out of the repeated collisions sprang the great liberal
movement, at first entirely the product of the universities,
particularly the National University of Peking. In 1916,
young Hu Shih, then a student at Columbia University, proposed in the magazine *Hsin Nien* (*New Youth*) the overthrow of the old literary language, terse but recondite, in
favor of everyday forms of spoken speech, a step of as great
moment in China as the shift from Latin to French, Italian,

and German in Medieval Europe. Upon his return to Peking University to teach, Hu championed the change by vernacular essays so impressive that an urge to literary reform swept the country, finding expression in everything from readable popular novels to mass literacy drives and understandable governmental decrees. Hu Shih's own *Outline of the History of Chinese Philosophy*, an outstanding literary achievement, was quickly reprinted eight times. More than any other effort, this shift of literary style demolished the barrier between people and scholar, and brought the people closer to participation in the problems of government and change. Meanwhile, Peking University was becoming the great center for harnessing Western and Chinese ideas. By the end of the decade, Peking was producing one graduating class of liberals after another. It invited foreign lecturers like Bertrand Russell and John Dewey. It was hospitable to the scientific method, encouraged personal and political individualism, stressed the need of nationalism. It brought new ideographs into the Chinese language, giving it a foundation for discussion of Western culture. Besides, it gave birth to a series of journals of political criticism and opinion: *New Youth,* first edited by the Dean of the Faculty of Chinese Letters, Chen Tu-hsiu, *The Renaissance,* edited by Hsin Chao, and later Hu Shih's *Independent Critic.*[9]

The few years preceding and following 1920 were the critical years in which Chinese opinion jelled. Peking University stood for the liberal position, that is, for open-minded efforts to seek an amalgam between China and the West; those of the intelligentsia who disapproved these efforts drew together against Peking ideas in a mildly cohesive conservative bloc. And before long there appeared still a third group. In 1920 a Russian agent was sent to China with the aim of converting the liberal movement to Leninism. He was very friendly, very intellectual, very much, in fact, like a professor; furthermore he arrived at a time when ideas

were most actively in flux. By 1921 the liberal movement had
not been converted to communism, but it had been split.

While there were three schools of intellectual opinion about
China's relationship to the West, there was not yet any concrete political program. Even the Communists, who had not
yet any mass basis, had none. Yet it was clear that China's
problems could not be solved in the absence of such a program. Some means must be found of bringing the country
together for co-operative action in the direction of change
and reform, whether it be the mild changes of the conservatives, the stronger ones of the liberals, or the upsets of the
Communists.

An attempt at a political program had been made by Kang
Yu-wei, in part through a rediscussion of Confucianism.
From a passage in the *Li Chi* he tried to derive sanction for
the gradual introduction of such notions as old-age care and
the abolition of the family. This program failed of popular
acceptance. Sun Yat-sen had put together his program of nationalism, livelihood, and democracy with its neat compromises between the old and the new, between the free market
and an authoritarian economy. His proposals had wide support, and Sun as father of the 1911 revolution, had wide support in his own person, but nothing had yet come of it. His
party, the Kuomintang, for a long time managed no more
than a tenuous existence in Canton, and Dr. Sun himself had
to spend much of his time in exile abroad.

Dr. Sun aimed to rid the country of war lords and to relieve it of foreign pressure, to promote industrialization and
improve the lot of the farmers, and eventually to usher in a
freely elected government that would be free from the taint
of nepotism and corruption. After appealing to various foreign countries, including Britain and the United States, for
support, he turned in 1923 to the Soviet Union, which dispatched Michael Borodin for counsel and advice. Under the

eye of idealist Sun, agitator Borodin, and a variety of Communists of various nationalities, there were united the Canton members of the Kuomintang and the members of the Communist party, an odd and inevitably temporary coming-together of opposites. Dr. Sun's Kuomintang gave the Communists a program to serve as the first rallying ground for general social revolution. The Communists gave the Kuomintang a Russian system of party organization and agitation. The Communists began to revere Sun Yat-sen. The Kuomintang began to adopt such labels as "the party above everything" and to arouse great sections of the country over the issue of antiforeignism. In 1925, Dr. Sun died while at Peking for medical treatment. His death furthered the movement rather than hindered it; he was all but canonized; and his ideas spread further than they had during his life.

In the summer of 1926 the armies of the uneasy alliance started north under the command of Chiang Kai-shek. By early spring of 1927, when the revolution had triumphed over the war lords of South and Central China, the two sides fell apart and took to attacking each other, first by word, then by intrigue, and later by force. The Communists and the Kuomintang left wing set up a capital at Hankow; the Kuomintang set one up at Nanking. The Communists wanted an extreme of antiforeignism and an immediate extreme of revolution against factory operators in the cities, foreign or Chinese, and against landowners in the country. They wanted no part of the Western-style merchants and Chinese bankers who had helped finance the Kuomintang. Chiang and his group, on the other hand, were primarily interested in the unity of the country; they were highly aware of the war lords quiescent in the South and still active in the North and West. They distrusted Russian Communism, and looked with alarm at the Communist preparations for armed revolution. They had welcomed bankers as allies and, while committed to land reform, did not wish to incur the active hostility of landowners. The split between the two groups was bloody; there were purges and murders. The Communists were forced out of Hankow into the countryside, where they set about building an army of their own. Change in China now depended on the Kuomintang.

The new Central Government inherited a country disrupted and depressed. The chief economic needs were more farm production, more roads and railroads, and a higher degree of industrialization. During the next ten years farm production did not increase much; the government was unable to undertake extensive restoration of old dikes and canals that had fallen into disuse; it did not build dams; it did not have the chance to convince farmers of the merits of new sorts of seeds and new methods of tilling. At the same time it encouraged more local action than had been shown in the preceding century, and it put its blessing upon public drives for farmers' credit co-operatives and for rural reconstruction. A start was made toward health and sanitation measures.

As for communications, modest gains were made in railway trackage; there was an increase of some two thousand miles, for more than half of which the Central Government was directly responsible. Payments were resumed on foreign railway bonds which had been in default during the days of political turmoil; the debentures increased greatly in value, and the outlook for new foreign financing improved with them. Very great progress was made in road building; a whole new network of highways sprang up. Two air lines were brought into the country. Several Chinese-owned steamship lines began operating on the Yangtze River.

Despite Dr. Sun's belief that the Central Government should be responsible for heavier manufactures, there was little increase in government-operated industry. Private Chinese capital was active, however, particularly around Hankow and Shanghai. Cottage industry increased, and even in the remoter provinces small shops teamed together for the simple assembly-line production of such things as flashlight batteries. The old two-level West-East system of economic life finally began to show signs of breaking down: there were now textile mills, power-generating plants, and small steel mills within China as well as within the treaty ports. There were actually successful Chinese corporations operating without benefit of the foreigners' law. So far as modernization of the Chinese economy was concerned, the ten years between 1927 and 1937 were the most important years in a century.

In the face of this modernization, traditionalists and reformers drew together into clearly demarked groups. Practically all Chinese, to be sure, shared a sense of their country's humiliation and a hope that it be removed. Practically all wanted the better government they had desired for many years. And practically all approved of such Western devices as could make their living more comfortable. But the active liberals—the ones who in varying degree wanted something more—were the students, the professors at the universities, many government officials and workers, almost all the professional men, many of the younger army officers, plus the modern businessmen and bankers from the large East China cities. The conservatives—the men who wanted nothing more than the minimum necessary to restore national respect —were a motley lot of landlords, provincial gentry and officialdom, not a few government officials, and most of the unreconstructed war lords. In this group, but not of it, was also the bulk of the Chinese people, who wanted nothing so much as to be left alone by officials, whether new type or old type, by war lords, by the old gentry, by the new intelligentsia, or by any other meddler, particularly tax collectors and conscription agents.

To the majority of the Chinese—to the persons who grew

the wealth of the country, fought its wars, transported its
wealth, and, in fact, did almost everything but enjoy well-
being in proportion to their labor—to this majority the word
modern—for which they created their own equivalent, *mo-
ten*—was a term that connoted something between uncertainty and skepticism. It stood for a way of life that posed
questions instead of answering them. It stood for something
outside the natural order of things: something that did not
simply happen but impelled instead. There was something
of rapidity about it that men who knew the slowness of the
soil distrusted.

The facts of change, however, were evident, and even the
village farmer accepted them. The town to which he carried his produce had altered drastically. Into the sequences
of the same-curved roofs, the repetitive play of lintels, the
harmony of façade, the never-ending variety of themes upon
a single architectural chord, unitive and understood by all
men, there were set square and ugly buildings, sometimes
flat-topped, to house new stores for cloth and hardware and
drugs. The main streets lost their intimacy; building lines
were pushed far apart so that where there had once been
space for two sedan chairs to pass there was now space for
two trucks. The people no longer crushed together in old
market-day fashion. Even the occupational pattern of the
city was upset: on the street of the leather workers there
were woodwork shops; on the streets of the embroiderers
there were silver shops. Old city walls had been breached at
many places and at others actually torn down.

In the countryside the word *road* once meant, except in
the North, where the transportation unit was a squat narrow
cart, a path two feet wide that meandered up hill, down valley, and around rice-field contours. Whatever moved, moved
on the backs of men or animals. Now there had come a different sort of road: a gash cut directly across the landscape on
which could travel trucks, busses, rickshas, carts. Each of

these vehicles greatly extended the mental and physical reach of the farmer by pushing out the frontiers of economical travel. A man-pushed cart can travel twice as far as a man-carried load before the costs of transportation—the food that men must eat in transit—consume the value of the product. A single ricksha puller can cover in three days a distance that took four days for two chair carriers and a luggage porter. Even these apparently small initial changes meant more and wider contact with the world outside and the end of complacent localism. The greater changes of motor trucks and trains meant for the localities served by them nothing less than a new economic order.

A Chinese farm, to be sure, looked very much as it had always looked. There was the narrow path, the stream edged with drooping trees, the green mounds of piled-up graves, and the bamboo clumps whence came material for the home manufacture of lathing, carrying poles, tool handles, rope, water buckets, clothes line, pipe stems, chairs, rafts, soy sauce pitchers. The *U*-shaped house itself, in the mud of its walls and the tile or thatch of its roof, still sprang from the soil it sat upon. The straw of the previous year's harvest still served families for shoes. The only steel products were pots, needles, and the tips of farm tools. The sculptured little plots of land had not changed, neither in the way they were hand-tended nor in the way they were cut up.

But the farmer knew that change was pressing upon the farm itself. He knew something about credit co-operatives; he was, to be sure, skeptical about such new plans for money, even though he hated the grip of the money lenders from which the co-operatives wanted to deliver him; but he was willing, when he had the chance, to try. He had heard about, even if he had not seen, new sorts of disease-resisting seeds, and he was skeptical about them too—foreign seeds, he feared, would not grow well in local soil—but he was willing, again when he had the chance, to plant a small corner of one field with them and watch what happened. He had known for some years about currency, the introduction of which was one of China's most drastic efforts to upset a localism that lived on copper cash and bulk silver. And he was highly sensitive to the considerations that influenced the prices he got and the rent or taxes he paid. To be sensitive to these considerations was to be sensitive to part of the basic plight of China in her sharp contact with the new West.

Meanwhile, the Kuomintang, the formal ruling oligarchy, had suffered the lot of many revolutionary organizations: confronted with power, it had sometimes misused it, sometimes failed to exercise it, sometimes used too much of it. Many of its members were no longer the liberal zealots they were in 1927. Some of them were anti-Western in bias and atavistic in thought. Some of them had used their posts to combine public government and personal spoils-getting. Some of them had used it to build more power. Some had attempted to control the thought of students and the opinions of journalists. Many of the most important party leaders showed little interest in the welfare of the people except in paper resolutions, much interest in a nepotism that reached down to county politics, where it most affected the people.

There were still no methods of inducing reluctant officials to pick up a job in their hands and take the praise or blame for it on their heads. There were still no extra-Confucian methods of checking up on the corrupt, save the occasional execution by top order of a particularly venal, particularly inept, and particularly weak rascal. The taxes were no longer farmed out—a great gain—but the purchases of the government had increased and the salaries paid by the government were modest. Graft probably decreased, but a century of disorder had made "reasonable squeeze" respectable, and some officials with a family tree full of relatives to support drew a fine line of respectability. Some prominent business families,

furthermore, turned this system around with even more upsetting results; they supported one of their number in government—in much the same way as they had supported him
during the Manchu Dynasty—and the government in effect
acted as a partner in private business.

Yet from this party no totalitarian rule emerged. China
remained a loosely organized country in which government
controls seldom worked. Since the times of Chin Shih Hwang
Ti, who twenty-two hundred years ago sought to his own
ruin to introduce rigid governmental controls, the Chinese
people had been remarkably free from the various autocra-
cies that were supposedly governing them. The Kuomintang,
indeed, could not be dismissed simply as a reactionary party
striving to maintain its own rule at *all* costs. It was the legal
creator and guarantor of modern government in China, and
in 1937 it had given China a decade of stability and continuity without which the country could not perhaps have survived. The Organic Law, which provided both for Kuomintang rule and for its transfer on the advent of constitutional
rule—for the party was to have tutelage over the country
only until the country could choose its own government—
was itself a tremendous advance in Chinese political thinking.

Kuomintang methods, to be sure, were often those of a
one-party dictatorship that still bore the marks put on it in
the early twenties by Borodin. Yet the power of this oligarchy steadily decreased. The old slogan, "the party before everything," soon fell into disuse. The party did not
maintain itself as an elite, and it did not purge dissident elements. It tolerated, even welcomed, such a variety of non-
partisan, well-educated men that by 1937 it was composed
of numerous factions, numerous nominal members, and
numerous liberals. Furthermore, it appointed to the Central Executive and Central Control committees—the organs
through which it supposedly controlled the government—

many independents who disapproved of the party regulars who officially appointed them. The result was a measure of decline of the controlling power of the party and a measure of increase of the autonomous power of the government. Once the party created the government, the government—somewhat like the universe pictured by eighteenth-century deists—tended to run itself. The political atmosphere of China was too strong for even regular party men to overcome.

The great undertaking of the government was the subjection of the war lords, a process that was still going on when war broke out in 1937. At first Chiang Kai-shek turned one general against the other, wrangled alliances to defeat third parties, then turned to fight his late allies. Later, when he had more force, he struck directly and hard. The war lords were playing a game with greater or less degrees of earnestness. Chiang was deadly in earnest. He struck fast. Once a war lord was subjected, however, he seldom disposed of the war lord; in 1937 most of his old enemies were not only alive but attached in some fashion or the other to the government. Not knowing what to do with Feng Yu-hsiang, a notorious turncoat, Chiang made him Minister of War so that he could keep an eye on him.

The process of bringing the Central Government to the distant provinces of China was no easy one. Until 1935, for instance, there was no Central Government power whatsoever in Szechwan, and the war lords Liu Hsiang and Liu Wenhwei—they were uncle and nephew—were hotly disputing who controlled what opium fields there. In 1935, however, the Communist armies, dislodged from Central China, made their way north across Szechwan. The Central Government offered troops to guard Szechwan; the frightened provincial authorities speedily agreed. The troops arrived, had no occasion to fight Communists, but did set up a big training center in the provincial capital of Chengtu. By the time war began Szechwan was within the Central Government orbit.

Unification of the country and confidence in the government made possible a second move of great importance: the China-wide introduction of one paper currency. China had operated on a system of bulk silver, copper cash, and some bank and provincial currency, but the currency seldom circulated much beyond walking distance of the issuing agency. The great measure of the success of the Central Government lay in the simple fact that the currency was planned, printed, circulated, and accepted by a people notoriously reluctant to put their faith in paper. Without currency it is highly doubtful whether China could have resisted Japan.

By 1937 the country was effectively, even though somewhat uncertainly, unified. Unification had involved confusion and turmoil. It had involved trying to keep students, inflamed by Japan's seizure of Manchuria in 1931, from precipitating incidents. It had even involved the kidnapping of Chiang himself. It finally involved a united front with the Communists, settled after 1935 in a few counties around Yenan in Shensi. In 1937 China was full of hope not felt at any time in her modern history. It was a hope of reform, of national strength, of victory, and of reconstruction.

Underlying this hope there was a weakness perhaps more important than anything Chiang or the Central Government or the Kuomintang had done or not done. China was still in collision with the West—not with the Western powers, for her diplomatic position had greatly improved, but with Western culture. Traditionalism and modernism were now living closely together, but an amalgam had by no means been achieved. There was no scale of recognized values common to all groups in the country. Consequently, political action resulted not so much from the will to act as from the possibility to act. Much that Chiang and the Central Government did was a simple barometric reflection of the internal Chinese political atmosphere. Each political decision

had to be measured against various diverse groups: the factions in the party that controlled much of the country's
wealth, the faction that controlled much of the machinery
of county government; the war lords, clipped of their power,
but still possessed of private armies; provincial governors;
secret societies like the Go Lao Hui, a group of plunderers
that controlled chief-of-police appointments in Szechwan;
the professional groups, who wielded a potent intellectual
influence; Communists; younger military officers; landlords;
and, of course, foreign powers. Chiang was limited also by
men around him who were not held together by a common
view of life. His astuteness consisted in his manipulation of
men and events to achieve the particular purpose of unifying China.

A true amalgam of West and East would have provided a
common view of life, but it is indeed questionable whether it
could ever have been *purposefully* achieved. It was something
that in a very real sense had to happen of itself. Before the
war, no Chinese could be sure what the new China would be
like or what it should be like. Would it be, horrible to contemplate, like Shanghai, which Lin Yu-tang called "an omi-
nous indication of what China may become." [10] Would it
become a replica of the West, which was certainly in depression, and which prominent Western thinkers were describing
as being also in decay? Was it not better to hold onto Confucius and Lao-tze than to decline and fall whilst attached to
the leading strings of another civilization? In this climate,
the liberals pushed the government on, the conservatives
strove to pull it back. The voice of the liberals sounded loud
and clear, but the liberals had not gone out to make revolution with Chiang as the Communists had with Russian
Borodin. Chiang, in fact, was given to distrusting Peking
University as a radical hotbed. At the same time he was
given to consulting the leaders of the liberal movement that

grew there. And he kept talking Confucius. Change had to come. But it had to come of itself.

China thus stood, neither altogether herself and certainly not yet something else, and hoped. She had experienced a decade of growing strength; now she faced a decade of growing crisis.

8

China Collides with Japan

THE DECADE OF MILITARY, ECONOMIC, AND DIPLOMATIC confusion between 1937 and 1947 may have been only a brief second added to the end of long years of history, but in terms of its psychological impact upon China, Japan, and the West, it may have lasted longer than centuries. The survival of an entire continent and an entire series of cultures, in a sense the survival of the West itself, hung on what happened during a period of brief but unbearably intense contact, which added a sense of terrifying urgency to the ever repeating problems of time past.

At the beginning of that decade China was more open to change than at any time before in her history. Change had thrown Japan into a state of tension greater than she had ever experienced. The first phase of the war, beginning with the attack on Lukouchiao, July 7, 1937 and ending with the attack on Pearl Harbor, December 7, 1941 indicated the inward cultural condition both of China and Japan, for in times of crisis a people seek out the particular resources that mean most to them. There collided two Eastern cultures that were themselves in inward collision with the West, and the nature of the resources upon which they drew and the degree

of outward success with which they used them forced the
minds of both the East and West into the condition from
which sprang failure: failure of one culture to meet another,
and failure of any one of the cultures fully to understand itself.

The China war started off in a manner highly Western.
Japan had studied foreign military practice, foreign army
organization, and foreign weapons. She had bought and
built in great numbers various instruments of war that most
Eastern countries possessed only for show. Only in the manner by which she launched the war was she Japanese, for the
decision was taken not by the top command but by officers in
the field: in somewhat feudal fashion underlings undertook
for their liege actions on their own responsibility that the
liege, now the Empire, could repudiate or support on the
basis of how well the action turned out.[1]

Japan's Westernization gave the action the look of high
propitiousness. By strength of modern arms she had the
whole of Manchuria as a home basis; by threat of arms she
had already occupied key areas of China. At Shanghai, for instance, she could moor warships in waters protected by international agreement, and in that city she controlled a large
slice of land on which she had concentrated arms, factories,
and soldiers. The event by which she precipitated war took
place not to the north of China's old capital, Peking, but to
the south of it at a place called Lukouchiao; the Japanese
had occupied the near-by railway town of Fengtai for over a
year.[2]

At Shanghai, in August 1937, the battle between the two
Oriental forces was fought basically on Western principles.
The two armies met head on and strength was pitted against
strength. The Chinese force was little more than a wall of
flesh concentrated along the river banks. It held for three
months against Japanese landing boats, armored vehicles,

aircraft, naval artillery, and heavy guns, but when a Japanese force landed at Hangchow Bay and marched to outflank Shanghai, the shattered Chinese fell back in confusion.

In North China the initial Japanese success was swift and the enemy spread out fanwise throughout the area north of the Yellow River. But before long the Japanese were in the position of men who think they see the summit of a mountain every time they climb over a foothill. In the year 1938 the Chinese no longer attempted frontal defense of the sort that had led to their slaughter at Shanghai. Instead they retreated, trading space for time. Japan's rate of march slowed and her soldiers, after a tardy finish to end-of-war celebrations, found themselves engaged in time-devouring skirmishes. After the fall of Hankow in October 1938, the war entered a long period of stalemate, during which Japan tried to bomb China into submission.

These were in outline the facts of the war. Behind the facts lay the psychological content of two very different minds. The Chinese were defeated when they tried to fight a Western-style war not only because they did not have the equipment for it but because they did not have a flair for organization, paper work, careful direction, and minute planning. The Japanese, on the other hand, were lost without meticulous plans. A plan, in fact, was even more important than success. All during the war, Japanese soldiers and civilians alike felt relieved if major setbacks were described as in accord with plan; without a plan they felt naked, exposed, and alone. Tradition had trained them loyally to carry out prescribed minutiae; if there was no complex code, no detailed chart, they ceased to function, and despair overcame them. In part the stalemate resulted from the fact that geography made it difficult for the Japanese to advance with heavy armament and from the fact that the armed strength of the Japanese made it impossible for the Chinese to advance without it. In part it involved dogged Chinese patience and a Japanese failure to follow through after an initial burst of success. "A Japanese army," a Chinese officer once said, "is like the easy-withering cherry blossom. It blooms at dawn, but when it fades in the evening, there is no color and fragrance is gone."

But in very large part the stalemate resulted from the fact that China fell back on traditionalism. What the Chinese lacked in machines and organization, they attempted to make up for in wits. They produced a vast and varied bag of tricks —infiltration, flank-depth defense, sidewise attacks, deception, disguise, flying columns, counterattack from the rear— each of which they used with endless variation. The Japanese, to be sure, understood these tactics intellectually, for they were based on a Chinese military tradition that went as far back as Sun-tze, who flourished some centuries before Christ. The Japanese had studied it themselves. Many of the tricks the Chinese used were described in detail in *San Kuo Chih* ("The Three Kingdoms") and *Shui Hu Chwan* ("All Men Are Brothers"), old novels that anyone could pick up in a bookstore. The aphorism so often repeated in the latter of these works, "If we cannot win by strength, we must use guile," could serve as a motto for the course of the war after the fall of Hankow in 1938.

The Japanese Army operated by rules, and the Chinese very early discovered how the enemy would react to any given series of events. It became possible for guerrillas to devise the most complicated ruses and stratagems with fair certainty that the Japanese would behave according to plan. Thus a guerrilla detachment could summon countrymen into the hills when a Japanese column advanced, station them in a broad semicircle, and set them to beating gongs and setting off firecrackers. The Japanese commander would halt, consider his exposed position, reason that there might well be a sizable force ahead of him, and call up reinforcements.

Meanwhile guerrillas would mine the road preparatory to attacking the supply columns when they passed by. When the reinforcements arrived, shaken and reduced in numbers and equipment, the guerrillas would retreat. The Japanese would follow, and once they were in full pursuit, half of the guerrillas would prepare an ambush in some narrow defile. Their companions, after drawing the enemy around the countryside until he was fatigued, would lead him into it.

The regular army adapted similar tactics to full-scale battles. Many times a Japanese attack, tipped by tanks and guns and covered by bombers, plunged into China's armies. The Chinese forces retreated, but their retreat swept them not before the enemy's main forces but to the flanks. A tank cannot be checked by a machine gun; rifles are no match for artillery; but if the tanks and guns are allowed to pass through, if they are countered by a steadily increasing defense in depth, if they are finally attacked from all sides in a manner different from that of previous battles, then tactics can serve as substitute for supplies. China retreated to conquer. At Shanghai, China learned the lesson of tactics. If the enemy's superiority in weapons be marked, frontal defense would only lose both cities and armies. Better to have the strength of sand than of steel. Just as sand absorbs the blow of hurtling shrapnel fragments, so a sidewise retreating army engulfs the thrust of mechanized units.

Battles, to be sure, do not have on the ground the simplicity they have on maps. No attack is so complex as a strategic withdrawal, while retreat to the enemy's flanks is far more involved than frontal falling back. If explanation be needed for the ability of the Chinese to undertake such complicated measures, it can be found in the two millennia of anarchistic co-operation behind the early battles of the China war. Besides, there was a tradition of military action that sounds singularly pacifistic to Westerners. Lao-tze put it thus:

The strategists have a saying:
> I dare not be a host, but rather a guest;
> I dare not advance an inch, but rather retreat a foot.

This is called marching without moving,
Rolling up one's sleeves without baring one's arms,
Capturing the enemy without confronting him,
Holding a weapon that is invisible.

There is no greater calamity than to underestimate the
  strength of your enemy.
For to underestimate the strength of your enemy is to
  lose your treasure.
Therefore, when opposing troops meet in battle, victory
  belongs to the aggrieved side.

The Japanese were by no means hoodwinked fools. They early began to develop stratagems of their own. They captured the booms that blocked the Yangtze River east of Hankow by a series of outflanking movements. Later in the war, in an effort to check Chinese infiltration, they tried to build up a system of mobile detachments operating on the flanks of their main forces, but in so doing they sacrificed some of the strength of massed firepower. They even modified their tactics of beeline drives toward objectives. To avoid being caught without supplies when their supply routes were attacked, they carried all they needed with them; but then they slowed their speed and weakened their striking power. They tried to bring up more men and more guns and more equipment to engulf the Chinese at all points, but the supply routes were long; traffic became snarled; and the Chinese forces exercised sufficient guerrilla control over rivers and roads to limit the shipment of material.

But the great Japanese handicap was inevitably psychological. The Chinese Army was composed of Chinese farmers, notorious individualists who had listened all their lives to storytellers reciting the details of old battles and old novels. The Japanese Army was composed of Japanese farmers, trained in obedience, who had absorbed a great deal of instruction about the glory of *Hakko Ichiu,* the honor of Yasukuni, and the prescribed methods of assembling and cleaning guns. Moreover, the Japanese, believers in aggressive attack, were accustomed to put most of their strength not into steady advances but into series of single blows. This predilection, common knowledge in the Chinese Army, was fitted in with Chinese tactics, and the Chinese regularly let the Japanese move their army—in itself an involved and tiring performance—almost all the way to an objective before launching counterattacks.[3]

In thus fighting Japan, China fell back on the inner resources of a long past at the very time that she was seeking to free herself of the compulsive grip of the past. It would seem, paradoxically, that traditionalism in this case actually encouraged reform. No one took to observing that Sun-tze had proved more valuable than Clausewitz. Such success as there was during the first phase of the war gave Chinese a new sense of confidence, a new respect and a new pride, a sense born of the country's being able to meet her own problems. China's survival seemed miraculous. Even in Europe, countries of advanced technical abilities were crumbling under the impact of aggression, but China was holding. The war lords, by and large, had stood firm. Wu Pei-fu, one of the campaigners of the twenties, was gaining respectability by refusing to kowtow to the Japanese in occupied Peking; Yen Hsi-shan and half a dozen others had submitted their armies to Central Government direction. Despite the loss of all of the modern cities, 80 per cent of the railway trackage, and almost all of the modern factories, China was not only still fighting but still checking the enemy. The government easily settled a crisis among rival factions in Szechwan that threatened to explode into fighting in the streets by insinuating

Chiang Kai-shek into the governorship of the province, and it kept fractious Yunnan from straying any distance from camp, even though it did not get that province entirely into camp. Special missions were sent to the tribespeople along the western and southwestern border, and they became unusually docile.

In this atmosphere of hope, the conflicts between new and traditional techniques eased. The war itself was a sort of amalgam of the old and the new—old tactics and new guns; old springs of emotion and new sorts of organization, from army squads to the Central Government itself; an old dislike for direction from above and a new feeling of unity. The new sense of confidence seemed likely to settle problems that the old sense of humiliation had not. In any case, the reform movement swelled during the first phase of the war. Tens of millions of persons had fled before the Japanese armies, many of them making their way, despite great privations, to distant West China. They brought with them the more modern habits of the East China cities, and many of them threw themselves into works of reform in an area where reform had theretofore touched only slightly. Credit co-operatives and manufacturing co-operatives were introduced—in 1939 they were big enough to take an order for five million army blankets—and small steel furnaces were put together. Mass education was preached and in many areas practiced. China was being brought closer together. The very fact that the war was conducted from a far-off and almost forgotten part of the country tended to swallow up the old North-South schism that had dogged China for some hundreds of years. New and younger officials were having their chance at a say in governing counties near the battle fronts; the older officials, too infirm or too cautious to operate near enemy lines, stayed close to Chungking (or in some cases turned traitor). In the politics of the country, these young men had as allies the younger army officers, whose older commanders were not spry enough to climb mountains. They were a cohesive group, graduates of Chiang's various officer schools, fiercely loyal to their Generalissimo, very serious about China's problems, very determined that China should become great.

These evidences of internal change occurred at a time of crisis far greater than was openly evident. China was strained for supplies. Until 1939 some materiel could be had from Germany, until 1941 some from Russia, who was having troubles of her own with Japan. But even with this help there were insufficient guns and bullets to go round; reserve stores were close to empty. The man-power problem was already acute; populous China, dependent upon all the people she had for tilling fields and transporting their products, could ill afford a big army that ate food instead of growing it, and ate it at the end of long supply lines that often required great trains of carriers. Furthermore, the government by 1940 was already paying for a good part of the war by printing currency. Cut off from the wealth of the East, the Ministry of Finance could do little but substitute inflation for taxation; and prices began to soar. The unity of the country, to be sure, was unbroken, but the political base of the government had undergone change; it lost not only the money of East China but the effectiveness of the East's support and got instead a mélange of West China war lords, local generals, rich gentry, and the bigger landlords, few of them over-friendly to reform. In addition, the united front with the Communists was uneasy; there had already been bloody incidents; Communist military activity had decreased and political activity had grown greatly. Communists took to denouncing Kuomintang conservatives, conservatives to denouncing the Communists. Finally, China was very obviously alone in the war; in the summer of 1940 she was cut off, except by air, from the outside world. She began to wonder how much longer she could hold out.

This wonder was confined to a very small group of government leaders in Chungking. It arose largely because of United States policy—or lack of policy—in the Pacific. This lack was to the Chinese the more remarkable in that the Pacific was one place where the United States had had a policy. It was not a positive policy of giving real aid in times of distress, but it was at least a policy of refraining from doing what the other powers did and of protesting when they did it. The American Minister to China between 1861 and 1867, Anson Burlingame, so impressed the Chinese Government by his efforts at sympathetic co-operation that they later made him their own first envoy to the Western powers. American policy so impressed scholar-statesman Tseng Kuofan, great official of the nineteenth century, that he remarked, "The American barbarians are not like the other barbarians; it seems they cherish no idea of trespassing on the sovereignty of China. They are good-natured and express their willingness to negotiate with China on the problems caused by other barbarians." It had long seemed only simple prudence for the United States to insist that the Asiatic arch stone be kept out of foreign hands, no matter whether the country was run by a collection of scholars, an empress dowager, a group of war lords, or a party of would-be democrats. The United States never belabored any Chinese government over problems of administration and reform, and in general acted the part of a man interested in the welfare of his neighbor but not interested in his neighbor's private business. This prudence found its final expression in the Nine-Power Treaty of 1922, engineered by Charles Evans Hughes, which agreed on the territorial, administrative, and political integrity of China—even though China, then lacking effective central government, was a battleground for contending war lords.[4] United States protests against the seizure of Manchuria in 1931 were the logical development of this policy, and the Stimson policy of nonrecognition of Japanese conquest was one of its fruits.

Now that a foreign power, Japan, was trying to seize China proper, Chinese government leaders watched the United States for new statements, new protests. None came for a long time.

In December 1937, the United States took its first step away from its old policy. The Japanese were in the first small phase of their big scheme of conquest and they were tormented by worry over how far the United States would let them go. They knew the gossip of Americans who were old China hands: that the China war and the China Government would fold by the next spring. But they remembered the knuckle drubbing, sharp although ineffective, that Henry L. Stimson had given them when they took over Manchuria in 1931.

The Japanese took pains to find out how far they could go. First, they demanded of the American Embassy in Nanking that the United States gunboat *Panay* be moved to a chosen spot to avoid possible accidents. Next, they followed the course of the vessel to its new anchorage, identified it from a patrol boat after it had been moored. Then, they attacked it from the air and sank it, together with two Standard Vacuum ships.

The Japanese found out what they wanted: the Americans did not intend to do anything about the war. Cordell Hull warmly advised the American public to keep its shirt on; it had shown small disposition to take it off. He promptly accepted Japanese regrets, and let three months pass before sending in the bill for damages. His concerns were the concerns of most Americans—how to keep everything American far far out of war's way. The State Department carefully instructed its consular and embassy personnel to run away from hostilities: to evacuate whenever necessary, and not to let Americans join up with either side. Claire Chennault, new air advisor to Chiang Kai-shek, was advised to get out of China and threatened with legal action if he did not. Such enthusiastic neutrality was highly encouraging to Japan.

This anxious unconcern set the pattern for the decade that followed. China was given little thought. The policy carefully built up by John Hay, Charles Evans Hughes, and Henry L. Stimson was quietly pushed aside at the first sign of its costing the United States any serious worry.

From the standpoint of timeless truth and its growth in the affairs of men, it may well have been that China should not have been aided and encouraged in violent resistance. It may have been that even the act of trying to repulse an invader would sow new seeds of evil that would before long yield a bitter harvest of new and more terrible dissensions and new and more terrible wars. It may have been that, given suitable encouragement, the Chinese, instead of waging a half-violent war, could have waged one that was nonviolent and thereby have prevented a bitter aftermath to the struggle with Japan. The psychological backgrounds of China, certainly, are not hostile to such nonviolence. But China had herself produced no Gandhi, and no American men of religion or men of politics had even broached a suggestion of nonviolence to the Chinese at a time when the suggestion would have been of some use. Clearly the State Department could make no such suggestion at all. Neither the Department nor the American people had the slightest conception of nonviolence as a weapon against aggression. Morals, strictly speaking, were not an element in policy.

But the position of the United States was defended in terms of morals. War, in the minds of the American people, was evil. From this proposition there was deduced the comforting idea that morality was served by keeping Americans out of war, regardless of what happened to anyone else. This was a counsel, clearly, not of facing moral issues, but of running away from trouble. Americans—and the State Department, which expressed their will—disliked war not out of a conviction that it violated the nature of truth and promised to destroy the peoples who took to it, but because it might affect their own tranquil night's sleep.

Even on the grounds of untroubled sleep, it would have been wise for Americans to concern themselves with China and to consider ways of putting out a fire before it became a conflagration that would rout everyone out of his bed. Clearly it was unwise to run away from the problem of war in the East altogether. But in the American mind the fact that the United States was running away was cloaked with the look of morality, and it was thus impossible to make United States policy responsive either to considerations of religious truth or to calculations of worldly wisdom.

Americans, of course, were warmly attached to China; the attachment was highly emotional. China was the brave little Belgium of World War II. It had unflinching Chiang Kai-shek, glamorous Madame Chiang. It was to be lauded in the press, aided by way of China Relief dinners, and prayed for in church. There was no question that China was angelic; even communist sympathizers, bemused by a united front, wrote rhapsodically about the Central Government. There was no question that Japan was diabolic. To be on the side of the angels without paying the costs of admission, the State Department fabricated a new and original policy, expressed by the term *moral* aid. That this produced nothing more than protests over the bombing of United States property and occasional protests over bombing of open cities, did not yet discourage the Chinese, who took it as a harbinger of aid to come.

In the summer of 1940, China hit her first great crisis. Government leaders had become discouraged in their hopes for American aid, moral aid being unnegotiable. The Japanese seized on the fall of France as a chance to start wangling their way into northern Indo-China and on the Battle of Britain as a chance to blackmail Churchill into closing the Burma Road. China was isolated. While Americans cheered Chinese resistance, Chinese officials calculated desperately the chances of their country's survival and whispered to each other their fears that an armistice might be necessary on the by-then advantageous terms Japan was offering. But Chiang refused to calculate. He would stake everything on the United States. The summer passed; there came the promise of American aid. The government caught its second wind, and the year 1941 was one of continued hope. Japan might represent a mountain, but the mountain was not going to get any bigger, and so long as they had tools in their hands, the Chinese were set to dig away at it. The great war slogan was not only "resistance" but "reconstruction," and the Chinese continued to look forward to a brighter postwar world.

United States diplomacy in those days still retained some of its traditional content. Ambassador Nelson T. Johnson sat with Chiang in the Generalissimo's house while bombs fell about them in Chungking. He brought promises of all aid short of war. Chiang made no demands, showed no disappointment. Johnson, amiable, scholarly, reticent about another country's business, no more discussed China with Chiang than Chiang discussed the United States with him. There was a sense of common aim and danger.

Token aid had already begun to arrive. Washington reacted emotionally to the puppet government of Wang Ching-wei in March 1940, and made Chungking a semipolitical loan of $20,000,000. When Japan occupied northern Indo-China in September, there was a remembrance of $25,000,000. In October Churchill reopened the Burma Road. The United States began to drop its policy of isolationist "morality" in favor of one of worldly wisdom. Early in 1941 there were enthusiastic special envoys from America. In March there was the promise of lend-lease to China. In the summer there was an embargo on steel and oil for Japan. It became clear that

Japan would either have to fight, give in, or slowly starve. Americans believed that the little men and women, playing at toy industries and toy battles, could not stand even a few days of really modern war.

Thereupon the Japanese Army moved into southern Indo-China, the first clear threat to countries other than China. Conversations went on with the Japanese in Washington; envoys Nomura and Kurusu suggested that the Japanese Army would move back into northern Indo-China if the freeze and the embargo were to be lifted. It became clear that only United States acquiescence in Japan's plan of conquest would remove the danger of war. At this juncture, representatives of Australia, Britain, China, and Holland—the A-B-C-D powers—were called together by the State Department to consider a suggestion for the American Army and Navy, who wanted three months more time for preparation against war, for a temporary *modus vivendi* with Japan. Australia alone agreed. China disagreed strongly. The suggestion was still in dispute when it became known to the State Department on November 25 that the Japanese Navy was moving southward in force from Formosa for an unknown destination. On November 26, Secretary of State Cordell Hull handed the Japanese envoys the United States decision: a general settlement only if Japan withdrew from China and Indo-China and recognized the Chiang government. Eleven days later Japan attacked the United States.[5]

9

Four-cornered War:
Japan and the United States

On DECEMBER 7, 1941, IMPERIAL JAPAN EXPLODED IN A dozen directions with all the fury of a volatile substance long pent-up and suddenly released. Bewildered, the West watched; stunned, the West began recasting battle plans. Aggression of such intensity was almost beyond British and American understanding, for Japan had of an instant committed almost her entire military strength and had chosen to proceed without sober military caution. The Japanese, for their part, cherished the glory of each day's advance and contemplated calmly—if they contemplated at all—the possibility of eventual defeat.

The assault took the form of an explosion, but the explosion proceeded from meticulous plans, logically based on tangible considerations of geography, economics, and standard military procedure. In part, these plans were the product of the experience of many years of war and intrigue in East Asia. But they were more than that; they were the product of constant thought about how to get the better of the Western powers. By the time the China war had gained momentum, the Japanese, making no secret of their aims, announced that their real enemies in the East were not yellow but white.

The direct sequel to the attack on the Marco Polo Bridge in North China was the attack on Pearl Harbor. For years the Japanese had been pointing out publicly that it was necessary to conquer China to conquer the world. The myth-clouded eyes of the West, like the guns of Singapore, were pointed in the wrong direction.

As early as 1930 the Japanese Army took political steps, beginning with the assassination of the relatively temperate Premier Hamaguchi. As early as 1931 it marched on Manchuria; and within a few years Japan began buying machinery suitable for redrilling destroyed oil wells. Long before November 1941, when the Japanese overlords dispatched their Pearl Harbor task force, they had built a war economy and had elaborated a philosophy of conquest. They had made *ronin* of the farmers and had drilled into their minds, already accustomed to the idea of acceptance, the traditional notions of bravery, and into their spirits, already attracted to glorious off-throws of restraint, the savage exhilaration of battle. The military had instructed raw peasants that they were gods and sons of gods. In the first year they taught the recruit loyalty: death rather than surrender. In the second year they taught him fury: murder before death. And they quoted the samurai story of the head that, when chopped off, jumped up and sank its teeth into the throat of the enemy. They insisted on "louding" exercises, wherein the lungs of recruits learned to bellow the cries of war. And they had sharpened their own tactical and strategic wits during more than four years of constant fighting in China. Experience in surf landings on hostile shores was provided by a series of raids on the China coast during 1940 and 1941, and maneuvers in Formosa and Hainan gave the troops familiarity with jungles.

In many ways, indeed, the logic of the war in the Pacific sprang from the logic of the war in China. For China had been in a position to outwit Japan. Japan now believed that

she was in a position to outwit the West. The very factors
that had led to stalemate from 1938 on in China appeared to
assure success against the Americans, the British, and the
Dutch. Japan's army, in relation to China's Oriental army,
appeared Western; but in relation to the armies of the great
Western powers, it too was Oriental. The limitations of her
economy forced her to choose between a few heavy weapons
and many light ones. In the main, she chose light ones: easy-
to-carry machine guns and mortars, comparatively small field
pieces, fragile but maneuverable fighter planes, and low-
caliber rifles. She even chose a lightweight sneaker instead
of a heavy boot. Light weapons, she reasoned, would give her
a great advantage in mobility and make it possible to play
tag with relatively immobile Western soldiers. Tactically,
Japan considered herself ready.

Psychologically she considered herself ready too. For more
than seventy years she had been learning from the West the
lessons of material might, and she had coupled them with
notions of obligation to a great emperor-god so completely
that she was overcome by an overpowering will to expand,
and by an equally overpowering sense of shame over the unreasonable treatment by other nations that appeared to stand
in her way. She felt herself strongly provoked.

In a particular sense, she was. Individual Western man in
his choices of egocentric estrangement from nature and from
his fellow man—choices which led to the outward manifestations of national wealth and national strength—was in a sense
as responsible for the war as any Japanese. The West was
not able, because of its own history, to teach Japan modernism without colliding with her. Western powers did not, of
course, stand physically in the way of Japan until 1941, when
it became obvious that she was threatening them, but Western ideas stirred wildly in minds still rooted in ancient
extremes and still chained to ancient duties. All obstacles,
thought the Japanese, must be overcome; all shame must be

swept away. The China war had begun in glory, but it had continued in perplexity and dishonor. Perplexity and dishonor could be relieved only by assault on the Western powers themselves.

For some time, however, the strategy of the assault was not clear to the Japanese. Attack on China was thought to be the prelude to attack on the Western powers, but China had refused—perfidiously, the Japanese fancied—to be conquered. Meanwhile the war in Europe produced attractive opportunities for action in the Pacific. Russia and Germany signed a pact; France fell; Britain was blitzed. But Japan did not attack. There was not one avenue to empire, but two. To conquer the world it was necessary to subdue China, but to subdue China it seemed necessary to conquer the world, at least to the extent of seizing the Anglo–American supply lines that fed Chinese armies. Japanese military policy from 1939 to 1941 veered repeatedly between agitation for more successful prosecution of the China war and demands for assaults elsewhere in the Pacific area, and cabinets were torn apart by the shifts of opinion. In the fall of 1941, however, it became clear that a military vacuum existed in the Pacific. The Japanese felt free to exploit it. They discounted American and British production, concluded that the great reaches of ocean would be more of a handicap to the British and Americans than the supply lines of China had been to them, and guessed that the United States would adopt a policy of Hitler first. Furthermore, they believed that the Americans were "insincere," that is, that they lacked spirit. By the autumn of 1941, the Japanese realized that the easiest way to finish China was to attack the great powers and to sever Chinese supply routes. The problem could be solved all at once. Once the Japanese realized this fact, the possibility of many wars became the reality of one war. They decided to strike.

It was not the sort of Western blow they had delivered at Shanghai in 1937. It depended on spreading confusion in every direction and then striking toward Singapore. It paid heavy dividends. Everywhere the Japanese found an almost perfect military vacuum. There were battles, but not a war; skirmishes, but not a campaign. The Japanese had as an ally Western weakness, miscalculation, and mistake. The United States had too little strength in the Philippines; the Dutch had too little in the Indies; the British had too little in Malaya and Burma. Java fell in part because its protecting fleet was not backed by adequate air support. Burma profited in no measurable degree by the experience of the areas that predeceased it. Although it was instantly clear that the first phase of the Japanese attack was aimed at Singapore, effective reinforcements never arrived; nor did they arrive in Burma. Only a few arrived in the Dutch East Indies. Of the three major Allied troop movements connected with the start of the war in the East, none was aimed at the actual line of Japanese advance. Six hundred thousand American soldiers were rushed to guard West Coast defenses, perhaps with the belief that since the unlikely had happened the impossible would happen next. Britain, at roughly the same time, began planning the occupation of Madagascar. And when Allied troops finally reached the Pacific theatre, they had to take defensive positions along the periphery of the battleground Japan had chosen. The Japanese saw their hopes made real; they had won their new empire at bargain prices. Their enemy was indeed "insincere," that is, he could not translate into action the will to act.

It was not only in her strategy but in her tactics that Japan appeared to dupe the West. Again and again she landed troops and outflanked British positions in Malaya by the same sort of maneuvers that she had used, years before, to outflank the booms in the Yangtze River. On land she infiltrated and encircled; she feinted in force in one sector and rushed flying columns through the lines in another. She marched down the Malay Peninsula in sixty-nine days. In

Burma the Japanese troops cut through the jungle, running by day through the Allied positions like salt through a sieve, and advancing at night in small columns. Everywhere the Allied front disintegrated and collapsed. The West undertook a revision of its old myths and reasoned that Japanese soldiers were unusual fighting men. Japan reasoned similarly: she saw her victory as the fruit of the Japanese spirit, Japanese "sincerity," and Japanese planned mobility.

But at the moment the Japanese seemed invincible, the Allies began to outfight them. In Burma, New Guinea, and Guadalcanal, Allied soldiers absorbed all the Japanese tricks and added some of their own. Groups of raiders were able to run loose behind the lines, tricking, confusing, and cutting off Japanese detachments, and at the same time upsetting supply lines and destroying food, fuel, and munition dumps. Japanese tactics no longer bewildered the troops, and before long, stalemate began throughout the Southwest Pacific. That stalemate was brief. Shortly after the Japanese advance ended, the Allied advance began.

By this time it was clear, to the Japanese as well as to the Allies, that the Western soldiers could outsmart the Japanese, and at the same time do what the Japanese had failed to do—shift a heavily equipped army as quickly as a lightly equipped one. Before the end of the second year of the Pacific War, the Japanese had ceased to regard enemy soldiers as confused weaklings and had begun to feel stirrings of respect for Western strategy, arms, and bulldozers.[1]

What was important to Japan's inward condition and to the nature of her cultural collision with the West was the method by which her high hopes were dashed down, the method by which her resources of matériel and spirit were overcome. The reason for her defeat—or at least what she took to be the reason—was bound to affect her mind sharply and deeply.

It is essential, therefore, to see enough of the war to suggest what that reason was.

Japan may have been embarrassed during the period of stalemate in the China war by what she thought was the heaviness of her equipment. In the Pacific she was embarrassed by its lightness, particularly since the superior mobility she hoped it would give her disappeared quickly. Her troops showed considerable tactical rigidity, even in land fighting. In New Guinea, for instance, they persisted in pushing attacks whose failure was evident soon after the beginning of action, and in launching new attacks on the basis of plans that already had failed. The plans themselves were often good; but the men showed little ability to improvise in the face of the unexpected. Furthermore, they failed to realize that encircling operations carried out in the midst of Allied troops left them encircled themselves—a fact of which Allied troops soon learned to take advantage.

The Japanese, to be sure, were not mistaken in many of the factors that encouraged their explosion throughout the Pacific. The main military effort of Britain and the United States was, as the Japanese had expected, directed against Germany. China was largely cut off from supplies. The length of United States supply lines did greatly increase the difficulties of Pacific operations and did considerably delay the development of United States striking power. And confusion, at times almost hopeless confusion, did hinder the initial Allied attempts to countermaneuver.

Yet in spite of all this, Allied operations in the Pacific increased in power. The United States, which carried the weight of the action, co-ordinated its land, sea, and air forces so that the three separate arms, despite divisions of command and even differences of opinion, generally functioned as a unit. In one area the forces feinted; in another they engaged the enemy and withdrew; in another they outflanked him by sudden troop landings and by naval maneuvers; and in still others they struck blows in patterns that effectively disorganized him. At the same time, safety was never sacrificed, as the Japanese had sacrificed it, to brilliance. No large Allied force, land, sea, or air, was committed to action under circumstances that did not promise fair certainty of success. Japan soon realized the worst: the enemy that could move fast was also heavily equipped with powerful concentrations of naval guns at sea, heavy artillery batteries on shore, huge fleets of planes in the sky, a mammoth supply system, and mountains of goods of all sorts. In various single operations United States forces, operating in a theatre half-way round the world from the main front in Europe, flung far more steel and explosive at the Japanese than the Japanese had used in their entire southward drive upon Singapore, Burma, and the Indies. Within ten weeks after capturing the island of Tarawa with heavy losses, United States forces were able to pound Kwajalein atoll with 14,000 tons of bombs and shells, and to drive ashore with relatively light losses. Two weeks later, they were able to seize Eniwetok and at about the same time to pound not only Ponape but also Japan's great naval base of Truk—and to keep up the pounding for two days, until not a single Japanese airplane could rise to attack.[2]

The measure of this power in part is the statistics of comparative losses: on Guadalcanal 40,500 Japanese casualties against 6,308 American; at Truk 201 Japanese planes to 17 American; in the Battle of Midway 14 Japanese warships to 2 American. In September and October of 1944 naval aircraft alone destroyed 2,594 Japanese planes.

In their conduct of the war, the Japanese labored under various weaknesses and various mismanagements. Behind their conduct, behind the war itself lay the habits of mind that made them decide what they did and carry out their decisions as they did. Nothing illustrates better the troubles in which these habits involved them than certain of the epi-

sodes of the Battle of the Philippines. Why they lost that battle is in a sense why they lost the war and why they started the
war. After the final fall of Manila, the battle for the Pacific
was irrevocably settled—no matter how long and how grimly
it might drag on. This finality came about because General
Douglas MacArthur, Third Fleet Commander William Halsey, and Seventh Fleet Commander Thomas Kinkaid turned
the island of Leyte into a death trap for Japanese troops, reinforcements, airplanes, transports, and escort destroyers—
and because during the first week of land warfare the Japanese committed most of their fleet in one of the biggest
engagements and one of the most lopsided defeats in naval
history. (They lost fifty-eight ships.)

What was cast was not a battle between the United States
command and a thin-faced Japanese field marshal named
Terauchi, known for his quick wits and his bald head. What
was cast was a battle between the men, the factories, and even
the histories and psychologies of two utterly different nations. Behind all the elements of MacArthur's command lay
the intangibles: not only the numbers of fighting men but
also their habits of mind; not only the numbers of guns and
planes and medicines and the countless other varied items of
supply, but also the mental and industrial organism built out
of everything that had happened to the United States in the
entire course of its history.

Nothing proved the strangeness of this strange battle more
forcefully than the dead bodies left on the battlefield at
Leyte: the Americans counted 74,261 Japanese corpses. The
American dead totaled 3,135. This astonishing ratio, 74–3,
could not be adequately explained by any of the rules by
which Western armies had ever fought: nothing so phe-
nomenally one-sided had happened in any campaign from
the Hundred Years' War to the battles of Napoleon, the frontal attacks at Gettysburg, the trench fights of World War I,
and the maneuvers in Europe of World War II. Why?

It was not a matter of courage: the Japanese fought savagely. It was not a matter of numbers: the Japanese sent in numerous reinforcements. It was not simply a matter of quantity of supplies: here Japanese equipment was plentiful. Terauchi had eleven armies and more than 800,000 men scattered under his command over the southern area of Japanese conquest, but he had not the intangible resources that MacArthur had. Behind him were not soldiers and sailors with an instinctive sense of machinery, gunnery, and maneuver; behind him were men who became rattled when chance interrupted carefully drawn plans. Behind him was an incompletely assimilated military tradition, whose fundamental ideas were foreign to his native culture—a storybook hodgepodge of imperial destinies and Japanese honor. The Japanese Army and the Navy were widely ignorant of the details of retreat—they had not studied the subject—and if retreat happened it had to be treated as something that had either not happened or had happened according to a nonexistent plan. When the men were fighting their hardest they were often fighting their poorest. They were fighting to preserve themselves from a peculiar form of Japanese disgrace, capture. They were fighting out of a frustrated national psychology that conceived of battlefield glory as a momentary fleeting reality—and that glory had been won three years before. They were trying to fight according to military rules and with military engines that had been created by the ancestors of their opponents. The consequence was inevitable. It was inevitable that even the chances of battle should play into American hands. In due time the consequence played itself out in almost freakish ways.

So far as United States action was concerned, the Battle of the Philippines followed the pattern already established in the Pacific. An immense quantity of matériel was put onto a vast fleet of ships and discharged with great force in maneuvers artfully planned and very astutely timed. The

United States plan was highly flexible. The whole attack was pushed forward a month and a half, and all the details of it altered when reports indicated reduced Japanese forces around the area of Leyte. When the attack finally erupted, it shot into the Japanese forces in a series of swift pincers movements, and after two months entrapped great numbers of men.

The Japanese response to the rapidly moving mountain of United States might was sometimes feeble, sometimes uncertain, occasionally bizarre, and at almost all times disastrous. The regular practice of the Japanese soldiery on the island of Leyte was not so much fighting the enemy as letting themselves be killed. The Japanese 16th Division, to be sure, received the message, "The Army has received the following order from His Majesty the Emperor: 'Enemy ground forces will be destroyed.' " But this call of duty only encouraged self-immolation.

Confronted by the weight and the force of the United States attack, the Japanese again and again sought opportunity for suicide rushes. At night troops regularly and madly charged United States combat teams bivouacked behind barbed wire; Americans had only to spray the wire with machine-gun fire to wipe out the attack. By day, the troops and their officers would regularly desert well-entrenched positions to run howling and screaming upon their enemy; Americans had only to hold fire until the rush had carried the Japanese within range close enough to annihilate them. Towards the end of the Leyte campaign, the Japanese even thought to block a final and victorious United States attack by means of a large but highly confused banzai paratroop attack. It was supposed to do no less than destroy all United States air bases, and it was to be followed by an attack by forces on the ground. But only two hundred to three hundred paratroopers reached the ground alive. Of one flight of fifty-one planes, eighteen were shot down. Some of the transports were lost and dropped their troops in remote areas. One plane flew over the airstrip at Dulag, dropped five paratroopers, and plunged into the sea. Another plane crashed two and a half miles north of the strip. Two planes attempted to land at the Tacloban strip; one was shot down, one crashed. The bulk of the force was dropped on the strips at Buri and San Pablo, which were being used only for liaison planes. At San Pablo the Japanese ran down the runway howling and shooting deliriously. One of them played a jew's harp, one a harmonica, another a horn as they charged. Other Japanese called out in English, "Hello, hello, where are your machine guns?" They burned two liaison planes, shot holes in a washstand, set fire to a jeep, and left an ammunition dump untouched. Everywhere the attack was quickly broken up and wiped out.

Banzai rushes were essentially convenient ways of discharging the obligation to live as if already dead and to die for the emperor. Suicide of this sort was the accepted manner of reacting either to an unfavorable military situation or to a breakdown of nerve. All it produced, essentially, was dead Japanese soldiers. The Japanese spirit insisted that all people preserve self-control in the face of disaster, whether flood, earthquake, bombing, or shelling; no noise, no matter how great the pain of mind or body. This article of honor cooped up emotion and made soldiers the more ready for suicide rushes after protracted shelling. The Japanese code also insisted on refusal to surrender, an insistence that made it impossible to drill security regulations into the heads of recruits. When a soldier was captured (usually because he was wounded and incapable of doing away with himself) he found himself in a situation for which he was entirely without preparation. By being a prisoner, he was no longer part of the Japanese spirit, and thus no longer Japanese; he had, in fact, acquired a new liege in the person of the country that captured him. Therefore it was only proper for him to spill out whatever he knew, however detrimental to the liege from whom he had just been cut off. It was proper for him to undertake translation, intelligence work, even propaganda broadcasting. Japanese prisoners were used generally through the Pacific area and definitely contributed to Allied victory.

Even the great naval battle of the Philippines turned out to be in essence a suicide rush. It was not, certainly, designed to be one; it was turned into one by Japanese fumbling and error. Three large Japanese fleets approached Leyte from different directions with the aim of wiping out the great concentration of merchant ships that carried the invading United States troops and matériel. One of these fleets let itself be caught in narrow waters to the south of Leyte by Admiral Kinkaid's Seventh Fleet; it was blown out of the water. Another of the fleets, made up largely of carriers, was crippled in the north by Admiral Halsey's Third Fleet. Since there were only two heavy United States naval forces in the area, and since each had been drawn away from Leyte, the third Japanese force should have had clear sailing. Between it and the ships and beaches at Leyte were Admiral C. A. F. Sprague's six jeep aircraft carriers (converted cargo ships, slow and unarmored), three destroyers, and five destroyer escorts. The heaviest gun was five inches. The Japanese fleet was made up of five battleships, eight cruisers, and thirteen destroyers. The battleships had sixteen-inch guns. Yet these ships allowed Sprague to lead them in a wild goose chase away from the beach at Leyte. They followed him around in the middle of a rain squall instead of blasting him when he came out of it, took hits from the United States destroyers and from the planes from the jeep carriers, and finally pumped three hundred salvos of the wrong type of shells into the United States ships, which they should have been able to sink at once. (The shells were set for armor plate; Sprague's ships were thin-skinned.) After almost three hours of unsuccessful engagement, the Japanese fled, possibly fearing the reappearance of elements of the main United States fleet. On its way home the force was decimated by air attack.[3]

Japan's failure in the field was matched by her failure at home. Her economy was not big enough for a really big war. It was not even enough for a really big empire. Abundance of empire, indeed, was one of Japan's problems. She had plenty of raw materials, for she had won access to areas that once supplied the world. But it is very possible to get sick from having to eat too much in too short a time, and Japan's predicament resulted in part from having been forced to bolt her empire too quickly. Her shipping was limited. If she gathered the full wealth of her empire, she could not supply her troops, in which case she lost the empire. If she supplied her troops, she could not exploit the empire, in which case she could not supply the troops protecting the empire. Soon her shipping began to disappear rapidly. As early as the fall of 1943 she was losing tonnage at the rate of 1,560,000 tons a year. In the single month of September 1944, she lost more than six hundred merchant vessels. By the end of the Battle of the Philippines she had not much more of a cargo fleet than she had a navy.

Japan ran into predicaments not only on the seas but in the factories. The underdeveloped industrial structure put a premium on man power and made it impossible for Japan, with a population greater than Germany's, to create an army one-half as large. The only way Japan could have freed more men for the army was to get more machines. But the only way to make those machines was to send more men into industry and fewer into the army. Strenuous efforts, to be sure, were made to get more men. Civilian industry and business were annihilated, but there still were not men enough. Quality of man power, furthermore, was even more of a problem than quantity. In large part Japanese industry was the product of foreign brains. "In the past," Koshiro Chiba, a shipbuilding official, frankly admitted, "our skills were mainly improved by study of equipment of advanced nations or study of models of foreign nations. But in wartime such studies are absolutely impossible." [4] There were well-trained Japanese engineers; but the industrial structure was weak in foremen and inventors. Neither fitted the feudal code, which discouraged initiative.

Pressures of ships, machines, and men did not of themselves produce economic crisis for Japan. The rate of attrition did. Seven hundred and forty-seven planes cannot be destroyed in one area in two weeks or 2,594 in another two months and be easily replaced. Cargo vessels, troop transports, and warships could not disappear at rates four times greater than shipbuilding capacity without straining the entire Japanese war apparatus. The apparatus gradually wore down. It wore down of itself; the rate of decrease of Japanese raw material stocks, the rate of decrease of production had started downward a considerable time before the B-29's started their mass raids; their downward curves appear to have been little influenced by actual bomb damage.[5] The economy itself simply wore out: roads, rail beds, streetcars, trains, houses, factory structures, machine tools.

The various economic predicaments meant that the Japanese Government had to hold the balances deftly between various ways of expending their war effort—raw materials or rifles, workers or soldiers, new plants or more planes. The success of the government's system of war organization was vital. Japan did not have the margin to muddle through. In this situation, Japan muddled and the balances were not deftly held. Too many people and too many offices sent out contradictory orders; too many kept competing for materials. There was never developed any effective over-all supervision of the economy. In the year 1943 alone, four entire departments were dropped out of the Cabinet; the central government tried to transfer certain functions to local government, but it also increased its machinery for controlling local government; the government reorganized itself drastically in the month of October; Tojo became Minister of Munitions as well as Prime Minister and War Minister; the government shortly after acquired a half interest in various key Mitsubishi and Sumitomo industries. Out of these changes there emerged the almost pathetic pronouncement that measures will be taken "with the view of establishing a system of responsibility for production."

The rulers of Japan had a common mind and a common aim, but in the everyday handling of matters of government they were not cohesive. The Army, to be sure, attempted to set up a monolithic structure whereby Japan was to be ruled in the forties in much the same way as Manchuria had been ruled in the thirties. There were totalitarian political organizations—the Imperial Rule Assistance Association and a more select group, the Imperial Rule Assistance Political Society—and the political parties, even the Black Dragon Society, went through the motions of dissolving in order to join them. But when a nation is exhorting itself to be traditional, it is difficult to become enthusiastic over innovations. The two groups began to split along lines of the old political parties. The Manchurian tail was never quite able to wag the Japanese dog. When Tojo was given greater economic control in 1943, industry had first to be appeased by the appointment of ten businessmen to a board of Cabinet advisors, each of whom held the Cabinet rank of *shinnin.* And in 1944 the Army had to give up Tojo altogether and agree to the appointment of six regular Cabinet officers of direct or indirect big-business affiliation. The Army even had to hand back the Greater East Asia Ministry, through which it ran foreign policy, to the Foreign Office.

Even within the two major groups of Japanese rulers there were groups and subgroups. Such Army men as Tojo, Itagaki, Sugiyama, Terauchi, Koiso, Araki, and Masaki—Japan's

top military leaders—were involved in a struggle for control
of military power by the cliques they were part of. Military
dissensions appeared openly at the highest levels of national
policy. For example, Sugiyama, then Chief of Staff, was selected as goat for the first major Japanese setback in the Marshalls and Gilberts and for the first American bombardment
of Truk. Tojo was selected as goat for the whole conduct of
the war up to the fall of Saipan. No sooner was he out than
Sugiyama appeared in the Cabinet as War Minister, and one
of his first official acts was to remove Tojo from the list of
active generals. During the war, government efficiency depended on merging the differences of rival groups and subgroups, but only success and mutual profit kept the coalition
harmonious. Crisis and failure did not bring them together.
While United States offensives pushed nearer, Japan was beset with conflicting counsels and contradictory off-stage directions.

If the armies were failing, the economy weakening, and the
government bickering, there was only one thing to fall back
on, *Yamato Damashii*—the spirit of Japan that, in the last
analysis, the Japanese had expected to win for them all along.
The battle was between "spirit" and crass materialism, and
it was inevitable that the "spirit" would win. Foreign Minister
Yosuke Matsuoka said, "The mission of the Yamato race is to
prevent the human race from becoming devilish, to rescue
it from destruction, and to lead it to the world of light. The
hidebound, material-minded civilization of the present generation has finally plunged the whole world into its present
welter of confusion. . . . Our Yamato race has a peerless
tradition. . . . Providence calls on Japan to undertake this
mission of delivering humanity from the impasse of modern
material civilization. Back to the Japanese spirit!"

This spirit, it was assumed, would triumph of itself,
whether by the operations of dead Japanese who had be-

come gods—an idea strong in the popular imagination—or
by the operations of a noble ethic directing the minds of soldiers and people. A writer in Japan's *Public Affairs* pointed
out that "As long as the Imperial Rescript upholds the racial
conviction that Japan is coeval with heaven and earth, America is doomed to be destroyed." This appeared to the Japanese mind to be an entirely correct proposition, not because
it bore logical analysis but because duty required belief in
anything uttered in the imperial name. The people of Japan
were troubled by the privations through which they had to
pass, but their minds were buoyed not by the idea that all
was going well but by the idea that everyone was doing his
duty. Hence the appeals to the people which at times went
so far as to underestimate Japan's position: "Enemy shipping can move where it will. The enemy can land wherever
they please due to their command of the sea and their gigan-
tic air force. On the other hand not even a single Japanese
ship can approach the decisive battle area. We have made
desperate attempts to rush ships through to the threatened
areas in the Southwest Pacific, but unfortunately all our ships
have been sent to the bottom. Our planes are outnumbered
ten to one. They have luxuries where we have not even
rice. . . ."

Such appeals did not upset or depress; they made the people work harder and think more controlled thoughts. Even
defeats produced little stir, they were atoned for by resigna-
tion: someone took responsibility; honor was saved, shame
defeated. What else was important?

The war began in an outburst of glory. A patriotic song
caught the mood of that brief moment:

> We will plant the rising sun flag dyed with our own
>   life blood on the farthest corners of the earth,
> In the far desert with its twinkling stars where the lion
>   roars beneath the trees.

We will drag the very crocodiles out of the Ganges,
      where it flows at the foot of the Himalayas.
The paper carp shall flutter high above the city of
      London.
Tomorrow Moscow and snowy Siberia shall be in our
      hands.
Our grandchildren shall raise a monument to us in a
      Chicago purged of gangsters.
And when our turn comes to cross the Styx,
      we will wrestle with the shades themselves.

The war ended on the eternal note of duty, restraint, frugality. No complaint; no regret; simple honor, simple obedience. The rulers of Japan knew that their defeat in war was complete by the end of the Battle of the Philippines. The capture of Okinawa only advanced the inevitable. The mass bombings only confused the mind without changing the heart. It was clear that there must be surrender, but where would come the formula that would make it possible to accept surrender as unconditional? For in the face of a new and terrible catalytic agent—Japan's first defeat in war—it was necessary to preserve the Yamato Damashii, the code of centuries past, more important to the Japanese mind than any factories, territories, or governments. The formula arrived at the same time as the atomic bomb. In the presence of the newest thing of science, there was put forth a great anachronism: the Japanese bowed and said, "Preserve the Emperor; we surrender."

To what causes did Japan lay her defeat? This was the great question put to her by the war, but at the end of war she was far too confused to answer it finally. Was it weakness in armed might or was it a weakness of inward reaction, a weakness of feudal response to a modern world?

Japan was defeated in fact by armed might employed by men of considerable personal flexibility and initiative. At war's end the Japanese could not have decided which factor seemed the more important. That decision could be reached only in terms of acquaintance with Allied military power near at hand—it could be decided, in short, only in terms of the way the Allies occupied Japan and the way they attempted to run it. How Japan then decided would determine the shape of her future. Psychologically, the Occupation became inevitably the most important part of the war.

10

Four-cornered War:
China and the United States

THE WAR IN THE ORIENT HAD FOUR CORNERS WITH EACH corner at one time or other at odds with all the others. Between 1941 and 1945 there was not simply one war; there were five. There were the big and dramatic battles between the United States and Japan, the slow, weary campaign between China and Japan, the brief hostilities between Russia and Japan, the undercover sniping between China and the partisans of Russia. In particular there was the United States cultural and political battle with China, which had as much to do with China's future as the war for the Pacific had to do with Japan's.

As 1942 began, the battle did not look like a battle at all. For some years the United States had been fond of China to the point of sentimentality, and for one year it had been planning and promising a great program of affectionate aid. Yet almost as soon as the United States and the Chinese Government became allies, the United States began to dislike the Chinese Government as emotionally as it once used to applaud it. The great opportunity for a cultural rapprochement became the occasion for a more severe cultural collision, shown on the one hand by a division of military counsel and on the other by a cooling-off of diplomatic relations.

The United States and Britain made one great moral gesture: the announcement of an end to the extraterritoriality system and treaty ports, to which Chinese reaction was immediate. The news reached Chungking on October 10, 1942, when the city had put on its best clothes and decked its streets with lanterns and green branches in honor of Chinese Independence Day. A crowd of 80,000 had gathered in the center of the city. Suddenly and unexpectedly Chiang Kai-shek appeared and, smiling, read the announcement. Great cheers came from the crowd; someone in the street proposed a resolution of thanks to the United States; it was greeted by another wave of cheers, and the motion was carried.

Wendell Willkie, who had been in Chungking that month, reported that in China there was a great reservoir of admiration and affection for the United States, but that the reservoir was leaking fast. He said that the United States had talked about production, but that some of the Allies had seen very few American arms.

The reservoir leaked fast. The trouble may have been too few supplies, but it was also too many advisors. The United States Government, on whom almost the entire responsibility for wartime East-West relations rested, in effect decided that what four-thousand-year-old China needed was an army of experts to put everything right: if you didn't know where to send a man, you sent him to China to make a survey. President Roosevelt looked at China—he said he knew all about it from his grandfather—and bespoke his enthusiastic confidence in getting the country put in order. The Burma Road became a place where a modern-day missionary met his friends. These men may not have been America's best missionaries, but they produced the biggest-scale intercultural contact in Chinese history.

Such an invasion was something new to United States policy in China, which had not before seen value in pointed discussion of the internal difficulties of a friendly country. Playing with the private affairs of foreign countries is impossible if one is not willing to back one's advice with material aid, regardless of cost. Unmindful of this impossibility, the United States took the position that a little American good sense and technical knowledge would make China a valuable ally of the United States and incidentally a strong and free country. Too polite for their own good, many Chinese did not object. But inevitably friction between China and the United States increased.

It increased not because of any lack of American good will. The army of experts made friendliness to China almost an article of faith. But very few of them were alive to what China was. They were the products of Western trends of thought which supposed the various peoples of the world to possess no inward, cultural, persistent characteristics, and which concluded that the characteristics of a people arose from guinea-pig reactions to quickly tangible and easily understood matters of climate, economics, politics, and what not. An acquaintance with the inward content of Chinese history and Chinese thought could not have been expected of most Americans in China: foreign policy, to the extent that its execution requires great numbers of men, cannot be conducted by persons of unusual flare or unusual training. It has to work through men of common general understanding and common general ideas. And common general ideas in the United States did not include awareness of the inexplicable psychological uniqueness of persons or of peoples.[1]

Consequently there was relatively little realization among Americans in China or in the State Department—even among those who spoke the Chinese language and had studied Chinese history—that China was in the midst of a cultural conflict of long duration between her own and Western ways of mind. There was little realization that China's problems arose out of inward reactions. Rather there was a belief that the outward problems could be settled by getting together all pertinent facts and forming sound unbiased conclusions from them.

The facts, of course, were myriad, and many of them were unconnected or even contradictory. But Americans had to draw conclusions from them and get on with their work. Yet in order to draw conclusions at all, they had to know which facts were important and which unimportant. This knowledge was impossible without a point of view. If facts be thought of as sand, some sort of filter had to be established to get only granules of the right size and shape. The filter, unfortunately, could be nothing other than myth. From it arose American conclusions about what was wrong in China and what ought to be done to right the wrong.

Thus the new advisors found many things in China to provoke fret. There were poverty and hardship, diseased bodies, and smelly night soil. Most farmers were illiterate; they were probably superstitious; they had no movies or radios and lived in flimsy houses with earthen floors. The American, not in anger but in sympathy, transferred to the Chinese all his notions of the good life of Main Street. The facts that filtered through the grid of his prejudices were evidences of his own hidden reactions. That these reactions took place in the storehouse of his subconscious mind only made his prejudices the stronger, for his subconscious mind was cluttered with a mass of notions about the good life— aims, principles, goals—all derived from his life as a child, youth, and adult in America. He was firmly convinced that he had no prejudices whatsoever, particularly the prejudice of blatant Americanism. Yet he had even imbibed distrust of such blatancy from his life as an American.

It was natural for him therefore to try to solve Chinese problems in terms of Western thought patterns. He advised big ideas, big plans, big industrial programs, or big governmental reorganizations. That his advice did not work did not force him to examine the advice itself. He examined rather the way the advice had been carried out by the Chinese Government, and he found himself nettled to find that it had not been carried out properly. He concluded that something fundamental must be wrong with a government that could let its people live in privation and superstition rather than follow carefully the advice that would make everything right.

The advice, indeed, was not followed. Ideas that were conceived in English had to be executed in Chinese, and Chinese culture could not speed up its powers of adaptation. But the only thing that seemed to explain this slowness to the American expert was the wickedness of the government of China. Besides, the more he looked at the government, the more he found to criticize: little democracy and something not a little like dictatorship. The sole legal party, the Kuomintang, had lost most of its enthusiasm for reform. The government was the same government that had been lauded as late as 1941, but it was now preoccupied with such basic questions as the problem of the survival of armies in the face of an enemy, and the problem of its own survival in the face of the maneuvers of semiautonomous generals and provincial groups. It was already so bankrupted by war that it could finance its armies only by printing money. It was worried over the Communists in the North, who had ceased spending their major effort against the Japanese, and who now seemed intent on splitting the whole of China.

A series of conclusions began to form in the minds of many Americans—journalists, political officers, and embassy men: namely, that a plot against the people existed on the part of the Chinese Government, which was hopelessly corrupt, not fighting the war, and not interested in fighting it. These Americans believed that the government was interested only in keeping and garnering strength against the Communists and in blockading them. The Americans noted that the Communists, on the other hand, talked for the people and against the landlords, that they were efficient in organization and noisy about democracy, that they did not emphasize ties to Russia, and that they were proposing a social order that appeared to rest on foundations some of which were highly attractive.

These observations were made within a particular mental climate, one favorable to large plans to win the war and secure the peace, one favorable to United States–Russian co-operation as the large plan of plans to prevent future wars. Furthermore, many thoughtful Americans had come to believe that outward organizations were the determining forces in human life, and that the efficiency of a system for organizing people was preferable to an absence of system in which people act as their own prime movers. Americans in general liked action; during the war the Russian nation and the Communist party of China were always doing something. The Communist party, furthermore, fitted its words to the stereotyped ideas of recent United States progressivism: centralized action, government controls, organization, efficiency, things lacking by and large in Central Government China. Besides, it seemed clear that the Central Government system, or lack of it, was wrong; therefore, the Communist system must be right. Although few Americans in China had any contact with the mass of the Chinese people, they liked them so well that they wanted them to be led and directed by the right system as opposed to the wrong system. Finally, none of the Americans was put in the position of attempting to direct the Communist party as they attempted to direct the Central Government.

These conclusions made a great stir in the United States. Broad charges, almost completely unsupported, were made in 1943 and 1944 not only by journalists writing for the public but by American officials talking privately: that the Chinese Government, thoroughly imperialistic, had designs on Indo-China and Korea; that no war plans could be mentioned to the Chinese army command because the plans would immediately be radioed to the Japanese (this despite the well-kept secret of the Doolittle raid on Tokyo); that the war was lost in China unless the United States withdrew recognition from the Central Government and gave it to the Communists; that Chiang Kai-shek's private life was irregular; and so on.

Such talk was not translated directly into official American policy, but it influenced it profoundly. The United States could hardly break with the government of an ally, but it could at least insist that the government form a coalition with its opposition. Active promotion of such a coalition became one of the chief ends of American activity in China—it became the new plan of plans to speed up the war, encourage reform, meet the needs of the people, and give hope for the future. All but a very few of the Americans in the field supported the plan warmly. Visiting experts and officers looked at the Communists in their capital city, Yenan, and were impressed by the slogans of production, co-operation, a progressive land tax, equitable rents and interest rates, and war against Japan. When the Communists hinted that they were simply a party devoted to the cause of reform and that they maintained an independent army simply to fight the Japanese and protect themselves against the sinister Kuomintang, the hint was quickly picked up. Many Americans in China and in the State Department at Washington were convinced that the Chinese Government had withdrawn its forces from the war with Japan in preparation for conflict with the Communist armies. Some of them believed that United States aid to the Central Government would have the unhappy effect of making it difficult to win the "agrarian" Communist group to friendship for the United States and making it possible that the friendship be given to Russia instead.

The growth of Russian Communism in China is a phenomenon that calls for discussion by itself. (See Chapter 11.) That phenomenon intruded itself so forcefully, however, into American relations with wartime China, that it calls for discussion as a part of the United States–Chinese cultural collision. It is doubtful, indeed, whether the sanguine views on the desirability of Chinese Communism and of the possibility of its friendship for the United States could have come about in the absence of myth. Myth made it possible to focus on certain facts and to overlook certain others. Among these overlooked facts (they were emphasized publicly by anti-Communists at the time, and they could have been verified at the time) were the following:

1. The cries of landlordism and of redistribution of the land was primarily a Communist technique of propaganda in China, not a serious approach to the prime problems of Chinese reform. The Communist charge was that some 80 per cent of the arable land in China was owned by 10 per cent of the people. Certain American experts considered the pattern of land ownership the crucial fact in recent Chinese history; the farmers, they indicated, were little better than peons; consequently, they warned, any industrialization in China, without distribution of the land to the people, would sit on a reactionary semifeudal base. These charges disagreed, however, with the best and most impartial statistics available, collected between 1929 and 1933 by a group of researchers directed by John Lossing Buck of the University of Nanking. The Buck survey indicated that of the total farm land in China, not 80 per cent was rented, as the Communists claimed, but 29 per cent. (United States figure, 44 per cent; Japanese figure, 46 per cent.) Two per cent of the Chinese

farmers were sharecroppers; of the United States farmers
9 per cent are Southern sharecroppers. Furthermore, average
rent from the land did not exceed the average rate of interest
on deposits in modern Chinese banks.[2]

It may be argued that tenancy increased in the decade following 1933, but it could hardly have doubled. The Buck
survey was made at a time when a long-term inflation of
prices had already tended to channel capital into land investment. Undoubtedly land reform was important in China; undoubtedly the landlords tended to control the better land;
undoubtedly there were serious local problems; undoubtedly
any move in China—or in any other country—toward a more
equal enjoyment of the world's wealth is highly to be approved. But to make a major social issue out of Chinese
land ownership was to do violence to reality, to hide other
reforms more urgently needed—increasing the productivity
of the land, introducing disease-resisting seeds, equalizing
the tax structure, and developing small industries, modern
banks, and credit co-operatives in the countryside, to name
only a few. And to describe Chinese farmers as peons is to
overlook the fact that most Chinese farmers considered themselves free men, and that the better-off Chinese families (who
divided their land among all their sons) not only rose from
the dirt but returned to it.

2. While the Communists approved publicly a policy of
coalition, particularly during the period of the united-front
line from 1937 to 1941, their actions did not suggest that coalition represented in any measure the limits of their aims. In
none of its statements, except those identifiably propagan-
distic, did the Chinese party suggest that it wished simply to
be one among a number of parties. Since 1927 it had been
an armed dynamic movement that had worked straightforwardly for control of all China. After 1937 it did not give up
its independent army. After 1942, it hoisted its price for co-

operating with the Central Government and showed no signs
of wanting to co-operate unless "co-operation" would put
it in control of such organs of the Chinese Government as
would make possible the eventual surrender by that government of its power. Furthermore, after 1941, no co-ordinated
support was given to Central Government military operations. Japanese advances helped the Communists rather than
hindered them: the Japanese subdued cities and communication networks and cut off the Central Government from
easy access to the unsubdued countryside, whereupon Communist forces moved in from the rear to organize the area politically and combine it into their own governmental system.

The Government troops supposedly encircling the Communists were not effectively encircling them: how account otherwise for the growth of territory the Communists held. These
Government forces were, in fact, holding positions taken at
the start of the war to hold the northwestern front against
Japanese attacks aimed at breaking through against Sian and
the railway to Hankow; true, any positions used to contain
the Japanese in North China served *de facto* to contain Communists, who were busy in the rural areas around and in
back of the Japanese garrisons. But strategic considerations
of the war against Japan required that Government troops
be stationed where they were, Communists or no. Similar
strategic considerations did not, however, require the Communists to shun not only major engagements but also
guerrilla assault on the supply and reinforcement lines of Japanese forces attacking Central Government troops. The Communist armies fought when they needed supplies, when one
of their government centers was threatened, or when the
Japanese made an infrequent raid into the countryside.

3. As for the supposed independence of the Chinese Communist party from Russia, the party publicly admitted to
dependence before the war and admitted to it privately during the war. Strength, the Communists kept insisting to one

another, came only from following the example of Russia. One of the great issues of Chinese Communism had for some time been the question of orthodoxy, and China had been one of the particular areas where the views of Stalin, Trotsky, and Zinoviev clashed. A regular succession of Moscow envoys had visited China to promote the strengthening of orthodoxy, among them Jacques Doriot and Gerhardt Eisler. The party had frequently been purged of heretics, among them its first head Chen Tu-hsiu, who was forced to resign in 1927, and his successor Li Li-san, deposed in 1931. Li Ta-chao, one of the party's founders, would probably have been purged had he not been shot by warlord Chang Tso-lin in 1927. On the basis of these facts it should have been difficult to ascribe independence from Russia to Mao Tse-tung, who, after all, came to power in the party over the expulsions and, in some cases, the assassinations of men whose minds resisted the blow-north-blow-south changings of the Russian Politburo. Indeed Mao adapted Chinese Communist strategy very exactly to these changings. In 1936, the united-front period, a time when the Russians were only too anxious to have someone else occupy Japan's attention, he argued for the release of Chiang Kai-shek from his Sian kidnappers. During the short period in which Russia sent supplies to the Government of China, he spent much of the party's effort fighting the Japanese and posted pictures of Chiang on the streets of the Communist capital of Yenan. The slowing down of his armies' efforts against Japan followed the nonaggression pact Russia signed with Japan in April 1941. As soon as Stalin began showing indifference to Chiang Kai-shek, which he did to American visitors as early as 1944, Mao spoke openly against Chiang; earlier he had taken down the pictures. Soviet Russia signed a second pact with Japan in 1944. Mao refused to sabotage a major Japanese offensive against China that came past his own front door a few months after the pact; he did not even attack Japanese supply lines.

Later on, when Russia began talking about United States imperialism, he mouthed the same words. Of his allegiances there was documentary record in his own writings. In *China's New Democracy,* written in 1940 and reprinted in Yenan in 1944, Mao insisted that Russian aid was indispensable to the success of the Chinese revolution, that in the future as in the past, success depended upon Russia, not upon Britain or the United States, and that if the San Min Chu I (the political testament of Sun Yat-sen) was not for an alliance with Russia, it was a reactionary San Min Chu I. Mao described the "new democracy" as "the dictatorship of the revolutionary classes," and explained further that there was to be no interval of "capitalist dictatorship," such as he said existed in Britain and the United States, separating the "new democracy" from the second stage of "proletarian revolution." In *The Chinese Revolution and the Communist Party of China,* written in November 1939, he said, "This new kind of New Democratic Revolution is part of the world proletariat socialist revolution, which resolutely fights against imperialism, i.e., international capitalism." To this frank statement there should be added a sentence from a resolution adopted by the Communist party in 1944: "The cooperation of the Chinese Communist Party with the U.S. is a temporary strategy."

What the United States position should have been in China is now a fruitless question. Nor is it fruitful to seek evidences of disloyalty to the United States amongst those Americans who believed in fact that landlordism was China's great evil, coalition its great cure, and Communist–United States cooperation its chief hope. There may well have been some Communist agents at work. But their work could not have had an important effect had there not been a widespread American ignorance of China and a widespread ignorance of the nature of communism. The climate of mind and emotion in which Americans worked in China was the important fact, and this climate encouraged myth. The myth grew constantly and at length became intertwined in practically every problem of joint United States–Chinese effort.

One of the chief problems was supply. Military goods came into China in insufficient quantity to meet the plans of any single commander.[3] In 1943 there began a three-way competition that put a great strain on the relations of Americans and Chinese. Early in 1942, Joseph Stilwell had been appointed Chief of Staff to Chiang Kai-shek at Chiang's own request—a position in which he gave counsel, took charge of lend-lease, but could not order around the Chinese armies. Stilwell, whom the Japanese had chased out of Burma in 1942, was training Chinese troops and hoping to drive a road back into China. Claire Chennault had been made Commanding General of the Fourteenth Air Force, successor to his early fighter squadron of Flying Tigers. Chennault was attacking Japanese coast and river shipping, supply centers, and troop concentrations. Stilwell believed that Chennault had spent great amounts of Burma Hump tonnage recklessly in stretching his forward air bases into East China. Chennault believed Stilwell was playing politics at the expense of the Chinese Army, which the air bases were supporting, and that he was wasting effort in northern Burma. For their part the Chinese supported Chennault and called vigorously, besides, for supplies and transport for their own troops, rotting all along the front.

In this situation a new factor appeared in the late spring of 1944: a group of B-29 bombers for use against the cities of Japan. The planes began eating up tremendous weights of bombs, gasoline, and spare parts. Competition intensified again. Chennault warned that he was short of bombs and ammunition in the face of probable Japanese attack through East China. Stilwell did not believe such an attack would develop, and the two men were at bitter odds when the fateful

summer of 1944 arrived. The Chinese were unhappy, particularly with Stilwell's control of lend-lease. Britain and
Russia, they said, handle their own supplies; why can't we?

The upshot of two and a half years of alliance was a confusion of command and practically no aid to the Chinese Army
itself, except that part of it fighting in Burma. The upshot
was also a coldness between most United States military men
and the Chinese Army. The two had little in common except
the enemy. An army that was loose in organization, that had
few supplies and practically no medical service, that had not
even watches to time attacks, and that kept on chattering
about the tactics of two thousand years before was no army
at all to men educated in the Western tradition.

While military relations were souring, so were diplomatic.
The Chinese were dismayed by the collapse of the prestige
of Western arms. Westerners were edgy; they found it difficult to admit that their own unpreparedness in Asia was the
cause of Japan's military success; they began to insist that
the Japanese had not been fighting in China during the last
four years but merely preparing; and the warm good will of
earlier days turned cold. A Chinese military mission took up
residence in Washington; no one came to visit it. Brigadier
General John Magruder, head of the first United States military mission in China, returned from Chungking to speak dis-
paragingly of Chinese military organization. When Chiang
offered to send extra divisions into Burma, London turned
him down. The State Department even proposed that Americans act as paymasters for the Chinese Army in administering
a five-hundred-million-dollar loan granted in 1942.

Not for the Chinese any longer the sop of good publicity.
The strain of war had led to increased corruption in China
and had weakened reform, and it was less easy to sing a song
of 1940. There were no longer any great air raids to catch
attention. Furthermore, the Communist party line on China

had changed—Russia's interest in keeping Japan busy with China disappeared when the United States came into the war—and changed with it were the reports of certain journalist sympathizers. As life in China became grayer and as prices went higher, Americans began talking about graft and disunity. They talked more feverishly about what they thought the Chinese thought. Truth was more and more made subsidiary to the will to believe and to the will not to believe.

In the critical summer of 1944, myth, increasingly the essence of the American reaction to China, almost became United States policy. It came closer to breaking China than had seven years of war.

By the time the first damp heat settled upon Chungking it was an article of faith among Americans that aid to the Central Government strengthened the wrong people—the conservatives. Many of the Chinese liberals tried to tell Americans that no aid was weakening them and buttressing the conservatives, who were saying that China had been thrown into turmoil without getting anything for it. But Americans by this time were discrediting some of the very group that admired them; prominent Chinese liberals who upheld the government were labelled reactionary. Furthermore, American denunciation of the government weakened the government in the eyes of other liberals, and it even pushed some of the more gullible toward the Communist party, upon which was the stamp of tacit United States approval, both through word of mouth and through the agency of the OWI, later to become the USIS, which reprinted stories from the United States and Chinese press that were either lukewarm toward the Chinese Government or cordial to the Chinese Communists. The Chinese Government, weak in public relations and over-polite in the face of Western criticism, found it difficult to counter such propaganda. Problems of war and criticisms by Americans combined to rob China of the great asset which she had developed during the first phase of war: self-confidence and hope.

Three groups of American actors took part in the crisis. First came the military. Chennault and Stilwell were not in agreement, but Stilwell had the say about where lend-lease should go; he was Chiang's Chief of Staff; he had the ear of Washington. And Stilwell was convinced that the Chinese war effort was tied up, not because of war exhaustion or lack of supplies, but because of anti-Communism. As early as 1942 he had wanted to arm Communists, march them across China, and put them into the fighting in Burma. Now he advocated arming the Communists and putting them and government forces under United States leadership.

The embassy, the second group, was headed by Clarence Gauss, who had come up in 1941 from Consul General at Shanghai to become Ambassador. He was working in accord with the prevalent State Department attitude—persuade Chiang that Chungking had to reach agreement with the Communists. He aimed to be very courteous and very correct, to be respected for frankness. He did not seek popularity with the Chinese Government: indeed, he took a low view of its ability to survive. The government itself paid more attention to the spate of such Washington-dispatched special envoys as Vice-President Henry Wallace.

The third group lived in one of the most bizarre journalistic institutions in the world, the Chungking Press Hostel, where they were housed by the Chinese Government and fed by the United States Army. This group, singularly cohesive, had abandoned an early uncritical faith in Chiang's government in favor of an admiration for the Chinese Communists. The journalists had the ability to do what no other Americans in China could do—talk out loud.

In the midst of a rising clamor against the government and in behalf of the Communists, the Japanese, reassured by a nonaggression pact with Russia in March 1944, moved ten divisions from Manchuria to the China front and launched an attack that cut through East China, overrunning Chennault's air bases and threatening at last to cut all China in two. Confusion and despair settled upon Chungking. The chief undertaking of Stilwell's staff was a publicly discussed plan for the evacuation of the city. Stilwell himself remained at the front in Burma. There were no general war plans at all. There were thirteen different and un-co-ordinated United States civilian and military intelligence agencies. Members of the United States embassy and members of the Chinese Government were on no better than formal speaking terms. The Chinese did not know American plans, did not know what supplies were available. In the field the Chinese armies were melting away.

In Washington, President Roosevelt suddenly took dismay at the thought of at least a million Japanese soldiers released from the battleground in China. He called in a military officer and personal representative, former Secretary of War Patrick J. Hurley, and dispatched him to Chungking along with Donald Nelson. His orders: to uphold the Central Government and keep its army in the field; to straighten out differences between querulous Stilwell and displeased Chiang.

Hurley had been in China in 1931 and had firm views on United States policy; he went to work with great energy. He disagreed with Ambassador Gauss, criticized him by cable to Roosevelt, began lecturing military officers, embassy officials, and newsmen. Simultaneously he began negotiations with Chiang, to whom he took an immediate liking, about the position of Stilwell. Chiang reluctantly agreed to make Stilwell field commander of all the armed forces in China. He agreed to the various attributes and authorities of the command. Hurley drew up a command chart, which both Stilwell and Chiang tentatively corrected and approved.

When the Stilwell storm broke one day late in September 1944, this document was under discussion at the Generalissimo's house in the mountains. Present were Chiang, T. V. Soong, Wang Shih-chieh, and other members of Chiang's Cabinet and staff. General Chu Shih-ming interpreted.

An orderly came into the room and spoke to Chiang.

Chiang said to Hurley that Stilwell was outside, that he had invited him in, but that Stilwell wished to see Hurley first.

Outside on the porch Stilwell handed Hurley a message for Chiang sent by Roosevelt from the second Quebec Conference through the War Department. It was in effect an ultimatum: United States aid would be withdrawn unless Chiang gave Stilwell exactly what Stilwell wanted.

Hurley said to Stilwell that he was on the point of obtaining what the President requested, and that an agreement even on details was at hand.

Stilwell said that the message must be delivered.

Hurley suggested that he himself explain the message to Chiang. The agreement otherwise might be disrupted.

Stilwell insisted that he was instructed to deliver the message in person.

The two men went back into the meeting. Stilwell announced that he had a message from the President of the United States to the President of China. He handed the message to General Chu.

In an effort to prevent public recital Hurley walked over to General Chu, about to start translating, and suggested that the Generalissimo would save time for himself and the meeting if he read the translation. Thereupon Hurley handed the translation to Chiang.

Chiang read the message. The muscles of his face tightened. He reached for his teacup and put the cover on top of it.

Stilwell asked whether that meant the meeting was closed.

Chiang's secretary said that the Generalissimo wished to be alone. Everyone moved out.

This quiet scene was the great political storm of 1944. In the next few days Hurley attempted to reconcile Chiang to Stilwell. After each conversation Hurley dispatched an *aide-mémoire* to Roosevelt, showing each to Stilwell before he sent it. Chiang was strongly resentful; the Americans, he said, wanted to take full command of the entire situation in China. He said emphatically that it was he who was running China.

On October 13, Stilwell proposed written concessions to iron out the impasse. Too late. Chiang had made up his mind. He angrily and dramatically refused to have anything more to do with Stilwell, no matter what the United States did. Anybody, he said, but not Stilwell.

Hurley went to his quarters to draft a cable to Roosevelt. In earlier cables he had indicated that the command was deadlocked at the top, with every army retreating, and that to break the deadlock he could not remove Chiang. He showed these cables to Stilwell, who said, "You're destroying me," and suggested alterations. At 2:00 A.M. Hurley wrote the final cable. The men, he said, are personally incompatible. The war is being lost. If the United States is defeated in China, all the angels in heaven swearing that Stilwell was right will have no effect on the verdict of history. He recommended Stilwell's withdrawal. At 6:00 A.M. he showed the cable to Stilwell. Stilwell was recalled.

China had meanwhile become ragged and worn out. She had served as a place for the United States to carry on a war, but she had been given little of the aid for want of which she had been fearful in 1940 of her own ability to carry on. The army lacked rifles, it lacked bullets—on some fronts there were only five bullets to a rifle and one rifle to three combat men. It even lacked spades to dig trenches and foxholes. It lacked trucks—there were only 6,000 in the country able to move,

the youngest of them 1941 models. Therefore it also lacked
food. To maintain life, the soldiers on many fronts had had
to turn themselves into farmers. Lacking food and transport,
the army lacked mobility. It lacked money; officers' salaries
were inadequate for families at home. Officer squeeze increased; soldier morale deteriorated. The army lacked doc-
tors, medicines. Above all it lacked arms, and to make up for
arms it had to maintain great numbers of men, whose cloth-
ing and feeding put extra burdens on a war-worn economy.

Inflation and malco-ordination were upsetting what little
production remained to China. Dealings between various
government ministries were disorganized. Steel production
was dropping toward zero; the National Resources Commission chairman could not produce because he could not get
customers at going prices; yet the Director of Ordnance was
operating arsenals at 50 per cent capacity because he could
not purchase steel; he could not get copper because inflation
had driven prices out of range of his budget. Because of an
ill-advised tax the Minister of Food was not getting enough
alcohol for the trucks that could be made to run. The trucks
that did get alcohol were tied up sometimes in carrying the
wrong things altogether, sometimes in carrying more of the
right things than modern production techniques required.
Private manufacturers were blocked from working capital
by inflation interest rates that ran from 65 to 150 per cent a
year.

Without inflation China could not have carried out a long
war; with it her strength to carry it out was measurably
sapped. The country suffered; individuals suffered: the intellectual who could not get enough rice; the farmer who could
not buy simple blue cotton for his clothes; the army officer or
the official who, unable to feed his family, resorted to graft;
the government man who found it necessary to hold six jobs
at once to get enough to eat. Production suffered: long-term
business operations like steel- or munitions-making became

difficult, a short-term operation like rice speculation became easy. Books and budgets and contracts and prices and financial standings went out of kilter.

The factors in the inflation were classic. The government, deprived of most of its peacetime revenues and confronted with wartime expenses, had to employ currency printing as, in effect, a tax on its people. Scarcity of goods was real: the coast of China had been blockaded for six years; China had lost her industrial cities and most of her transport; she had drained off men from productive work on farms and in cities into fighting, road building, and airport constructing. Demand for goods was just as real: savings in the Orient usually take the form of precious metal or goods or food; paper money flooding in from government expenditures put more money into more pockets; uncertainties as to the future forced liquid capital into goods; the expenditures of the United States Army and of United States soldiers, who changed their greenbacks into Chinese currency at open-market rates, were heavy; hoarding and profiteering, twin agents of inflation, were omnipresent. No OPA system could have been applied to China, a country loosely organized politically and economically, a country with probably the freest of the world's free markets. Here China's weakness proved a source of strength. Weak in machines to create army or civilian goods, weak in controls to keep prices at artificial levels, she was strong in her agricultural economy, which gave her great lasting power and resilience. No industrial country could have survived more than a few months of China's inflation.

Political deterioration, marked in the summer of 1944, increased in the autumn, chiefly because Chinese politics had changed so little during a time when military and economic affairs had changed a great deal. The government was subjected to political pressures more severe and was forced to effect political balances more tenuous than any in recent

years. Backward-looking elements in the Kuomintang kept
pushing measures repressive to reform, assembly, and free
speech; liberal voices in and out of the government and in
and out of the party seemed to be ineffective. It is a truism
that reform decreases whenever war begins, and that graft
increases. At the time of China's greatest wartime crisis, the
war had been going on for seven years. The surface of China,
for a long time poor and shabby, came to look poorer and
fuller of patches.

The government, struggling to keep up morale, attempted
to tighten internal censorship, but the attempt only made
criticism more vocal. Even in Chungking small merchants,
farmers, and artisans talked freely in teashops, while government men, professional people, and teachers talked not
only frankly but heatedly in their homes. At a meeting in
Chengtu, capital of Szechwan province, a leader of one of the
minor political parties, speaking with great freedom, cried
out, "You must talk and shout and talk and shout until you
get freedom to speak." The meeting was reported in detail
in a local newspaper; nobody was molested. The *Ta Kung
Pao* once published a sharply critical article on Chungking's
mishandling of Honan famine relief entitled, "I am looking
at Chungking, but I am thinking of Honan." The newspaper
was suppressed for three days. It appeared on the fourth day
with a lead article explaining its suppression and repeating
details of its criticism. Chinese newsmen, experienced government officials, and even moderate university professors began
more and more to be influenced by the argument that their
government was black and the Communist government
white. The educated groups were hardest hit by inflation.
They had little to eat, little to wear. Illness and malnutrition
made new and heavy inroads in the health of their families.
In universities the active tuberculosis rate increased sharply.
The persons who had once thought themselves the flower of
modern Chinese life began to feel that they were worse off

than weeds. They found themselves dependent upon the government for simple subsistence.

Suddenly, however, there came a quick resurgence. Perhaps the very violence of the Stilwell affair cleared the air. In any case, during the ten months following, there appeared some of the few bright spots of the ten cloudy years. The armies held and then began to grow in strength. In spring 1945, there were successes on the eastern front and for the first time in many months the straw-shod soldiers sang. The government proposed specific measures of reform; liberals found a stronger voice in its councils.[4] The official conduct of Chinese and Americans became measurably more cordial. The soon-forgotten reasons for this improvement were more aid and less advice.

The withdrawal of the B-29's freed needed supplies. More matériel and more airplanes to transport it were sent to China. Monthly tonnage over the Burma Hump began to mount. By June 1945, it hit 80,000 tons, in addition to 10,-000 tons over the road and 13,000 through the pipeline. It became possible to plan an autumn 1945 drive through South China into Canton.

As supplies went up, political advice went down. Lieutenant General Albert C. Wedemeyer, Chiang Kai-shek's new chief of staff, locked up the file of the Stilwell affair, declined to be informed about it, and refused to talk politics. He insisted that United States opposite numbers meet with Chinese opposite numbers, that there be no United States secrecy about materials and plans. The Chinese showed indications of willing co-operation. When Wedemeyer asked for reinforcements from government troops supposed to be encircling Communists in the North, the reinforcements were promptly dispatched.

Ambassador Hurley, meanwhile, spent more effort being friendly to the Chinese Government than in being critical.

He tried a one-man flyer at solving the Kuomintang-Communist schism, met rebuffs on both sides, and, although he took Stalin's word that the Communists lacked Moscow backing, thereafter refused to tolerate talk that the United States should arm the government's opponents. In fact, he started a campaign to reverse the entire trend of American opinion in China. In this campaign he had the advantage of a belief in traditional United States–China policy; he had the disadvantage of the entrenched body of prejudice of other Americans, to which he reacted with not a little fire. He summoned meetings of all United States agencies in China—military, economic, diplomatic, and intelligence—and lectured the assembled representatives until they became disgruntled, irate, and, in some cases, sincerely aghast. Few men were convinced. Some relapsed into silence—in Hurley's presence; others refused to agree and were promptly recalled.

But when the lid was clamped on in China, steam blew off at home. On their return to Washington from China, the men whom Hurley had got rid of insisted more strongly than ever on the correctness of their anti-Chiang views. And when Hurley returned for a visit to Washington in the winter of 1945, the late George Atcheson, Jr., then acting head of the embassy, dispatched an argument for arming the Communists with which every official of the embassy agreed. (The same George Atcheson, later transferred to Tokyo, responded to the direction of MacArthur with enthusiasm and ran interference for the Occupation against Communist maneuvers in Japan before he was lost in a plane in the Pacific.)

Things were more serene in Chungking during the winter of 1944–45, but they were considerably more troubled in Washington. Manchuria had suddenly become a great and secret word in the State, War, and Navy departments. The new China hands were in favor of an influence in Manchuria other than that of the government it belonged to. Even men once anxious to get supplies to China now thought complacently of Russian penetration into Manchuria: it would be a token of United States–Russian co-operation; it would encourage the Chinese to domestic reform. There was strong talk, *sotto voce,* from the State Department about forcing Chungking to terms with the Chinese Communists. There was wide agreement that China needed a Tito in the form of Communist leader Mao Tse-tung, instead of a Mihailovich in the form of Chiang Kai-shek. There was a new force in the world, experts pointed out, and the world's future depended on warm Russian-American co-operation.

Out of this atmosphere came the February 1945 secret agreement at Yalta between Stalin, Churchill, and Roosevelt. It pulled Russia into the Asiatic war, permanently detached Outer Mongolia from China, and gave to Russia rights she had seized in Manchuria before the Japanese seized them in 1904–1905: a pre-eminent interest in the port of Dairen and the two main Manchurian railways, and control of the naval base of Port Arthur. The agreement required China, not represented at the conference, to come to terms on these points with Russia.

This document not only upset a previous agreement at Cairo, which promised the return of Manchuria to China, but cut to pieces whatever was left of traditional United States policy in China, never before formally disowned. It was a trade of territory that did not belong to the United States for a Russian promise of participation in a war in which Russia would, in any case, be anxious to participate. A note from President Truman, containing its provisions, reached Chungking at the end of June 1945, and Foreign Minister T. V. Soong and, a little later, Foreign Minister Wang Shih-chieh went off to Moscow to the thankless job of negotiating a treaty they were already compelled to sign. They wrung out a few extra concessions, particularly a statement that Russia would recognize and support only the Central Government, but back home they could not mention the Yalta agreement aloud: Russia was not yet at war with Japan.[5]

This pill had just been forced down the Chinese throat when the American government produced still another. At the end of July, there was dispatched to Chungking for urgent consideration by Chiang a United States plan proposed by General Stilwell: the landing of the U.S. Tenth Army north of Shanghai, the supply of arms to a million Chinese Communists, the capture of Shanghai, and the clearing of the Yangtze Valley—a great coup for the Chinese Communists. As soon as Chiang saw the plan, he became enraged and refused to see any American for days.

Precisely at this turn General Wedemeyer found himself forced to consider the imminence of final victory. He took stock and immediately after V–J Day presented a set of proposals to Chiang. A vacuum existed; the question was who should fill it and how it should be filled. MacArthur's first general order had directed Wedemeyer to move Central Government troops for the re-occupation of Manchuria and North China and for the acceptance of the Japanese surrender. Wedemeyer added together all the elements in Manchuria: Russians, Chinese, Communists, plus Japanese arms. He saw the impossibility of filling the vacuum with forces available.

First he recommended that Chiang himself request a five-power guardianship by China, Britain, France, Russia, and the United States over Manchuria to prevent unilateral action on the part of any nation or group, the guardianship to end whenever the Central Government requested.

The Generalissimo did not accept the idea. For one thing, he had hopes that the Russians would stick to their word in the agreement reached on the basis of the Yalta decision: support of the Central Government. In particular, he realized the blow to China's prestige if she admitted the need for a guardianship.

Wedemeyer next recommended that seven American divisions be sent in to aid in the surrender. To this Chiang readily agreed. The idea was sent to the Joint Chiefs of Staff, who sent it to MacArthur. MacArthur, facing the entry into Japan, said No.

Thus ended one chance for a peaceful future for China. Soon Communists armed by the Russians with Japanese arms appeared throughout Manchuria.

11

Four-cornered War:
Russia and China

THE CULTURAL COLLISION OF RUSSIA AND CHINA BEGAN FAR later than the collision of China with Britain and the United States. There was indeed political collision in the last half of the nineteenth century, but the Russian way of thinking was scarcely known in China until 1920, and then almost altogether in its Communist form.

This way of thinking was, of course, far more complex than a simple faith in Marxism, as interpreted by Lenin in the course of an actual revolutionary situation and as amended by Stalin in the light of actual experience of government. It had tenacious roots in what Russians for many generations conceived their destiny to be, what they considered their political mission, what they believed their relationship to life, to truth. The nature of Communism as it affected China cannot be grasped without indicating these intertwining roots and without recalling certain familiar facts about Russian culture.

Outwardly, the great fact of Russian history has been expansion. During the history of her territorial growth, her

lands now expanded, now contracted, but ultimately increased. Relations with foreign powers consequently loomed
large in her national life. As early as the reign of Ivan the
Terrible, Russians found it advisable to purge an entire feudal class at home, the better to gird for war abroad. The
governments of the Czars were ridden by an almost path-
ological desire for national security and by a driving belief
that it was their function to accomplish the continuous and
glorious expansion of the state.

This state of mind was linked intimately with the fact of
frequent wars. The first half of the nineteenth century, for
instance, saw Russia as a participant in eleven: war with India, with Persia, the War of the Third Coalition with France,
war with Britain, with Turkey, with Sweden, the invasion by
Napoleon, a second war with Persia, a second war with Turkey, the taking-over of Poland, and the Crimean War. In
1914, as his price for fighting in World War I, Czar Nicholas
demanded territories roughly comparable to those Stalin
secured after victory in World War II.

When there was not the fact of war, there was the tool of
diplomatic intrigue. Consider Russia's maneuvers in the Far
East. In 1860 Russia was able to prod China into ceding the
Amursk region and the left bank of the Ussuri River, territories through which the Trans-Siberian Railway now runs
and in which Vladivostok is located. Some years later, attempts were made to push Japanese influence out of Korea;
interestingly, a Japanese proposal to set the thirty-eighth
parallel as a dividing line of influence was spurned. Between
February 1896 and February 1897, the Korean king actually
took up residence in the Russian embassy and followed Russian dictates in return for Russian planning of a Korean army,
which, the Koreans hoped, would protect the independence
of their country. The Russians, however, overreached themselves in their dictation. The Koreans turned to the Japanese

in order to weaken the Russian influence that they had attempted to use originally to weaken the Japanese, and the center of Czarist maneuver in the Far East thereupon shifted to northern parts of the Chinese empire.

At this time, Russia considered her sphere of interest in China to be not only such outlying provinces as Mongolia and Sinkiang and Manchuria itself, but also such provinces as Hopeh, Shansi, Shensi, and Kansu—all of China north of the Yellow River. After the Boxer Rebellion in 1900, she had almost complete control of Manchuria, and she was building the Chinese Eastern Railway as an avenue of quick access to Vladivostok and Harbin. This control, exercised in the face of British and American disapproval, at length produced umbrage from Japan. Russia attempted to force China to sign a treaty giving her all power in Manchuria, except for formal title, but China refused, and protest mounted from Japan, who considered Manchuria her particular preserve. Russian retreat seemed inevitable, and Russia in fact signed an agreement to remove her troops to northern Manchuria and agreed upon a timetable of departure. The first date of departure came and went; a second was set; it too passed without Russian withdrawal. In February 1904, Japan launched a war in which she was victorious in little more than a year. Defeated, Russia lost control of all Manchuria except its northern fringes; but a coalition with Japan followed the war with Japan, and Russia's power grew in Mongolia and in Sinkiang.

In part, this expansionism was the consequence of fear that some neighbor or other along Russia's stretched-out borders might rise to attack. Russia has indeed been given periodically to the fear that there is somebody under her bed, perhaps because she has been so much given to crawling under other people's beds. But the maneuvers of Czarist Russia in the Far East were hardly limited to those of a political Peeping Tom.

These were the outward events. The inner, more decisive events lay in the evolution of the Russian way of thinking. From the middle of the nineteenth century to the rise of the Soviet Revolution, a great and confused ferment of ideas possessed Russia. That this ferment was linked in some manner to the revolution that followed it is suggested, first of all, by the number of reasonably exact prophecies of it that were made many years before the revolution took place. In *The Possessed,* written between 1870 and 1872, Dostoyevsky described the psychological flavor of a small conspiracy of atheists and nihilists in a minor city that compares frighteningly with the actual cell activity of the Russian Revolution—or, for that matter, of revolutionary Russian Communist activity anywhere in the world today. His portraits of the leaders Stavrogin and Verhovensky, aside from the depth of inward conflict with which Dostoyevsky endowed them, are current portraits; so too are the portraits of the subordinates: Lyamshin, a sniveler ready to follow the loudest voice; Fedka, very certain of the correctness of the revolutionary views, completely tight-lipped when under arrest; Shatov, disillusioned by the party but caught and finally crushed in its coils; even Kirillov, an atheist who believes that he can kill God by killing himself.

Dostoyevsky drew a psychological likeness. The poet Lermontov, an active Slavophile during the early nineteenth century, wrote the following apocalyptical vision:

> The day will come, for Russia that dark day
> When the Czar's diadem will fall, and they,
> Rabble who loved him once, will love no more,
> And many will subsist on death and gore. . . .
> Dawn on the streams will shed a crimson light,
> And then will be revealed the Man of might
> Whom thou wilt know and thou wilt understand
> Wherefore a shining blade is in his hand.[1]

That prophecy could be so exact suggests that the inward complex of mind and emotion that made the Russian Revolution was in existence long before the fact of the revolution itself, and that it put upon the official theories and the outward actions of the Soviet régime certain characteristics that were bound to be of great importance when the new Russia came into contact with her neighbors. First, perhaps, of these characteristics was messianism. This sense of destiny, to which all but a very few of the vocal Russians of the nineteenth century gave witness, could be as mild as Dostoyevsky's warm feeling of the uniqueness of the Russian spirit, or it could be as extreme as the demand of certain Slavophiles that Russia should mother the world for the world's own good. It has been a characteristic of the Russians (wherein they are not unlike the Japanese) to talk far more than most other peoples of what it means to be a part of one's own country. The ideas of Hegel were warmly received in Russia essentially because they were ideas of the *vocation* of a people. What saves Russia saves the world.

But what saves Russia is ideas. The urge that has existed in many countries to go forth and do actual daily work against injustice existed in Russia only in rudimentary form; only infrequently did persons of liberal cast go out to visit the imprisoned or the victims of oppression. Rather they argued *ideas* that would rid Russia of oppression and injustice altogether. Russian thought during the last half of the nineteenth century is witness to a deep and unquestioned faith in the power of intellectualism. School boys, as Dostoyevsky pictured them, heatedly argued the nature of God and the universe. Their elders with few exceptions carried on the same argument. If only there were the right theory, the right dogma, the great idea, social salvation would inevitably follow.

For many intellectuals the great idea centered around the hope of freedom, the freedom of each individual within some sort of brotherhood, some community, some *sobornost* (literally togetherness) that would give the individual inward sustenance. Thus, Kropotkin's and Tolstoy's anarchism; thus, too, Dostoyevsky's profound understanding of the unique, suffering, tragic human being, called to assert the truth that he is a person. But along with the ideal of freedom there grew the exactly opposite ideal of the power of society. By its very abstract nature Russian thought was cut off from popular understanding. The people could not respond to the ideas of the intellectuals; they could not comprehend such abstractions; nineteenth-century Russian literature abounds with instances of miscomprehension by peasants of plans aimed at their improved well-being. The conclusion that emerged more and more from the confusion of ideas of prerevolutionary Russia was put very succinctly by Belinksy the philosopher: "People are so stupid that it is necessary to bring them to happiness by force."

To a group of intellectuals charged with a sense of mission and willing to bring people to happiness by force, the intellectualism of Karl Marx had immediate appeal. Indeed, one of Marx's first supporters anywhere in the world, was, somewhat to Marx's own annoyance, a squire from the steppes named Sazanov. The Marxian analysis, after all, is one which holds that the world moves and acts in accord with certain intellectual formulations, and that its historical progress must take place upon an intellectually charted map. Marx, furthermore, wanted men to be altruistic and free, so free that they would live in an anarchistic society, empty of external restraints, to which the individual would contribute according to his abilities and from which he would take according to his needs. To achieve this end, it was necessary to study society abstractly, to reduce the elements of which it is composed to formal concepts, and to discover which concept was valid in terms of an analysis of history. Marx's great concept, of course, was the determining power of the economic conditions of

life. Change economics, and you change men. Appeal to the
proletariat, convince it that it is being exploited, and it will
see that its selfish class interests require a struggle for material benefits, which, when the struggle is won, will make possible the disappearance of all classes.

The struggle was indeed won, although it was more a
struggle by a determined group of intellectuals than by a
group of proletarians, but the halcyon anarchistic society did
not result. This failure did not, however, provoke in Russia
any wide questioning of the basic rightness of the Marxian
idea. It was necessary in Soviet Russia to promote differences
in income and class in order to maintain the production of
goods and food necessary to social survival. It was necessary
to make stronger and stronger appeals to the interests of productive groups and to impose increasingly stronger powers of
government. In Russia, Marxism ended by justifying the imposition of more external controls on man than any of the
bourgeois social thinkers, so despised by Marx, had theretofore been called upon to defend. This imposition was defended by the Belinsky-like argument that it is permissible to
force people toward their own good.

The fact that the good might be some distance off was
not of great importance to the Soviet intellectuals. The good
life of Communism came to occupy a place in Russian thinking somewhat comparable to the idea of the second coming in
Christian theology. It was a long way off, but it was inevitable, and it made necessary in this here-and-now certain acts
of faith and certain methods of behavior. Marxism, in its Len-
inist-Stalinist form, presented Russian intellectuals with a
motive. It presented them also with one world-saving idea,
and made possible the erection of a single series of dogmas
behind which the nation could altogether be united.

Certain of these dogmas appear more Russian in coloration
than Marxist. The belief that the outside non-Russian world
is fated historically to fly at the throat of Russia whenever

possible is a belief to which the Czars were not strangers. The substance of the mutual recrimination of Stalin and Churchill in the twenties could, except for differences in language, have been uttered a hundred years earlier.

CHURCHILL: We have a band of cosmopolitan conspirators gathered from the underworlds of the great cities of Europe and America in despotic possession of still great resources.

STALIN: The Soviet people will never forget the violations, robberies, and military invasion which were inflicted on our country a few years ago by grace of English capitalists.

The historic inevitability of the victory of Russia's brand of faith was one which the nineteenth-century Slavophiles would not have shunned. The theory of the "inevitable contradictions" of the capitalist world, which would lead to the bloody exhaustion of all other powers, would have given comfort to imperial prime ministers. And, in somewhat more genteel speech, such a prime minister might have said with Lenin: "Against the advance of the predatory Germans, we utilized the equally predatory counterinterests of other imperialists. We resorted to maneuvering, dodging, falling back, which are obligatory in all wars. . . ." Even the war scares that have periodically seized Moscow, often without basis in fact, have a somewhat traditional character, as, for instance, the imagined crisis in 1927 that was to produce war any day with Britain or the fear of war with Japan in 1933. Such traditionalism, far from weakening Marxist dogma, simply gave it more strength.

Upon these dogmas Lenin and Stalin erected a remarkable superstructure. They provided Marxism with a system of organization and a method of strategy. The system of organization, resting on the introduction of an army of political agents, carefully graded by rank, into every element of social and economic life, made possible perhaps the most complete top-to-bottom control of a nation's life in modern times. The method of strategy made possible the extension of the Russian system elsewhere in the world. It included not only techniques of propaganda (in particular, the deliberate use of the lie, justified by reference to the Marxian denunciation of honesty as a bourgeois concept) but also techniques of warfare. Lenin, Trotsky, and Stalin were not only men who had fought an extensive civil war; they were also close students of military strategy.

After 1920, when Communist missionaries began bringing the new dogmas to the Chinese at the University of Peking, China appeared to move out of political collision with Russia at the same time that she moved into a cultural collision with her. The Soviet Government, which had formally renounced all ties with the past and which indeed believed that by breaking with the methods of Czarism it had become the one government genuinely concerned with the self-determination of peoples, made a total renunciation of any special interests in China in a declaration to the Peking Government on September 27, 1920:

> The Government of the RSFSR declares null and void all treaties concluded with China by the former Governments of Russia, renounces all seizure of Chinese territory and all Russian concessions in China, and restores to China, without compensation and forever, all that had been predatorily seized from her by the Tsar's Government and the Russian bourgeoisie. . . . All Russian citizens residing in China shall be subject to all the laws and regulations obtaining in the territory of the Chinese Republic and shall not enjoy any rights of extra-territoriality. The Government of the RSFSR renounces any payments by China as indemnity for the Boxer uprising.

This largesse resulted not simply from a devotion to theory expressed which was reflected also in promises to Persia and Afghanistan; it was also the consequence of a measured view of strategy for Communist success in Asia. Necessary to success, according to dogma, was conflict between the imperialist powers. And in 1920 Lenin was persuaded that war between the United States and Japan was at hand. Indeed, he even planned to grant substantial economic concessions to the United States to stir up conflict to hasten the war. He wrote:

America and Japan are on the eve of a war and there is no possibility of preventing this war, in which there will again be ten million killed and twenty million mutilated. [America and Japan] are going to spring at one another because Japan has quietly worked during the imperialist war and taken almost the whole of China, whose population is 400 million. . . . The American imperialists say, We are in favor of a republic, we are for democracy, but why did Japan steal from under our noses more than her share? [2]

This somewhat inaccurate piece of military intelligence was coupled with the notion that the countries of Asia were on the verge of an uprising against Britain. Furthermore, Russia's gift was not as free as it sounded. Soviet theoreticians made clear that self-determinism must always be sacrificed to what Stalin called "the right of the working class to its dictatorship." It was entirely correct, according to Soviet dogma, to be ready to take back what had been unconditionally given.

The involutions of Soviet policy were not at that time readily evident; they were indeed only beginning to be worked out in the Soviet Union itself. To Chinese intellectuals seeking some method of national salvation, the one great fact was Russia's renunciation of special interests or privileges in China. Furthermore, Russian intellectualism was not without appeal to Chinese intellectuals, alert to the traditional place of the scholar in society. Much of the discussion of how China should come to terms with the West was carried

220 Collision of EAST and WEST

on in terms scarcely less abstract than the discussions which preceded the Russian Revolution. While the Marxian analysis was antithetical to either the Taoist or Confucian strains in the Chinese mind, many intellectuals welcomed such antithesis; they were impressed alike by the final Marxist aims of a free society in which the individual, not the Confucianist family, would be the unit of worth, and by the Marxist provision of an actual method by which social change could be brought about.

When the Chinese party was founded in 1921 its leaders and members were intellectuals, some of them from the University of Peking, some students returned from France. Its first head was Chen Tu-hsiu, once Dean of the Faculty of Chinese Letters at Peking; one of its prime movers was Li Ta-chao, librarian of the University. A figure of importance was Li Li-san who had founded a Communist group among Chinese students in France, one of whom was Chou En-lai, later chief publicity man for the Communists in Chungking, now Foreign Minister. Among the members was Mao Tse-tung, who was studying at Peking and working as a clerk. As a liberal, he impressed his fellow liberals as being very able, very serious, very cunning; not a little unscrupulous, and very well versed in the psychological reactions of both the Chinese rich and the Chinese poor. He came from a poor family, but married the daughter of a scholar who recognized his ability. At the time of his conversion to Communism, he was a vegetarian and a disciple of Tolstoy.

Upon this group and upon the Comintern fell the chore of determining how Marxist-Leninist principles could be used to father a specific strategy of revolution in China. Until 1924, little was accomplished. The Chinese masses themselves showed no disposition to act according to Marxist-Leninist principles. But in 1923 Dr. Sun Yat-sen began negotiating with the Comintern for assistance in his nationalist revolution, and in 1924 the members of the Communist party were

admitted into the Kuomintang. The basis of accord between
the Soviet representative, A. Joffe, and Dr. Sun emphasized
nationalism. Their joint statement read:

> Dr. Sun Yat-sen holds that the Communist order or even the
> Soviet system cannot actually be introduced into China because
> there do not exist here the conditions for the successful estab-
> lishment of either Communism or Sovietism. This view is entirely
> shared by Mr. Joffe, who is further of the opinion that China's
> paramount and most pressing problem is to achieve national uni-
> fication and attain full national independence, and regarding this
> task he has assured Dr. Sun Yat-sen that China has the warmest
> sympathy of the Russian people and can count on the support of
> Russia.[3]

Precisely what goals the Comintern and the Chinese Communist party were pursuing in this alliance is not clear. The
aim may have been a progressive infiltration into the Kuomintang and a taking-over of the nationalist revolution from
within. Between 1924 and 1927, the Communists were indeed increasingly influential in the high places of the nationalist movement; they were using Russian funds to stir up
nationalist agitation and antiforeign violence in the large
cities. On the side, they became leaders in aggressive trade
unionism. Dr. Hu Shih has suggested that, given the emphasis of Joffe on nationalism and the zealousness of Chinese
Communists in stirring up antiforeign, particularly anti-
British opinion, the Comintern may have hoped to provoke
intervention by the great powers and thus provoke the imperialist war, necessary according to dogma for the final victory
of a Communist revolution. Indeed, intervention almost became a fact after the March 1927 attacks on foreigners, foreign property, and consulates in Nanking. (The men in
charge during the attacks, General Chen Chien and Political
Commissar Lin Tsu-han, are now prominent Communists.)
The early coalition of Kuomintang and Comintern oc-

curred at a time when Stalin, at work on an over-all strategy which made Russia the base for world-wide revolution, was at increasing odds with Trotsky. Stalin may have seen possible victory in China resulting from working from within the Kuomintang, or he may, at the same time, have seen the opportunity for an imperialist war which, by being fought far away from Russia, would have weakened Russia's enemies whilst it prepared the ground for revolution. Trotsky was not of this opinion. He voted against co-operation with the Kuomintang and called it co-operation with the bourgeoisie and an obstacle to the rise of a purely Marxist workers' party. Trotsky wished instead for immediate uprisings in such places as Shanghai and Canton, the creation of soviets, and the forming of a Red army. Co-operation with the Kuomintang continued, but Moscow's instructions to the Chinese party became increasingly confused; one set of cables would call for easing agitation against landlords, while another would call for arming workers and peasants in view of "the treacherous and reactionary policy of the rightist members of the Kuomintang." [4]

Events did not necessarily prove either Trotsky right or Stalin wrong. But the coalition in China was abruptly and bloodily terminated, and not on Communist initiative. Chiang Kai-shek, successor to Sun Yat-sen as head of the Kuomintang, was already suspicious of the Communists, against whom he had already effected one minor and unnoticed purge. On April 12, 1927, Chiang took the occasion of the antiforeign attacks in Nanking to begin general and violent suppression of Communists in Shanghai, whether Chinese or Russian. Promptly thereafter he set up a government in Nanking and announced that the government in Hankow, where Chinese Communist leaders and various members of the Kuomintang less critical of them were grouped, would have to come to terms. Shortly the Hankow government did fall apart; the Kuomintang members of it did come to terms.[5]

This turn of events became the occasion for a blast from Trotsky against Stalin's policy of Communist-Kuomintang coalition and contributed to the downfall of Trotsky himself. It became also the occasion for a fresh view of Communist strategy in China. The immediate call of the Comintern was for a general revolution under the slogan, "All power to the peasant unions and rural committees," of which the only practical consequences were a few strikes, an uprising in Canton that was put down in three days, and a series of abortive attacks on cities by troops who had remained loyal to the Communists. These events resulted, it would appear, from Stalin's maneuvering of Zinoviev, head of the Comintern, into ordering actions whose failure would ruin Zinoviev's own influence.

Russian advisor Borodin went back to Russia, where he was labeled a deviator and put to unimportant duties. Chen Tu-hsiu was removed as head of the Chinese party (he was finally read out of it in 1931). Denounced by Russia for reasons they knew not, many Communists either joined the Communist opposition or drifted over to the Kuomintang. The reason the Comintern gave alike for the purges and the defections was "error" on the part of the Chinese party: inconsistent political line, lack of revolutionary zeal, opportunism, matters for which the Comintern was itself responsible. A deeper reason lay in the fact that many members of the Chinese Communist party were more concerned with what they thought to be the truth of Marxist Communism than with what they thought to be sound Russian policy. For some years after 1927 the party itself was shot through with Trotskyism. In 1930 Li Li-san, then leader of the party, was even ready to criticize the Comintern publicly: "As soon as the Chinese Communists seize Hankow, we will be able to speak a different language to the Comintern. . . . Loyalty to the Comintern is one thing; loyalty to the Chinese Revolution is something else." The Comintern declared that "Comrade Li Li-san has permitted himself to toy with the worn-out theories of all the rightist and leftist renegades of Communism," and attacked him for failure in his attempt to capture the city of Changsha. Three months later, Li was taken off the Central Committee of the Chinese party and forced to leave China for Moscow.[6]

In the Soviet Union itself, the grafting of Marxist branches onto Russian roots was not an easy process; it was one during which most of the early Communists died, and one in which many years were required to work out an over-all revolutionary strategy. In China the process was even more difficult, for the Chinese party was not grafting branches onto Chinese roots but transplanting whole Russian trees, not essentially adapted to the Chinese cultural soil. The culture of Russia may have been twisted, even distorted in one direction by Communism's rise to power. But Communism in Russia took to itself many traditional ideas, and the Russian spirit, one imagines, is still inwardly embroiled in the old issues of the individual and the togetherness, the final nature of the universe, man in the form of God and God in the form of man, however different the images in which the old issues are now conceived and expressed.

In China, however, Communists had to work out a revolutionary strategy in a terminology that was closer to that of Czarist Russia than it was to that of Republican China. This process went on particularly during the years between 1930 and 1934, which marked Mao Tse-tung's rise to power within the Chinese party. Mao's strategy—responsible for his rise—centered around the nourishing of a Red army; it called for agrarian revolution, then concentrated largely in the province of Kiangsi, and aimed against landlords and rich peasants, from whose demise came a considerable part of the party's money and supplies. Mao's later accounts of the history of this period, detailed as concerns army stratagems, have the same fuzziness as the Comintern's as regards over-all policy. Of the 1927 debacle, he wrote: "The capitulators in our Party's leading organs voluntarily abandoned leadership of the masses of peasants, petty bourgeoisie, middle bourgeoisie, and especially abandoned leadership over the armed forces causing the revolution to fail." He righteously condemned using "ultra-Left, erroneous policies toward the petty bourgeois and middle bourgeois elements as our Party did in the period from 1931 to 1934. . . ." On the other hand, during the period following the breakup at Hankow, Mao acted with an aggressiveness that apparently displeased the Chinese Central Committee, who criticized Mao for activity against the rich peasants, and pleased the Comintern, who criticized the Central Committee and bade them follow the injunction, "Confiscate the landowners' lands, arm the peasants, create soviets." [7]

By October 1934 Central Government forces were able to dislodge from central China the Chinese Communist armies under Mao and General Chu Teh and send them off on a remarkable six-thousand-mile long march to the neighborhood of Yenan in the northwest, where the armies arrived in October of 1935. Although fewer than twenty thousand were reported to have survived, a strategy of conquest had at last been set. The broad strategy of this conquest was simple; Stalin summed it up in one sentence which Mao quoted in *The Chinese Revolution and the Chinese Communist Party:* "The special characteristic of the Chinese revolution lies in the fact that it is an armed people fighting an armed counter-revolution." In other words, the Chinese Red Army is the basic element of Communist strategy in China, and the expansion of territory through its operations is the key to success. This strategy had been tested during the years in Central China; after 1934 it was far more important than any particular doctrines about the roles of the urban pro-

letariat or the rich peasants or the so-called middle capitalists, doctrines which could be tailored to suit immediate
propaganda needs.

Mao wrote that

> . . . because of the unbalanced nature of Chinese economic
> development (the rural economy is not entirely dependent upon
> the urban economy), and because of the vastness of China's ter-
> ritory (there are immense spaces for the revolutionary forces to
> fall back on), and because of the disunity and conflict existing
> within the anti-revolutionary camp, and because the main force
> of the Chinese revolution, which is the peasantry, is under the
> leadership of the Communist party: so there arises the great
> possibility that the Chinese revolution will succeed first and fore-
> most in the countryside. . . . It is incorrect to ignore the prin-
> ciple of making and establishing revolutionary bases in the
> countryside, and it is equally incorrect to ignore the need for
> strenuous work among the peasants, and the need for guerrilla
> wars.[8]

To establish such a strategy within the framework of a
system of dogma that emphasizes the dissatisfaction of an
urban proletariat as the prime mover of revolutionary success is no small undertaking. It would seem unwise to
imagine, however, that the strategy was Chinese in the sense
that it was an indigenous response to Chinese conditions. It
was rather an application to the particular situation in China
of the most suitable stratagems that could be found within
the theory and practice of the Russian form of Marxism. The
civil war in Russia, for instance, provided an example in the
widespread use in a Red army of peasant troops.

Not only was there a settled over-all strategy by 1935;
there was also an established system of tactics, well described
by four Red army slogans:

> When the enemy advances, we retreat!
> When the enemy halts and encamps, we trouble them!

When the enemy seeks to avoid a battle, we attack!
When the enemy retreats, we pursue!

These tactics were not unlike those used on a larger scale during the Sino–Japanese War by the armies of the Central Government after the abandonment of Western-style positional warfare. Not unlike the tactics described by Sun-tze or by Lao-tze, these tactics represent the genuinely Chinese element in Chinese Communism. (They represent, too, it might be observed, the diabolic use to which great and dynamic philosophies of life are occasionally put.) It is significant that they fit, however, the concealment strategy of Lenin, the civil-war ruses of the Red Army in Russia, and even the tactics employed by Russia, a country of spaces vast enough to match China's, in fighting against Napoleon in 1812. Dr. Hu Shih reports, moreover, "that leading Chinese Communists attributed the success of the Long March to what Stalin had taught as 'the strategy of retreat,'" a matter which Stalin had taken up at some length in *Problems of Leninism,* wherein he laid down tactical principles very comparable to the slogans of the Chinese Red Army.[9]

After the Sian kidnapping of Chiang Kai-shek in 1936, the look and the slogans of the Chinese Communists underwent change. In September 1931, they had denounced suggestions of "a united front against the external enemy," namely Japan, as "ridiculous, absurd, and lying inventions," [10] although they called for resistance to Japan. Up to the time of the Sian kidnapping, the Chinese Communists had not yet been able to fit into the united-front line that was being advocated by Moscow, there being no party in China they could unite with. The Sian kidnapping, however, did afford a basis for unity of a sort. Chiang had been kidnapped by Chang Hsueh-liang, son of the old Manchurian marshal Chang Tso-lin, and by Yang Hu-cheng, generals who were supposed to

be getting rid of the Communists once and for all, but who
were in fact working out a so-called "United Anti-Japanese
Army," which was to include the Red Army. Two facts became clear during the kidnapping: first, that Chiang's anti-
Japanese sentiments were stronger than his public diplomacy
had led anyone to suspect; second, that Moscow's pro-Chiang
views were as strong as anyone might have suspected in the
light of the friction Russia was experiencing with Japan. It
appears evident that the Communist delegates who were present in Yenan argued for Chiang's release; it appears evident
also that Moscow ordered them so to argue. A small "United
Anti-Japanese Army" could not have involved the Japanese
Army to a degree sufficient to reduce the danger Japan presented to Russia. In Moscow, *Izvestia* denounced the kidnapping the day after it occurred.[11]

The Chinese party's attitude to its switch-about was set
down in *The Tactical Line of the Chinese Communist Party*,
written by Chang Hao:

When the December, 1935, Resolution was issued, the policy
was "Fight Chiang and Resist Japan." Now it is "Ally with
Chiang and Resist Japan." If we want to resist Japan, we must
unite with Chiang. If the Communist Party wants to secure
greater victories, it must fight Japan.

In the Sian Affair, Chang Hsueh-liang and Yang Hu-cheng and
the other militarists were really more interested in opposition to
Chiang than in resistance to Japan. The Communist Party saw
this clearly and used all its power to advocate a peaceful settlement. . . . Therefore our tactical line was: "Peaceful settlement
of the Sian Affair!" and "End all civil wars!"

Because the Chinese Communist Party is an International Party
and the directives we received from the Third International also
said that a peaceful settlement would be right and profitable, it
was decided that for the greater benefits of the future, we must
have peace.[12]

One of the consequences of the switch-about was that the Chinese Communist Party agreed not to call itself Communist and that it united its army with the Central Government *in name*. This change in nomenclature confused various foreign observers, among them the British Ambassador to China, Sir Archibald Clark Kerr, who began to see in the Communists an agrarian party led by men not unlike the British Labour pioneer, Keir Hardie.[13] Of more important consequence, however, was the maintenance of an independent Red army and the expansion of it whenever possible. Fundamental Communist strategy was never altered. This strategy, in fact, became all-important after American entry into the war, when danger to Russia from the Japanese forces in Manchuria considerably lessened. Communist power in China grew. In April 1945, Mao told the Seventh Congress of the Communist Party that ". . . our regular army has already expanded to 910,000 men and our people's militia force has increased beyond 2,200,000 men." As for the area controlled by the Communists, Mao said that it covered areas ". . . extending into nineteen provinces and containing 95,500,000 people." [14] The upshot of the united front with the Central Government was the conquest of large areas of Central Government territory and their subjection to rigid and effective Communist political and economic control.

Communist strategy in China had fumbled, misstepped, experimented, reached first principles, reached final principles. Now it was ready to be put to work on a grand scale.

12

Aftermath in China

At the end of the international war, the communist party of Russia found its interests singularly united with those of the Communist party of China; this unity was symbolized by the simultaneous presence of their respective armies in Manchuria. The Chinese Communists, for their part, had a covetous eye on the area as a base for supplies and pressure against the Central Government. The Russians entertained happy memories of the days at the beginning of the twentieth century when their railroad ran across Manchuria to Changchun, thence to Dairen and Port Arthur, there to serve the naval and merchant vessels of the Russian fleet —days when theirs was the real power throughout the Manchurian countryside. In 1945 a Russian best seller, allowed to run seven hundred pages by paper-short Moscow, concerned itself with the old Port Arthur and with the dastardly Japanese, who with the connivance of treacherous Germans defeated the patriotic Russian forces.

The Russians did their best in Manchuria by occupying it before the Japanese had a chance to surrender, but international nicety (at that time still important to Russia) required them to leave what was, after all, the territory of their ally China. In this withdrawal they maneuvered with care. They dismantled an enormous quantity of factory machinery and shipped it home to the Soviet Union, a step which could hardly have met the secret wishes of Chinese Communists. These wishes were met, however, by the slow departure of the Russian Red Army, with incidental and occasional violations of a timetable agreed upon with the Chinese Government, so that trustworthy Chinese Red armies could be at the spot when the Russians cleared out. Russia also undertook to see captured Japanese equipment into the same trustworthy hands. Thereafter, she gave Japanese arms, which she was in a position not only to capture but to manufacture, together with Manchurian and Korean troops trained in Siberia.

From these beginnings and from the territory which the Chinese Red Army had been able to capture and organize during the war, the Chinese Communists within four years were able to take over the whole of China proper and during the year following (1950) to launch a drive on Tibet, to move hundreds of thousands of troops to Manchuria, and to intervene against United Nations forces in Korea. Perhaps the most astonishing fact of this astonishing success is that Communist conquest meant a sharp break in the Chinese way of life and that, in the cultural collision between China and Russia, Russia overwhelmed China in the space of only three decades.

So utterly contrary to Chinese tradition were the political slogans and the political organizations of the Chinese Communists that there would almost seem to be involved a case of what Arnold Toynbee calls cultural suicide. There is an abrupt end to the ancient ideals of the free and quiet life when, instead of a magistrate in each county, there is an active political agent in every village, when there is an absence not only of freedom of speech but even, as Hu Shih has remarked, freedom of silence. There is an abrupt end to the Confucian ideal of an orderly country arising out of har-

monious personal behavior. There is an end even to the study
and teaching of Chinese philosophy, ancient or modern. Since
the victory of Communism, Chinese intellectual journals have
argued the rejection of the old philosophy, which put personal behavior before the social environment, in favor of
Marxian determinism, which sees personal behavior as the
result of outward material conditions. Many scholars have
publicly confessed their error in holding to the idea of personal freedom and have seen that true liberation rests with the
dictatorship of the peasants and workers.[1]

That Communism sounds very similar whether it is translated from Chinese or from Russian is indicated by Mao Tse-
tung's *On the People's Democratic Dictatorship,* published
in July 1949:

We are quite different from the political party of the bourgeoisie. They are afraid to talk of abolishing classes, state authority, and party. But we openly declare that we struggle hard precisely for the creation of conditions to accelerate the elimination
of these things. . . . We cannot eliminate the state authority
now. Why? Because imperialism still exists, the domestic reactionaries still exist, and classes in the country still exist. Our present
task is to strengthen the people's state apparatus, which refers
mainly to the people's army, people's police, and people's court.
. . . The domestic crisis of America is very grave. She wants to
enslave the entire world. . . . At the present time, rulers in
Britain and the United States are still imperialists. . . . Suppos-
ing that these countries are willing in future to lend us money
on the condition of mutual benefits, what is the reason for it?
It is because the capitalists of these countries want to make
money, the bankers want to gain interest to relieve their own
crisis. . . . Internationally, we belong to the anti-imperialist
front headed by the U.S.S.R. . . . "You are dictatorial." Yes,
dear gentlemen, you are right, and we are really that way. The
experiences of several decades amassed by the Chinese people tell
us to carry out the people's democratic dictatorship. That is, the
right of reactionaries to voice their opinion must be taken away

and only the people are to be allowed to have the right of voicing their opinion. . . . Our experience may be summarized and boiled down to a single point—the people's democratic dictatorship based on the alliance of workers and peasants and led by the working class (through the Communist party). . . . The Communist party of the U.S.S.R. is our best teacher." [2]

The Chinese Communist régime has been a patient pupil culturally, prescribing Stalin's *Dialectical and Historical Materialism* as a new basic textbook, ordering out of textbooks "reactionary theories on heredity promoted by Mendel, Weismann and Morgan" and ordering in "the progressive theory of Michurin." "The backward aspects" of the theory of relativity are to be eradicated, along with the "reactionary theories of Eddington and Heisenberg." Politically the régime has been remarkably absorptive of Russian-coined phrases: "American imperialism has now taken the place of Japanese imperialism"; "The Korean people are now standing in the first line of defence in the war against aggression." Similarly, the régime prates about United States enslavement of "satellites in Western Europe," warmongering, and the protection afforded the world by the Russian veto in the Security Council.[3] Such notions, of course, are propagated in such form only for those Chinese who can read, but an important fact of Chinese Communism is its pervasiveness throughout the entire social structure: education begins with political organization of the farmer or the worker.

The Communist régime was not so popular that many Chinese did not vote against it with their feet, when it was still possible to use feet. Until the final collapse of the Central Government armies in North China, many millions of refugees poured out of the Communist areas, by no means all of them rich. The number of them was highly uncertain; at the end of 1947, it was said to be thirty-three million, a figure that probably should be viewed with distrust, but even if there were only half as many, they could not all have been landlords; there are probably not that many well-off people in the whole of China and certainly not in the poorer agricultural area of North China, inhabited by only slightly more than a hundred million people. Furthermore, since the victory of the Communists, there have been, according to their own admission, notably by Mao Tse-tung in June 1950, various armed attacks from anti-Communist forces on the mainland. Finally, as late as the fall of 1950, it was observed that there was more evidence of feeling against Russians on the streets of various large cities than there was against such Americans as were still resident.

Against these indications of unpopularity there should be ranged the elementary fact that the Chinese Communists won a civil war, that they were actually welcomed with relief in many cities, even by bourgeois elements who, according to any sort of Marxist analysis, should have been plotting against them. Furthermore, it is evident that the party, even before it was victorious, contained a strong core of Communist believers. It would not otherwise have been possible to begin to undertake the political organization of China.

This core of believers consisted first of a limited number of intellectuals and political leaders caught as enthusiastically by the Russian variety of intellectualism as were the first leaders of Chinese Communism in the early 1920's. These men were joined during the forties by the more naïve or the more disillusioned students, in particular those who hankered to be the John the Baptists of China's political reform. A third group was made up of young villagers, fretful under old-fashioned and not-yet-changed village and family rules, who saw in Communism a way of breaking out into a larger life. A fourth group was made up of persons who literally had nowhere else to go: the lost, homeless, landless, jobless, who had been tossed up and thrown about by a generation of war lords, international wars, and civil wars. Of this

group the most numerous part consisted of soldiers from one
disbanded army or another who were left without occupation, without food or the means to get it; without family,
without land or any other form of security. For persons in
such a tragic position, working with the party or fighting
with the Red army offered at least a chance for keeping alive
and a hope of a turning-upside-down of things that might
give them a position in life—a situation caught in the Chinese
phrase, *chiung-ren fan-shen-liao,* poor man coming to the top.

The existence of a committed Communist core in the
party and in the army does not by itself offer reason sufficient
to explain the conquest of China. The great ally of Communism, very much as Marxist theory would have it, was war
—war exhaustion and postwar demoralization. The Central
Government had to carry a burden that the Chinese Communists did not: the financing and supplying of many millions of men for a period of eight years, a continuous struggle
unmatched in length in modern history. The war had been
financed by an inflation that kept professors and their students starving literally for years; supplies had at the same
time become so scant that many of the officers and the men
in the armies had been vegetating along the front for years.
The government, to be sure, could not be blamed for being
in office throughout a desperate period of war and diplomacy.
Poverty and war exhaustion rather than evil intention were
to blame for most of the profiteering and corruption that
was rife in the country.[4] Exhaustion was to be blamed for
much of the weakness of the government ministries: there
was no national wealth left to be put to constructive effort.

Furthermore, the government's failure at reform—its lack
of concern over civil rights, its attempts at control over students, its occasional arrests of even genuine liberals—had been
paralleled by the partial success of reforms: a constitution,
elections, and, perhaps more significant, popularly elected
provincial councils. These reforms could not, however, loom

large against the fact of war debilitation. Nor could they off-set the fact that the Government was unable to raise some compelling standard around which the country could rally. China's debilitation was not only military and economic; it was also psychological. At the end of the war it would have been even more difficult than at the war's beginning to com-bine traditionalism and Westernism in an admixture of ap-peal to the various groups in Chinese life and to the various strata of the Chinese mind.

Confronted with the fact of debilitation, the minds of many Chinese hostile to Communism were actually intrigued by it. Confucianism had long endorsed revolt as proper and necessary whenever dynasties fell into confusion and corrup-tion—or simply into bad luck. With all the strength of the subconscious mind, most Chinese, from water carriers to pro-fessors of engineering, still accepted revolt under such cir-cumstances as a moral obligation. Furthermore, the Chinese Communists very shrewdly contrasted the "harmony" they insisted prevailed in their midst with the "confusion" that prevailed elsewhere. Their propaganda had in it a little of something for everybody from the displaced soldier to the unsettled businessman.

Here, however, the Chinese content of the Chinese Com-munist revolution ended. Without a defined strategy of attack, without material Russian help, and without Russian counsel in exploiting a revolutionary situation, the Chinese Communists could not have come to power. The war had given the party great opportunity for growth and for the perfection of its fundamental strategy of armed expansion; the Russian capture of Manchuria gave it supplies and a vast operating base. As for the revolutionary situation, it devel-oped along a psychological pattern that resembled in many respects episodes of the Russian Revolution—and, indeed, the episode of nihilistic creation of confusion described in Dostoyevsky's *The Possessed*.

First, the strategy. Expansion presented serious problems, for the party had to keep strict control of increasing numbers of peoples, and control meant not only a network of secret police but a vast network of agents, whose faithfulness was assured by putting one set above another. An agent had to be inserted into each captured community, and the agent had to be given means of subsistence, which in rural areas meant land; slogans of land distribution were thus robbed of much of their appeal to people not yet under Communist control. Furthermore, the pressures of civil war squeezed Communist China: there had to be heavy taxes and requisitions of crops and cottage manufactures; volunteering for the Red army had to be forcefully encouraged in certain places. And in certain places the party had to resort to the old war lord trick of growing opium for the sake of quick cash: the opium was smuggled across the lines for sale in Government China. Furthermore, there were some difficulties arising from the suspicion and supervision Russia inevitably gives to her servants. This suspicion led to a degree of separation between North China Communists and Manchurian Communists, among whom there reappeared from Moscow the once-rambunctious, once-deposed leader of the Chinese party, Li Li-san. Some of the party faithful found it difficult to accept the Russian version of divide and rule.

None of the problems was as great as the strategic opportunity. The Communists, secure in their own areas by reason of top-to-bottom organization, had only to concentrate their forces to destroy this or that city, mine, factory, or railroad and thereby to weaken further a government already weakened by war, while the Government had to stretch out its forces to guard the country's productive assets. The Communists were in a position to muster strength at one place, attack, destroy, and depart, confident that Government troops were too spread out for effective counterattack. This procedure was outlined by Mao Tse-tung in *Turning Point in China* (originally, *The Present Situation and Our Duties*).

1. First strike scattered and isolated groups of the enemy, and later strike concentrated, powerful groups. 2. First take small and middle-sized towns and cities and the broad countryside, and later take big cities. 3. . . . The holding or taking of cities and places is the result of the annihilation of the enemy's fighting strength, which often has to be repeated many times before they can be finally held or taken. 4. In every battle, concentrate absolutely superior forces—double, triple, quadruple, and sometimes even five or six times those of the enemy. Under specific conditions, adopt the method of dealing the enemy smashing blows . . . , aiming at the destruction of a part of the enemy and the routing of another part so that our troops can swiftly transfer forces to smash another enemy group. Avoid battles of attrition. . . . Replenish ourselves by the capture of all enemy arms and most of his personnel. . . .[5] [In Chinese civil wars defeated soldiers have of necessity to go over to the conqueror if he will have them; otherwise they would lack means of keeping alive.]

The first result of these tactics was to wear down Central Government troops who were seeking to recapture Manchuria and to upset the economic life of the large cities by shutting off rail lines and sources of goods. In Manchuria Chiang responded by hanging on to advance positions with dogged and almost ritualistic persistence—it was as if he would give up all of China before he would give up any part of it—and before the battles for North China his armies were seriously weakened. The battle for Manchuria was over in November 1948; on January 31, 1949, Peking was occupied. On October 1, Mao proclaimed a People's Republic of China with its capitol at Peking. By November 30, the Red Army had captured Chungking in the Far West. Meanwhile the great cities of China had fallen, practically without battle, one after the other.

The key to this abrupt collapse was careful exploitation

of the revolutionary situation. The Communist armies had been so maneuvered as to appear invincible; their blows had been so patterned as to confuse wildly the economic life of the cities and the morale of the Government armies. A feeling of hopelessness and helplessness spread throughout the country, helplessness before communism, helplessness before inflation, helplessness before starvation and violence. In this situation Mao berated only a chosen few persons whose names had been put on a war criminal list; he spoke with careful, although not necessarily frank, emphasis upon the part that even the businessman, the petty bourgeois, and the middle-class landlord could play in the new democracy. As a consequence, officials, businessmen, and gentry went out, once the conviction of helplessness had settled upon them, to parley the surrender of their cities. China appeared suddenly to give in before Communism.

Whether this giving in meant the end of Chinese culture or only its temporary eclipse cannot be known. Communism in China has two great and powerful weapons: first, the Russian technique of organization (far more effective than even the tyranny of Chin Shih Hwang some two thousand years ago), which, unlike inefficient tyrannies, provides a method of issuing orders at the top with the certainty that they will be obeyed everywhere at the bottom; second, the Russian technique of the lie, which unlike inefficient lying, provides a method of systematically playing upon the mind and emotions of a people until they treat as truth what may either be fact or fact's exact opposite, depending on what a small group of men conclude the people should react to and how they should react to it. (The lie was of particular use in 1950 in fomenting antiforeignism.) Finally, Communism has the benefits of Russian example, counsel, and guidance, not to mention the presence of numbers of Russian administrators and technicians that may run into the tens of thousands.

Against these strengths stand a measure of armed opposi-

tion and whatever may be left of four thousand years of
history. There are besides the old long-term weaknesses: a
paucity of administrators and technicians, and an insuffi-
ciency of food and of man power that will continue until a
greater measure of.industrialism comes into being. There
are also the dogmatic rigidities of Marxist-Stalinist theory, a
weapon of some use in overthrowing the government of a
rural country and in instituting an efficiently rigid totalitarian society, but hardly an instrument for seeing even the
simple facts of what is going on elsewhere in the world.
Dogma makes few fresh contacts with reality. It opens China
to the risk of unlimited war and unlimited defeat in a world
which offers certainty of the world triumph of Communism
only to believers.

For the present, however, there is the cold reality that the
nation of the greatest historical bulk in the world—almost
half a billion people, more than four thousand years old—
gave in to a culture in most respects alien to it. It would seem
that the Chinese people could no longer, when hard pressed,
go on trying to work out their salvation freely; that is, to
work it out amidst uncertainty of mind, confusion of spirit,
and trying and terrible poverty. A great and lasting truth of
Chinese culture was its lack of government fetters. A great
hope of the past century was that this Chinese truth could
merge with Western truths in an amalgam that would keep
China free and at the same time make her strong. It may be
that the hope was dashed because, after a century which had
greater conflict than it had hope, China could bear no more
collisions of cultures. It would seem that the growth of Communist dictatorship in a country militant for two millennia
against controls of any sort was possible only to the extent
that Chinese culture—weakened by its repeated collision
with the West—no longer possessed vitality.

It has been argued by some Westerners that, however

distasteful Communism may be to them personally, China needed something of the sort to rid herself of the confusion of the last hundred years. The fact, therefore, that the Chinese Communists were able to set up a government and a police system is thought praiseworthy by some persons, and various of the régime's social measures are called achievements. Social measures, however, are important not simply as things in themselves but as means to particular ends; and it would seem that the social measures taken in China so far have had ends of much the same sort that social measures have had in Russia: total state power and increased capacity to wage war. The disappearance of graft and corruption, for instance, indicates not so much that China has been given a fine new morality and a good government as that she has been given a police government and an efficient spy system. Graft and corruption are present to some degree in any country which operates from the conviction that it is as important to protect the innocent as to detect the guilty—an operation which permits many guilty persons to go free. Corruption is not present in Communist countries (where graft is, of course, theft against the state) because detection of the guilty is considered of far greater importance than protection of the innocent. When simple suspicion is grounds for punishment, graft vanishes; but innocent persons vanish also.

It has been suggested also that Communism in China represents nationalism and a resurgence of the Chinese spirit. Nationalism is indeed a slogan of the Chinese Communist party. It has been since the 1923–27 coalition with the Kuomintang. The Communists have described their nationalism as a drive against colonialism and against the interference of imperialist powers in China; the chief target during the twenties was Britain and during the thirties, Japan. Since World War II the chief target has been the United States, described by the Communists as very similar to Japan:

There is no difference in nature between the policy of American imperialism toward China and the policy of Japanese fascists toward China, although there are differences in form. The venomous treachery of means employed by American imperialism, however, surpasses that of Japanese imperialism. . . . The self-defense war now being waged by the Chinese people against Chiang Kai-shek and American imperialists is in its nature a war for the motherland. It is an all-national war obtaining the support of the entire nation.[6]

Such reasoning, which lacks basis in objective fact, is an essential deduction of course from Marxist-Stalinist dogma, which makes it an article of faith that the United States, the most considerable non-Communist power in the world, is all black while Russia, the most considerable Communist power, is all white. Dogma makes it possible to overlook on the one hand the fact that the United States meddled extensively in Chinese affairs only between 1942 and 1947 and that its meddling took the particular form of criticism by its officials of the government of Chiang Kai-shek and of some degree of praise, at least, for the Chinese Communists. It makes it possible to overlook, on the other hand, that Russia has been seeking and winning territorial power in China since 1860, that Russian forces made off with most of the machines of Manchurian industry, and that Russian armies occupy Chinese cities in Manchuria. Dogma of this sort is perhaps more correctly viewed as a source of political and military morale and as a device of propaganda rather than as a belief arising out of distress over the plight of Chinese culture confronted by the Western World.

The public pronouncements of Communist leaders make it appear that they see China in a student-teacher relationship to Russia. More important, both their words and the actions of their régime make it appear that their fundamental enmity is towards Chinese culture itself, towards any trace of living or even thinking according to Confucian or Taoist patterns.

In the cities intellectuals are prodded towards public recantation of what is in effect the last four thousand years of Chinese history; farmers are brought together in the countryside to discuss the very un-Chinese virtue of obedience to a network of village agents, and they are forced to meet conscription and food levies considerably more onerous, it would seem, than any during the past century. In short, while it is certain that the Chinese Communist party is zealous for rigid and efficient control of China, it is not at all certain on the basis of its actions, that it is equally zealous for the material lot of the mass of the people. As in Russia, livelihood of the people appears to be secondary in importance to the strength of the state, and to be therefore a matter subject to manipulation for the greater aim of party power.

Indeed, unless it be believed that a system of organization is the chief end of man, the rise to power of the Communist party of China can be described only in terms of the dictionary definition of conspiracy: a combination of men for an evil purpose. (That the conspirators are convinced of the rightness of their purpose does not of course, make the purpose right.) The conspiracy, indeed, was the combination of a few men very skilled in the application of Marxist-Stalinist strategy to a situation provoked by international war, and very determined in their belief that Chinese culture should be supplanted by Russian. Were these men Chinese? They were by birth, in language, and in certain of their habits; but they had undergone a conscious change not simply in political affiliation but in cultural allegiance. On the other hand, most of the Chinese sympathetic to Communism, including probably the mass of the members of the party, were Chinese in allegiance. The great majority of them, certainly, knew little more than the rest of the Chinese people what they were being led into. Their knowledge both of Marxism and of Russia was scanty. There were few published accounts of Russian society; there were few translations of the main Communist

writings. *Das Kapital* has not yet been fully translated into
Chinese; there is a 152 page translation of Engel's condensa-
tion, of which copies are scarce. Stalin's *Problems of Leninism*
and *History of the Bolshevik Party* were the party's chief
study manuals. Many party members saw the movement to
which they adhered simply as one attacking the old management of Chinese culture; they saw it as a movement towards
national and personal liberation, and, paradoxically, towards
the achievement for China of some of the material benefits of
Westernism. Among the sympathizers many took the view—
expressed by Chang Hsueh-liang just before the Sian kidnapping—that perhaps Communism would be a good thing to
have temporarily since it would enable China to clean house.
This view rested, of course, on the unfortunate misconception
that Communism can be got rid of at will. What the sympathizers did not realize was that Communism would not only
clean the house but lock the door.

For the leaders of the Communist party were engaged in
the technique of the total take-over. They had a strategy not
only for military but for cultural battle. This strategy dictated that the cultural battle should for a time progress slowly,
that the party should appear to minimize its differences with
tradition, that it should proclaim itself as only one of a coalition of anti-Kuomintang parties, that it should make great
promises to workers and to farmers, and that it should at the
same time hold out a friendly hand to intellectuals, small
capitalists, landlords of middle-sized holdings, and even foreign businessmen and missionaries. Once, however, the police
system was set up, the cultural battle quickened. As late as
November 1950, many missionaries in China were convinced
that they had freedom to carry on their work; by February
and March of 1951, some of them had been jailed, many of
them had been publicly denounced, most of them had tried
to leave China, and all of them had been subjected to new
and confining restrictions. As soon as the Communist régime

had sufficient internal power, it not only struck hard at Westerners but also forced upon Chinese the alternatives of change
in cultural allegiance or unemployment, imprisonment, death.
The Communist strategy of cultural conquest was flexible; the régime was careful not to push at any given time
beyond the limits of its power. But the strategy was inflexibly
progressive; as power grew, pressure grew. By the spring of
1951 the cultural battle was near success at least of an outward
sort in the cities, by their nature relatively easy to control.
The greatest battles were yet to be fought in the countryside.

During the final years when Communism was coming to
power, China's Government seemed unable to speak effectively to the people, to give them new hope and enthusiasms,
to give direction to the great economic and political flounder-
ings of a tired but not yet worn-out country. There was even
difficulty in explaining to American officials in China what
the Central Government wanted to do, what it was up against,
even what the Communists were doing. Occasionally Chiang
was goaded into stating grievances, more often goaded into
silence; generally he hid his thought and possibly his perplexity behind a Chinese affability.[7]

The last gestures of the United States–China drama were
all anticlimax. The war had been won. Central Government
China, jubilant for the moment, her good will warm, welcomed Americans as partners in a better future. Admiral
Kinkaid took the United States fleet into Shanghai, a city
that had just become Chinese for the first time in a hundred
years, while Chiang Kai-shek refused even to talk to the British admiral in Chungking. "I asked America to co-operate,"
he pointed out. At the war's end the United States opportunity in China was still great.

It was an opportunity to pull together a stricken country,
not by giving advice, but by giving aid. It was an opportunity

to stop lecturing and start discussing, as one equal with another, principles of freedom of speech, person, and press—ideas of appeal to a people who inclined toward a maximum of freedom from government. The United States had not seized opportunity earlier; it had used principles to damn the Chinese Government rather than save it. Now it threw the opportunity away. Americans were not aware of the opportunity; the Chinese were unable to tell them of it.

The opportunity was thrown away silently. There were United States troops in China, charged by international agreement to aid Chinese forces in receiving the Japanese surrender, and there were cries in the United States to bring the boys back home. The State Department made no comment and forbade its ambassador in China to make one. There were the brushes and jockeyings of the coming full-scale civil war: no comment. T. V. Soong was in Washington seeking aid for China: no comment. The press talked about civil war and the venal Chiang government, and asked what America was doing in China anyway: no comment.

Into this silence there finally erupted Patrick Hurley, home from China for discussions with the State Department. In progress was a public statement; in progress also was a private disagreement between the Ambassador, not a man to hold his tongue, and the functionaries of the State Department, never a group to change its mind rapidly. Nettled, Hurley suddenly lost patience, resigned his post, charged that he and the country's China policy had been sabotaged by State Department career men. The resulting Senate investigation brought angry words from Hurley; from Secretary Byrnes it brought a promise that the State Department would really say something. From Truman it brought the dispatch of the Marshall mission. And it brought China into full public and, therefore, into political controversy.

What was finally said openly to the new emissary, General George Marshall, was in some ways the same as what had been said secretly by President Roosevelt to Ambassador Hurley: support the Chinese Government, but try to effect a coalition between it and the Chinese Communists. But in one vital respect it was new: give no aid to the government unless it settles its differences with the Communists. Secretary of State Byrnes tried lamely to insist that this had been the policy all along.

This policy that appeared so attractive at the time insisted that a government friendly to the United States be forced to terms with armed rebels friendly to Russia. The Marshall mission failed, therefore, before it began; the very statement of its purpose was the statement of the inevitability of its failure. It was foolish to assume that what the Chinese could not compromise, the United States could.[8]

It took a long time for the failure to be recognized, and even when the facts of failure were recognized, the causes of it were not. Marshall set out with great dignity, integrity, and firmness to work for unity. Marshall not only had an impossible problem to solve; he had to try to solve it under the burden of an impossible conception of Chinese politics. The Chinese Government raised no storm of warning. Chiang said only that he had been dealing with the Communists for twenty years, but that Marshall wanted to try: so we'll try.

Unity did not come. Now the Central Government would renege, now the Communists. The Communists would make use of truces for troop movements, even ask for truces when their military position became unexpectedly weak. Marshall's only possible pressure was pressure on the Central Government: the holding back of an air program, the holding back of ammunition to fit the United States guns with which the Chinese were equipped. Nobody in Washington seemed to object that pressure was one-sided. Loans that had been granted China were tied up in red tape. The United States, to be sure, still had the greatest good will and it backed its good will with the money that went into UNRRA.

But this money, by United States insistence, went mainly into works of immediate relief rather than into works of rehabilitation that could provide basis for any lasting relief. The Chinese Government was even criticized for selling UNRRA goods to soak up currency and check inflation.

Precisely at this time the United States was weakening men it itself considered progressive. United States pressure had put General Chen Cheng into his position as Minister of War in 1944. He wanted army reform and used as an argument United States insistence that cutting down the size of the army was prerequisite to United States aid. He got rid of 250,000 officers and the men under them. Suddenly, however, on the renewal of civil war after one of the periods of truce, General Marshall stopped all United States aid. Chen Cheng immediately lost influence, almost lost his job. Fellow generals criticized him sharply: "You wanted an efficient army, not an inefficient one. Now you haven't even got an inefficient one to fight the Communists." It was not until the summer of 1947, when soldiers in Manchuria were almost out of bullets, that Chen Cheng received aid from United States Army surplus.

United States pressure on the Central Government was effective in that it gave the Communists reason for negotiating without any necessity for reaching agreement. Only Russia could apply pressure on the Communists. Instead she gave aid, particularly arms of Japanese manufacture. Yet confronted with evidence that the Communists were indeed Communists, United States policy makers still refused to believe. The fact did not fit the point of view. The myth continued that it was particularly important for the United States to win the allegiance of an "independent" revolutionary movement in China. When Marshall finally admitted the failure of his mission, he still was convinced that there must be a "liberal" element in the Chinese Communist party, that a group existed to which the United States could appeal.

This misconception may have been due in part to the blan-
dishments of Communist negotiator Chou En-lai, an old Communist noted for being skillful, evasive, and charming. He
played for a time the role of the sad, neglected young girl
in the Chinese theater, and in this work developed a wistful
sincerity that served him well in talks with Americans during
the war and after it. But in far greater part it arose from the
political climate of America-in-China. The failure, however,
did not change the climate. Marshall came home bitter. He
was bitter not about ideas Americans had about China but
about the ideas that Chinese had about China. In China he
had suffered the first great failure in his life. Meanwhile, the
price of Communist demands for taking part in a coalition
government were steadily going up. In July 1947, the Government, held back until then by United States pressure,
finally announced it would treat the civil war as a civil war.

Thereafter, United States policy, when it found time to
glance at China, saw a confusion that existed largely in itself.
Some men wanted to send advisers to China but no money;
others wanted to send money but could not see how to get
the advisers. Some said to give no help to China so that Russia will be disliked because she does give it; others said, do
not worry, for if the United States doesn't have enough to
help China, neither does Russia. Still others said, wait hope-
fully for signs of Titoism. More attention was given to adapt-
ing the changing facts in China to the previous policy than
in framing new policy. This adaptation led to the keeping
private of a public report for which Lieutenant General
Albert C. Wedemeyer had been sent to China—the report
called for full support to the Central Government—and it
produced a white book on China in 1949, but it was more
fruitful of confusion than of concrete results.

Little effort was made to clear this confusion away. Policy
makers made no more effort than they had made in 1937 to
examine the old policy of Hay, Hughes, and Stimson. For ten

years the old policy had been scuttled whenever it came into conflict with any other desires or even whims, so that it survived only as a waterlogged relic. The policy was upheld when it involved no price: it was easy to promise Manchuria back to China. It was upheld verbally when it involved other countries: it was for the sake of British, Dutch, and United States territory, as well as of Chinese, that Hull refused to bend to Japan in 1941. But it was pushed aside whenever anything else came along: whether Russian interests in Manchuria, or American desires to redo the Chinese Government, or British desires for greater military aid in Europe.

Eventually Chinese patience began to break. One man said, "You have raised a tiger from a cub and then walked out." Hu Shih quoted the *Book of Rites:*

The Chi nation was suffering a great famine. Chien Ngau prepared food by the roadside, waiting for the hungry to feed themselves. A hungry person appeared abruptly, his face covered up . . . his sandals tied to his feet by strings. . . . Chien said, "Pshaw, come to eat!" The hungry person looked up sternly at Chien Ngau and said: "I have come to such a pass only because I have refused food offered in disdain." He thanked Chien for the offer, but abstained from taking any food and was starved to death in the end.

In China the reservoir of good will had all but run out. By the end of 1947 only a miracle could have given China fresh strength. The time for effective aid was long past.

The State Department, seeking for something to do, found nothing. The problem of China as it concerned the United States was literally in the grip of history. Much of the discussion, furthermore, was literally in the grip of politics. After 1947, well after the date when a new approach to policy towards China might conceivably have been effective, certain political persons who had not theretofore shown particular interest in China found China a convenient weapon with which to belabor the Washington administration. They made the regrettable error of laying the mistakes of the United States in China, not to an historical situation or to the American people as a whole, but to a small group of government officials. This attitude made it the more difficult for officials to know what to think privately about China or what to say publicly. They clung somewhat precariously to the belief that somehow the United States would have to come to terms with what still seemed to them a new force in Asia. Yet this belief collided with a series of unpleasant surprises, culminating in Chinese participation in the Korean war and in an invitation to Chinese Communist representatives in December 1950 to negotiate, which ended not in negotiations but in wild Chinese denunciations of the United States.

These surprises were inevitable. So, in a sense, was the dismissal of General Douglas MacArthur from his commands in Korea and Japan, a dismissal which resulted from his views on a third area, China. Concerned with his own command, the East, he came in conflict with American, English, and European policy-makers who were concerned with the West. A dramatic question was put, the same tragic question that underlay many years of history and that centered around the particular direction—Asia *or* Europe, East *or* West—in which American aid should be committed. Because he said East, MacArthur was dismissed by men who said West. This question, of course, should never have been put; the problem was East *and* West. Carefully balanced aid was necessary for both areas, whatever the cost. But the history of East-West collision during the decade between 1937 and 1947, determined by the history of centuries past, remained a rigid determiner of actions, attitudes, and decisions. Myth and misunderstanding had led to the writing off of China in 1947, and in 1951 Asia seemed of no more weight in the Western-held balances of history than it had four years earlier.

13

The Occupation in Japan

AT WAR'S END JAPAN WAS TIRED OUT AND RUN DOWN.
Trains and streetcars were broken and decrepit; roads were
worn and rutted; in a country devoted to tidy neatness, there
were dirty clothes, dirty buildings, wherever there were
clothes and buildings left. In the cities there were vast and
unbroken stretches of rubble, and even in untouched villages there was shabbiness. Japan, in these circumstances,
was confronted by one of the greatest of catalytic agents,
defeat in war.

The manner in which this agent worked depended upon
the Allied Occupation of Japan, for practical purposes an
American Occupation, and the Occupation itself stemmed
from a great initial jolt, an experience so profound that its
cast fell everywhere upon the decisions of the occupier and
upon the reactions of the occupied. The moment of that jolt,
which lasted no longer than a motor ride from a suburb to
a city, was inevitable in terms of what preceded it, and what
followed was inevitable in terms of the jolt. It made of the
Occupation no matter of foreign roar-and-rule over a group
of defeated Orientals, but a highly adroit meeting of highly
different cultures.

The essence of the jolt was that nothing happened. An

unarmed and unescorted transport plane approached enemy Atsugi airfield. Japan, defeated, was yet an armed camp, containing no fewer than two and a half million trained troops and seventy-three million propagandized people. The plane landed; General MacArthur and his staff were ushered into cars. Through all the evidence of a nation's torment and fatigue, the little convoy of cars continued to Yokohama, guarded only by enemy police. And nothing happened.

The discipline of the Japanese held. When ordered to fight they had fought. When ordered to welcome the Americans they had welcomed them. They were confronted with a handful of conquerors—monsters, according to Japanese war propaganda. To these conquerors they bowed.

The long-term aim of the Occupation was to find means of altering the Japanese way of mind so that it would never again contemplate war. The bowing affected deeply the manner in which that aim was to be pursued, for it indicated a native tractability and discipline, qualities which seemed to argue well for the reform of Japan. The policies and the acts of the Occupation came, indeed, to be based on those qualities. It would, of course, have been possible to proceed far differently. The occupying Americans could have stepped to one side and let Japan suffer violent and undirected catharsis, wherein the Japanese might or might not have risen up against an emperor and a system of aristocracy by which they had always been docilely led. And this catharsis might or might not have given Japan the revolution from below that she has never had, might have cracked the old pattern of duty, loyalty, and restraint. But the landing of United States forces had been effected without loss of life because of the very discipline that bound the Japanese to their leaders. Hence, after Atsugi, the great issue for the United States of whether or not to deal with the Emperor, of whether to promote slow reform or quick catharsis, became the simple issue of whether to have order in Japan or disorder.

The decision was inevitable and what followed sprang from it. Order in Japan still meant deep-rooted feelings of duty and obedience, self-restraint, and self-abasement in the presence of one's betters; it meant the name of the emperor, keystone of the arch of discipline; it meant the Shinto religion, buttress of the emperor's name; it meant the continuity of the Japanese Government, the breaking of which might upset the pattern of disciplined Japanese political behavior. It did not mean that the institution of the emperor could not be reshaped, the Shinto religion not be purged, the Japanese Government not be reformed. But it did mean no sudden loosening of the underpinning of the Japanese mind.

The landing jolted the Japanese no less than the Americans. The very words used to discuss the conquerors changed. Where once they had been spoken of in patterns of speech used exclusively for mean inferiors, suddenly they were discussed in terms reserved for exalted superiors. Never questioning the principle of dispensation from above, the Japanese in effect welcomed the Americans as their new overlords. They had been ordered to—and their welcome sprang from motivations little different from the motivations that led them into war. Just as the war had represented at first a glorious, however channelized, outburst from the austere restraints of peace, so peace provided a glorious, though still channelized, outburst from the horrors and restraints of the last years of war. In wait for the Occupation lay the intemperate love of novelty of a people who traditionally do little that is new, the wild zeal of a people who frown on even mild excesses of behavior as bad taste.

As soon as the United States Army made it clear to the Japanese that it would play fast and loose neither with their women nor with their emperor, that it was, on the contrary, to show high liberality and high concern for the improvement of the Japanese lot, there broke out manifestations of sincere enthusiasm somewhat admixed with shrewd fore-

thought. The Japanese people became avid for the facts of
the war, and they speedily became convinced that their leaders had betrayed them and that the Americans had saved
them. General MacArthur's popularity became so great that
most of the Japanese spoke of him with reverence, many
considering him a deity, some referring to him as the rein-
carnation of the founding god, Emperor Jimmu. The name
of the Occupation took on a magic-like quality: the mention
of it was enough in some cases to institute any action, reverse
any action, or stop any action. Many Japanese began to look
to the Occupation as a protector against their own government, and started deluging its branches with letters of complaint. Newspapers lectured the Government on being fair
to General MacArthur.

Some of the Zaibatsu monopolists came forward with a
plan for partially putting themselves out of business. The
House of Peers, without any United States pressure, took it
upon itself to abolish peerage. The Japanese Government
undertook a purge of its members considerably more drastic
than the Americans asked, disqualifying no fewer than 425
of 600 members of the House of Representatives. A Minister
of Home Affairs, head of a tight dictatorship, began divest-
ing himself of authority. War criminals, convicted of brutality
to prisoners of war, thanked United States military courts
for the fairness of their trials. For the first time members of
the Diet began to write legislative bills. In the first elections
66 per cent of all the women, theretofore possessors of no
legal or civic rights, obediently went to the polls. An imitation Town Hall of the Air regularly drew six thousand claim-
ants for the three thousand seats in Hibiya Hall. A schoolgirl
interrupted class to sing songs. Rebuked, she said, "Everything is free now."

Small stalls on the Ginza, Tokyo's main shopping street,
briskly sold toy jeeps. An eagerness for papers, magazines,
books, ran all through the country: books on the United

States, specimen election ballots, treatises on local government, textbooks on science, primers on civics. A Japanese-written biography of General MacArthur became a nonfiction best seller and an American-written potboiler about an affair between an American correspondent and a Japanese movie actress topped fiction lists. The Japanese Government insisted on translating *An Outline of Government in Connecticut.*

This enthusiasm, to be sure, threw Japan into confusion. It lacked any exact sense of direction, often any concrete object. There was a readiness for change without an understanding of why there should be change. There was an excess of receptivity, but there was also highly restrained behavior. Since the Japanese were accustomed to considering not social principles but social relationships, new principles were accepted in terms of the old pattern of obligations. Consequently, the confusion remained orderly. There were not even scattered actions against the occupying forces, and only Communists lifted their voices against the Emperor. But Japan had thrown herself into a state of flux that offered to the Occupation its great opportunity to pursue its basic objective—the fundamental reform of the nation.

Japan continued in flux. No government found an effective pattern of rule: one cabinet after the other sought one; one cabinet after the other failed. Principles did not become sharply defined. There were a thousand political parties, more than a score of them large enough to elect Diet members. New names appeared everywhere. Of these names, Suzuki, president of five hundred twenty thousand railroad workers, was typical. At war's end he was a switchman who, like fourteen of the fifteen men on his executive council, had never before belonged to a union. When seventy-five thousand girls and boys were to be discharged from the railroads, Suzuki threatened a one-day general strike, stood his ground, traded words with the Prime Minister and the Minister of

Communications, won his point, and beat a Communist effort to call a strike after the issue of the strike had been settled. It was typical of the confusion of the labor movement in 1946 that he lost half his union during the negotiations and won it back afterward.

Since very little of Japan's surface life was fixed, the great question of the Occupation was how it should become fixed. It was clear that the mental patterns of the past lent themselves to aggression in economics, in politics, and finally in war. So long as unthinking obedience to overlords remained part of the Japanese way of living, so long as there existed a sober and more than puritanic restraint in daily life that resulted in infrequent but violent explosions of bloody excess, so long as the quiet life of the home provoked an almost gastric appetite for big business, big politics, and big imperialism abroad—so long would the Japanese problem remain unsolved. Japanese zeal alone would not solve it. In the nineteenth century Japanese zeal over the Westernization ordered by the edict of the Emperor Meiji was great, yet Japan selected only such surface Western techniques as adapted themselves to strictly Japanese use. In the seventh and eighth centuries A.D. Japan set out with great ardor to make herself Chinese, adopting everything from women's headdresses to the social philosophy of Confucius and the written characters of the Chinese language. Yet these were no more than drapes arranged about an unchanged body social. Japan's tendency was to import much, but to reject those techniques and ideas, particularly ideas of freedom, that failed to harmonize with her inner and unchanging convictions.

The task was to open the Japanese mind to what it had rejected. It fell upon the general staff of the Occupation, known by the magic name of SCAP, initials that stood for Supreme Commander for the Allied Powers, but that came to mean the relatively small group of Americans in three or four downtown Tokyo office buildings who watched the progress of the Occupation and charted its course.

Initially SCAP was a missionary enterprise. Unlike American groups then operating in China and Korea, it was often dynamic, and almost always evangelical. Its message was by no means imperial. SCAP was uninterested in Allied economic penetration of Japan, uninterested in long-term Allied control of the country; indeed, its chief efforts were to make control unnecessary. It preached the good news of the United States of America—with due deference to the equally good news of the British Commonwealth and the smaller democracies. It was interested in the conversion of Japan to democracy and in the basic reform of her way of life, and talked of representative government and of the equality of the sexes much as American missionaries have always talked in the Far East, but on a much vaster scale.

In this talk the person of General Douglas MacArthur loomed large. Unlike his predecessor, Commodore Perry, who surrounded himself with an aura of more than Oriental splendor, General MacArthur immediately undertook to avoid show. On one occasion, when the Provost Marshal tried to clear the streets for a MacArthur trip, he was rebuked. Only two sentries were set to guard the old embassy building in which MacArthur lived. When he entered an elevator in his Dai Ichi office building to find, for the first time, a Japanese already inside, he overwhelmed the man by insisting— over self-abasing protests—that the man ride along. The news spread, and the Japanese generally were overwhelmed. But MacArthur preserved at the same time an unapproachability that helped keep his currency high. He granted formal audiences and appeared in public only long enough to get from the door of the Dai Ichi Building to his black Cadillac sedan. This strengthened the sense of obligation incurred, most Japanese felt, by his favor to them. Like the Emperor, General MacArthur was put into the class of higher obligations.

This man and the men under him concluded that Japan could be led in the direction of democracy only by breaking Japan up. The country was quickly stripped of armies and arms, defeated generals co-operating with Americans in the dispersal of a force put together by the labor of many decades. The country was next stripped of leaders. This purge was not punitive, as were the war-crime trials; its aim was to sweep clear the old aristocracy of Japan and to make room for leaders of a new sort. It was, moreover, highly thorough. It cast from national life not only men who were unduly zealous over the war or unduly oppressive but also those who simply held important posts during the war in such varied fields as government, industry, banks, political parties, unions, cultural associations, radio networks, movies, and newspapers.

The Occupation turned next to the big combines, in which the economic life of the country had been centered. Zaibatsu securities were frozen; the personal wealth of the big families was frozen also; and the Japanese Government was ordered to develop antimonopoly plans. Gradually there appeared a program for stripping the families not only of say in but of ownership of their combines, and for preventing the rise of new economic overlords. On October 8, 1946, the Big-five Zaibatsu families formally surrendered their securities under terms that would leave them only a small fraction of their former money. SCAP and the government continued to seek means of redoing the entire Japanese economy. The combines, once separated, could not be permitted to come together again. There would have to be antitrust legislation, reform of the commercial code, reform of the banking acts, reform of the patent acts. Crippling of the Japanese industrial machine by removal of plants and equipment would have to be pushed.

While this destruction was in progress, SCAP undertook

to encourage the Japanese to do their own reconstruction. To the end of developing a democratic initiative lacking in the Japanese mind, General MacArthur insisted that SCAP refrain from directing that something be done and prod the Japanese into doing it themselves. More than 90 per cent of the Occupation's early activity was handled in informal conference between Americans and Japanese. When the Japanese asked for formal orders, SCAP usually refused them. When the Japanese asked permission to raise such ticklish issues as repatriation in the Diet, they were answered, "Why do you ask?" When the Shidehara Government fell into straits, subsequently to collapse, SCAP's government section declared itself off limits to the Government so that there could be no inference that the Occupation was trying either to keep the Government alive or to kill it off. MacArthur thus sought to avoid the pitfall of trying to establish democracy by edict.

Even on delicate conservative-progressive issues SCAP managed by and large to tread delicately. It did not criticize the Social Democrats, not even the radical wing of the party; undertook no concerted antilabor maneuvers even when workers threw management out of factories and ran the factories themselves. SCAP made a point of dealing with equal good will with more progressive youngsters and more conservative oldsters. And at all times SCAP worked through a popularly elected Japanese Government. There was no attempt to direct that government for particular political ends. SCAP operated on the democratic premise that whenever possible the Japanese should run themselves.

The Japanese Constitution, for instance, came into being without the issuance of a single Occupation order or directive. There was talk with SCAP's government section; there was research on every constitution in the world; there were occasional nudges in the direction of freedoms and decentralizations that would have made the forebears of the Japanese blanch. But each draft and redraft of the document was written by Japanese; the Prime Minister himself wrote the no-war article. When the draft constitution was prepared, it was given two full months of free and sometimes violent debate in the Diet, all of which was widely publicized. Three articles were amended, three deleted, and one added. SCAP insisted to the Diet that it could do anything with the Constitution it wanted to.[1]

The result of this restraint on the one hand and gentle prodding on the other was a document that provided for perhaps the most representative government in the world. It ensured as many freedoms as any other constitution. It even prohibited wire tapping, restricted the use of confessions in courts of law, and permitted any person acquitted of crime to sue the state. It provided for a completely representative upper house. It forbade public office to any but civilians (for whom a new Japanese word had to be invented), completely renounced war, arms, and armies, and hamstrung the emperor.

As the Japanese watched these activities, the aim of the Occupation came to be summed up for most of them in a single word—democratization. Lacking experience in democracy, they thought the word meant what had already happened to their country. They were inclined to think that it meant elections as contrasted to appointments, although there was some realization that it was something more complicated. SCAP had already illustrated to the Japanese a number of very concrete democratic procedures, whose effect on the Japanese mind could be summarized somewhat as follows:

Democracy meant various freedoms from government and various dispensations of law that the Japanese never before had. It meant a somewhat disquieting equality of persons that made the head of the house no more important before the courts than the wife of the youngest son. It meant a rigid-

ity of law supposed to block the whims of rulers, and a fairness of trials supposed to prevent the sadism of police and
the careerism of prosecutors, formerly dependent upon Tokyo for existence and advancement. It meant a fragmentation of government, so that the links that bound towns and
prefectures to the government in Tokyo snapped. It even
meant that the people, not Tokyo, should have the say in
purging their officials and schoolteachers.

It meant a new and somewhat confused view of the
Emperor, who became less of a remote deity and more of a
personalized father—a transformation the Japanese tried to
effect with not a few misgivings. The Japanese remained
tied to him by the bonds of duty; they felt even an affection
for him, growing out of sympathy for the man who had to
lose face by ending the war. Almost all of them felt profoundly and eternally indebted to him for ending it—and
overlooked the fact of his declaring it. Most of them recognized that it was no longer improper to criticize him, and
that newspapers were not guilty of crime when they remarked that he did little but say, "Ah so." Yet when a Japanese picket paraded before the imperial palace with a sign
implying that the Emperor had no concern for the people's
lack of food, he was promptly arrested for libel (*lèse majesté*
being no longer a crime) and sentenced to prison, whence he
was released not by law but by the *noblesse oblige* of the
Emperor, via a general amnesty on Constitution Day. The
Japanese remained uncertain about what precisely to think
of the Emperor—he was a sort of god who had lost his deity
—but they wanted at least to respect and follow him as the
symbol of the country. And this too seemed like democracy
to the Japanese.

Democracy meant also a new sort of education. It meant
a new set of textbooks in such subjects as history and government written in a very different style by Japanese clearly
new to the old Ministry of Education, which was essentially

a device for funneling propaganda. It meant no textbooks on the ethics of Shinto but, instead, a handbook on civics. It meant that teachers, lowly functionaries, were allowed to see the directives of mighty SCAP, indeed that SCAP insisted that they read them.

Democratization meant in addition the ruination of landlords and the breakup of land, which tenants and part tenants (69 per cent of the farming population) once rented in exchange for 50 to 60 per cent of the crop, a system of bondage to which moneylenders chained them tighter. The reform bill of October 1946 allowed owners to rent only a little over two acres of land and to till only about seven acres, and it forced them to sell off, via the government, their extra land at easy rates. It set up also new regulations for credit and for such tenancy as would remain.

Most unusual of all, democratization meant a wildly active and much confused labor movement, very inexactly based on United States unionism. Four million workers were unionized in the first twelve months of the occupation—almost half of the total nonfarm working force (13 million minus four million urban unemployed). Labor's reaction to this sudden rise resembled the delirium of a man whose fever shoots up rapidly. Only one million of the four were covered by collective bargaining agreements and strikes were frequently mishandled and bizarre. Electricians twice carried out a five-minute blackout; train engineers blew their whistles in concert for one minute; a theatrical troupe went through a play in pantomime and spoke no words; there were hunger strikes, sit-down strikes; production-control strikes, and a variety of others. The labor movement became the most signal illustration of democratic initiative in the whole of Japan. It did not spell democracy exactly, but it spelled it large.

If democratization meant all these things, it meant to the Japanese a sharp break with their past. The break appeared

so great that Japan acted at times as if she had been jolted to
the core and abruptly started off on an entirely new way of
life.

The Occupation remained a military one, and as such it was
inevitably involved in paradox. Military organizations are in
the business of issuing orders. Besides, SCAP's democratic desire to have the Japanese do the job was confronted by the
occasional unwillingness or inability of the Japanese to do it.
The Japanese Government, through which SCAP effected
democratization, was the most progressive Japan had ever
had, but it was still far from an ideal instrument. While it
sometimes carried out Occupation suggestions and directives with more exuberance than SCAP ever anticipated, it
quite as often dragged its feet. Old mental habits died hard,
and warm adherence to the *idea* of a loosening of centralized
controls or of a breaking-up of Confucianist family law was
no guarantee of consequential action. The government was
still run by the Japanese bureaucracy, in addition to the
Cabinet and Diet at any time in control. Like any bureaucracy, it tended to resist change. Furthermore, few Japanese
were quite sure what change was. To many of them it did not
seem a far step from the conservative party (called liberal—
and actually liberal in relation to pre-Occupation politics) to
the radical, but not communist, branch of the Social Democrats. The life of the Japanese had been so highly channeled
that it remained difficult for them to breathe the heady air of
relative freedom without either fearing it or becoming drunk
on it. That fear, mostly subconscious, made the bureaucracy temporize on occasion, an activity in which it was not
overly discouraged by either liberal or social-democratic governments. These governments, however, through free elections did represent the people. They also represented in
varying degrees their essential conservatism. In dealing with
the sometimes reluctant dragon of the Japanese Government,

SCAP dealt also with the inner reluctance of the Japanese people.

In cases of entrenched reluctance, the only resort was to directives (1,172 in the first twelve months of occupation alone), on which the Japanese were at times so ready to lean that they treated suggestions as dictates—a situation complicated by the fact that it was impossible for them to tell in many instances, whether SCAP would crack down or not. SCAP at times undertook with one hand what it guarded against doing with the other.

Reluctance was by no means the most important fact in this paradox. It was essential, for instance, to keep Japan as a nation of measurable industry; otherwise many millions of people might starve. Industry needed buttressing and got it from SCAP. Even more important was the United States conception of Japan not as a country in itself, a house, as it were, to be swept clean for its own benefit, and incidentally for the benefit of other nations, but as an adjunct to general United States foreign policy. Policy appeared to demand that the United States have a friend and potential ally in Asia. Until Americans tried to eat Chinese pears and found their teeth set on edge, China was the friend and the ally, and policy called for her to be strong and united. But during the war United States policy first lost faith in China and then all but lost interest. Japanese docility and industry made Japan the new friend, the new potential ally.

The first indication that the Japanese were becoming America's chosen people in Asia came from General MacArthur himself in a speech on September 2, 1946, wherein he remarked that Japan should be a Far Eastern bulwark of democracy. After that speech, the Occupation, while still concerned with the reform of Japan, became increasingly concerned with the strengthening of Japan. The fact that much in Japanese society needed to be broken down confronted the fact that strength required that much of it needed to be built up. The more monopolies were broken up, for instance, the more was the Japanese economy upset, the more was unemployment increased, and the longer was delayed the day when foreign and domestic trade could find the right volume and the right balance for the needs of the country. Were SCAP to have been favored by the miraculous arrival of that day, the course of the Occupation would have followed the channels of reform altogether, but it was SCAP's fate to encounter problems of purges, politics, religions, education, and democratic decentralization precisely and necessarily at a time when the Japanese economy was seriously out of kilter—and when United States policy seemed to require that it be in kilter.

While SCAP's early controls in some fields were extremely loose, not only in politics but even in industry—the manufacture and allocation, for instance, of such items as glass and paper—in others they were extremely tight. When it came to fertilizer, a great need and a great lack, SCAP did almost everything but run the plants. Its controls over coal, critically short, tightened continually through 1946 and 1947. By the end of 1947 control of Japanese industry was considerably tighter than the wartime control of United States industry. The Economic Decentralization Law, passed during the winter of 1947 was an American document—it had to be translated into Japanese—and its passage was secured, very probably, only because SCAP would have forced it through had the Japanese balked at approving it. Japanese who were prepared to embrace free enterprise with fervor were not a little upset to discover that the oxygen of freedom was being mixed with the anesthesia of control. The amazement was shared not only by up-and-coming businessmen but by various political men, including not a few socialists, who saw free enterprise as a radical means of redoing Japanese society. They were at times troubled that their economy was not so much getting redone as rebuilt.

Rebuilding the economy meant inevitably rebuilding the direction-from-above prejudices of the Japanese mind, out of which it grew. Before the Occupation, business was run, not by a number of persons, but by a small group of business-men, militarists, and bureaucrats, whose activities were so collective that it was difficult to tell where business ended and war and government began. This group handed down joint directions for the rest of Japanese society to adjust to.

SCAP may not have liked this way of life, but it could not afford to jettison it. It was impossible for more than a year to do away with the control associations, avenues of Zaibatsu direction of war production, because some working means of control of industry had to be maintained. The associations were therefore abolished in name, "democratized" to the extent of electing the officers whom the government once appointed, and left pretty much as before to handle priori-ties and allocations. (The little fellow had more say than before but still seldom spoke up.) It was even necessary to retain the notorious wartime Neighborhood Associations, despite all their connotations of police spying and govern-ment propagandizing; to have abolished them would have been to abolish the only established system of rationing.

It was necessary not only to keep old forms of overlord control, but even to institute bigger and more efficient ones. The old system of economic manipulation, designed to fit the changing notions of the Japanese ruling group, was cum-bersome. Price control, for instance, was scattered through various agencies responsible to various ministries. SCAP, therefore, prodded into existence in Japan a superagency, the Economic Stabilization Board, of a sort that concentrated in one individual's hands more formal power than the Japa-nese had been accustomed to giving anyone, with the excep-tion of Tojo. It fell heir, for instance, to the duties of the old control associations. The lot of its director was not easy. His power was more theoretical than real, and SCAP frequently had to give him informal backing and prodding. His problems, furthermore, were complicated by the fact that no system of control could give the Japanese people and Japanese industry their survival requirements. It was necessary therefore for SCAP and the government to wink at most black markets, whose prices attracted away from the farms food that would be eaten there had only legal prices been paid.

Price control was but one problem of many. SCAP had to propagandize efficiency—and responsibility—both to government and to business. Meanwhile, it had to try to reform their inner workings. But this reform produced upsets, both economic and political. Extensions of the purge of wartime leaders, for instance, got seriously in the way of industrial and political recovery, and after going fast with the purge, it became necessary to go slow. It became necessary to go slow with the breakup of large industrial combines. It became necessary not to let Japan find her natural level of industry and her natural sources of raw material, but to increase both the level of industry and the quantity of raw materials. American officials, consequently, began to scour the world for more goods for Japan. Certain parts of the Occupation began to take a dim view of the turmoil connected with the labor movement: it kept the country disorderly.

The Occupation jolted, but it also soothed Japan. The great question was whether the Japanese were jolted hard enough to be forced out of their old patterns of life. Did the jolt penetrate deeper than the surface of their minds and emotions?

The forms of language express the deep and almost unconscious convictions of a people, and the Japanese language has not changed. It is still impolite to disagree with anyone, particularly with SCAP. It is still unthinkable to swear; profanity still does not exist. There is still an entirely different pattern of speech, even entirely different words, for speaking of various grades of inferiors and superiors. Women, inferiors, still speak in word forms different from those used by men.

Techniques in art and methods of house building similarly reflect basic conclusions about how life should be lived, and Japanese art and architecture are still devoted to a rigid simplicity and restraint, which bottle up thoughts and emotions. Duty and obedience—in a word, discipline—remain the deep-rooted concepts with which the Japanese view every facet of their existence. Their lives are still as disciplined as their paintings, still as restrained as their No and Kabuki plays, still as austere as their chairless and bedless rooms.

In religious habit there has been little change. The Emperor still announces important news to his ancestors. The new constitution was officially promulgated by imperial rescript in the Diet, but it had, in a sense, already been promulgated by telling it to the dead. Shinto religion, whose hard core is, if not emperor worship, at least state worship, was purged of ultranationalist doctrine and separated from the state, but much more than the simple nature worship of folk Shinto still goes on. It is remarkable how little face has been lost by the deities who were supposed to protect Japan. The deities, it is now widely agreed, really had nothing to do with the war in the first place; their names were wrongly invoked by the men responsible for the war. Buddhism has shown few signs of new strength. Christians are still scarce. Meanwhile Yasukuni, where are enshrined the souls of the men who died in Japan's wars, still survives, and most Japanese still look to these deities as more than ordinary immortals. Violence remains so awesome to them that a warlike departure from life gives special position to the dead and requires special appeasement from the living. The emotional foundations of Shinto have not altered.

Nor have the neo-Confucianist ideas of family and national duty that the Japanese continue to embrace. Younger brothers still follow older brothers, women men, sons fathers, and in like manner the low follow the high, and all follow the Emperor—and SCAP. Freedom is a condition that pertains to persons, but as yet the Japanese exist as persons only dimly. They exist rather as groups; even in the handling of problems political and economic, SCAP seldom finds a responsible individual; it finds a body of men, tied together by a network of loyalties based on age and position that even purges and anti-Zaibatsu measures have not broken up. The greatest resistance to change comes from groups most strongly attached to Confucianism. Furthermore, as the Occupation goes on, the early enthusiasm changes into the restless and somewhat bored restraint that is always the essence of Japanese life. It is significant and unfortunate that the Occupation delayed almost three years in launching a program of cultural contact, in particular the publishing of Western books, and that the program did not become large.

The specific dangers of Japanese traditionalism are the twin ones of totalitarian government and aggressive war. The old fondness for excesses of arms, while at present overlaid, is not uprooted. Furthermore, totalitarianism in Japan could be as easily of the so-called left as of the right: Communist overlords would fit Japanese mental predilections as well as any other. If totalitarianism be seen as a circumstance attendant on the spread of feelings of confusion and uncertainty among a people, the conflict of aims of the American Occupation hardly contributes to long-term democracy in Japan.

Japan is still in flux. It requires effort to maintain traditional habits of mind side-by-side with Western methods of machine manufacture, popular elections, radio broadcasting, movies, and even cabaret taxi dancing. No conscious effort is now being made to preserve Japan's mental insularity, and the Japanese way of life is being slowly but powerfully subjected to outside assault. There is a new enthusiasm for personal money getting, and this sense of individualism may transfer itself to other parts of Japanese life, or it may simply breed another group of wealthy families. There is, in particular, the rise of the labor movement. There is nothing Shintoistic or Confucian in the demands of workingmen for better conditions and higher wages. A rise in workers' wages promises to redo much of the Japanese economy. In a Japan in which wages are high, it would not be easy to support either heavy-industry expansion or a Zaibatsu of the old sort.

What is more, no new set of overlords has yet emerged in Japan, except SCAP. In the past Japan went through periods of disorder in which no one knew who the overlords were but in which no one questioned the principle of overlordism. SCAP's insistence that Japanese life be strengthened, not broken up, made of SCAP a sort of ad interim ruling class and General MacArthur a sort of ad interim deity. Japan, so long as it remains traditionally Japanese, requires a center around which the country and the government can operate. The center was provided by the Emperor and by MacArthur until his abrupt dismissal in April 1951, which left an immediate vacuum.

How will the Japanese fill this vacuum? Will the emperor, old arch stone of the old system, fill it alone? Will a different American general help fill it? Will the elective aristocracy of the democratic system become a class to which the Japanese will chain themselves as firmly as they have been chained in the past? Or, most dangerous of all, will Japan Westernize herself to the extent that she embraces a totalitarianism of right or left, a sort of Western system which will least disturb her ancient patterns of mind?

As late as 1947 the vast social experiment begun at Atsugi airfield could yet have led to an amalgamation of those patterns with Western patterns and could yet have broken the old bonds of obligation and restraint. But by making cultural change in Japan subordinate to foreign policy (in part the consequence of United States distrust of Central-

Government China), the United States made it more likely that the great surface changes in Japan would not initiate deeper reactions. The lesson that war and occupation have taught the Japanese, in the last analysis, is might. Japan may now well imagine that it was not her mental rigidity but her lack of strength that defeated her. How imagine otherwise if an occupation of conquerors shows such solicitude for her strength? She may well conclude that it is not ideas, not religion, not any practices of freedom or equality—not these but might that she has to learn from the West.

The possibility that she would so conclude was strengthened, certainly, early in 1951, when she was engaged by the United States in peace discussions about her rearming herself in order to play the role of a counterbalance to Russian strength in the Far East. The country which had been carefully and constitutionally stripped of preparations for war was now to be coached for the familiar role of a great power in the Orient by means of preparations for war.

But if might is indeed the conclusion that Japan is drawing from such lessons from the West, the confusion of mind into which she was thrown by MacArthur's dismissal may lead her to question which force in Asia is mightiest, and to wonder whether she should attempt to counterbalance Russia after she becomes a free agent. If MacArthur's Eastern orientation in the East-West issue was so strong as to lead to remarks that Washington had ordered squelched, and if Washington's Western orientation was so strong as to lead to the kicking out of one of the main props of the Japanese social system, then Japan may conceivably conclude—to her own and the West's misfortune—that the might of the United States is not something on which she can count, and that she must look elsewhere.

14

Confusion in Korea

THE PRICE OF CULTURAL COLLISION IN ASIA HAS REGULARLY
been exacted on the battlefield. The first price of the collision that took place between the years 1937 and 1947, themselves years of war, was levied upon the West in a particular
battlefield that abuts China, touches Russia, and looks across
narrow straits to Japan. In Korea, Russia and the United
States had earlier found themselves coproprietors of an occupation probably more unpopular than any in recent history.
In the diplomatic wranglings over Korea the United States
had suffered a series of far-reaching defeats. And in Korea, the
United States, by way of the United Nations, finally found
itself at war.

At the conclusion of World War II, the country seemed to
give promise of eventual peace and plenty. Korea has more
area and people than Greece and Turkey put together. Its
scenery is tumbling and rough, its rice hollows fertile, its subsoil moderately rich in minerals. At the end of the war, it
owed neither external nor internal debt. It was in a position
to produce enough gold to back its currency and to pay for
some of its imports. Since the Japanese had owned most of
the wealth, there was opportunity of a sort that has seldom
existed on earth—a complete redistribution of land and fac-

tories. Furthermore, the country, which combines low-roofed
houses, antique temples, steel hotels, and a north-temperate
climate could have become a haven for tourists and a locus
for foreign investment. It could, in short, have become the
model state of the Orient. But by the end of 1947 Korea was
worse off economically than it was under the Japanese. The
Russians were contentious, the Americans ill at ease, the
Koreans destitute and irate.

The outward sign of the country's suffering was a pleth-
ora of foreigners. After forty years of exploiting, the Japanese had left, to be sure, but they left Korea stripped of
goods, its soil mined, its fertilizer plants shut down, its trees
cut for fuel, its economic patterns disrupted, and its fishing
fleet decimated. Japan furnished technicians and managers,
thereby stunting Korean industrial growth; Japan furnished
government and education, thereby outraging the Korean
spirit, a complex entity, neither Chinese nor Japanese, that is
politically fiery. When the war ended, the Russians moved
in from the north and the Americans from the south, and the
thirty-eighth-parallel demarcation of their zones was an am-
putation with instant economic effect. Both armies arrived
with the slogans of liberators, but they stayed as occupiers,
and the Korean spirit was outraged afresh. Korean refugees
from North Korea and Japan—two million of them—poured
into the South. In the South food became scarcer; soap,
matches, and light bulbs disappeared; the South found itself
lacking coal, newsprint, power, and fertilizer. It found itself
full of United States officers and officials who knew nothing
of Korea, acting as heads of government bureaus, as mayors
of towns, as executives in ex-Japanese businesses, and as experts in fields ranging from art to education. It did not
accept them happily, and political disquiet compounded
economic debility. The Koreans wanted to eat; they wanted
to be free. They blamed the Japanese; they blamed the Russians; they blamed the Americans.

Korea was, of course, a particular witness to an Orient in transition: Chinese culture played a great part in its shaping, for Buddhism and Confucianism admixed with native Shamanism are the chief ethical and religious forces, and Japanese pseudomodernity has altered much of the economic life and launched Korean nationalism. Furthermore, Korea is a particular witness to the economic troubles of that transition: the United States Occupation undertook a thorough economic survey to find out what the southern half of the country needed for filling the promise that Korea appeared to hold out.

The Occupation found a well that very much needed priming. This well had been fitted to the currents of Japanese economic life in such a manner that the North sent raw materials to Japan and the South sent rice; in return both areas were handed a modicum of Japan-finished products. These products were all-important to the Korea economy, and the finding of new sources of them for a time appeared all but impossible because of war exhaustion and the thirty-eighth-degree split. Korea, to be sure, is overwhelmingly agricultural; three-fourths of her people are farmers. But farmers themselves need industry—if only for tools and fertilizer—and non-farmers starve without it. In 1946 in South Korea alone there were 3,700 plants employing more than fifteen employees apiece, along with thousands of cottage industries, which turned out furniture, brass work, cloth, lacquer, bread, candy, baskets, and the like—enough of them to account in normal times for 25 to 40 per cent of all South Korean production. But South Korean industry was equipped mostly for making finished goods. The raw materials, except for some graphite, tungsten, and gold, were in the North, and industry was starved for materials that were not crossing the thirty-eighth parallel. Even the soil was starved; Japan converted to war production the plants making fertilizer, and for ten years the Korean farmer got none; besides, the plants were in the North. Needed, the United States Occupation concluded, were raw materials, fertilizer in great quantities, a large irrigation project, forest products, marine materials, canneries, railroad equipment, simple machinery, medicines. South Korea's eight large and twenty small textile plants, which turned out before the war over two hundred million yards of cloth a year, lacked cotton, wool, worsted, repair parts, dyes. There were six power plants, which had had no repairs for four years and could not produce their rated 197,600 kva; there was an 80 per cent complete hydroelectric plant, started by the Japanese, that could not work without further materials. Even with it working and even with power from the North, there still would not have been power enough; wanted, the Occupation concluded, were two steam plants. Elsewhere there were patterns of tangling shortages: almost no railroad ties, rails, repair parts, telephone poles, wire, oil, gasoline, kerosene, lubricants, greases, and wax.

The Korean cultural pump needed priming also: textbooks, teacher training, special personnel, radios and films, libraries—six million dollars' worth of them by United States estimate—enough to create a new school system and an entire set of new textbooks, both of which were once entirely Japanese. It would have provided also the technical training highly important to a people long held subservient. For special training in both administration and technology the importation of specialists was essential. It was clear that unless Koreans were quickly and intensively given new skills, the managerial hiatus brought about by the exodus of the Japanese would last a very long time.

The meeting of these needs could, of course, have been carried out without reference to international politics. But it appeared all during the course of the Occupation that every United States plan had to be fitted into the long-distance game of wits that was being played across the thirty-eighth parallel. Furthermore, United States acts and refusals to act had as background more than half a century of singularly uninspired United States dealings with Korea.

The record looked good at the start. In the nineteenth century the United States insisted that Korea be treated as a completely independent power and that she be free of any trace of the younger-brother status that she maintained with China for a millennium and a half. It presently appeared, however, that this insistence sprang not so much from United States devotion to Korean independence as from pique and bewilderment over China's semi-Confucian international system, which depended on cultural similarities and notions of virtue rather than on any of the devices of Western politics. At the end of the Russo-Japanese War, the key to which was control of Korea, Theodore Roosevelt felt no qualms in awarding Korea to Japan as a protectorate, a relationship that Japan quickly turned into outright colonialism. The United States did not object. Until the Cairo Declaration in 1943, Korean independence was no concern of American policy, although individual Korean revolutionists found haven in the United States. Cairo, however, called for a free and independent Korea, and Potsdam, to which Russia later subscribed, reaffirmed Cairo.

At the end of the war Russia and the United States met in the middle of Korea. Precisely why they met at the thirty-eighth parallel remains mysterious. It is said that it was a military decision on the spot, but the Russians arrived ten days before the Americans. It is said that it was another of the Yalta jokers, and that the split was a matter of formal high-level agreement. And finally it is said that the decision was made in Washington. But whatever is said, the decision reflected the then-current enthusiasm that saw Russia as a state pleasant to do business with.

The end of the war and the deportation of the Japanese were considerable enough events to obscure for a time some of the consequences of this misstep, but shortly the misstep was followed by another. Confronted with an unyielding barrier at the thirty-eighth parallel, Lieutenant General John R. Hodge sensibly urged that the barrier be dealt with at top levels. The top levels set up a joint commission to work out a provisional government, in the course of which they not only tacitly formalized the thirty-eighth-degree split but also brought in the word "trusteeship," a condition, they declared, that was to continue five years. The Koreans were angered by the fact; they were horrified by the word, for the Americans who had proposed it at the Moscow Conference of 1945 were unaware that it could be translated into Korean only as Japan's word "protectorate" had been translated. The Korean sense of outrage speedily translated itself into parades, demonstrations, speeches, denunciations. Meanwhile the Joint Commission was carefully sabotaged by the Russians, who showed little disposition to work for the all-Korea government agreed upon at the Moscow Conference.

This indisposition took the form of a Russian insistence that only such persons and parties as approved of trusteeship could be part of a government, a qualification met by no one anywhere in Korea except the Communists, who in 1946 changed their political line in the very middle of a parade in Seoul that began against trusteeship and ended in favor of it. The indisposition was furthered by refusal to have any more than formal dealings with Americans—General Hodge sought vainly for months for co-operation with his Russian opposite number. The sole significant instance of interzone communication was the interchange of northern hydroelectric power and southern food and electrical equipment.

For a long time United States policy, framed by a State-War-Navy committee with the help of reports from the field, saw no alternatives to a single-sided attempt to make the

Joint Commission a success and to a sincere effort to provoke minimum Russian irritation. Unfortunately, it saw internal Korean politics as an adjunct to the hope of doing business with Russia. What seemed necessary within South Korea was a coalition of Communist front and anti-Communist parties that would not antagonize Russia and weaken the Joint Commission, although it was already defunct. This notion (it is not unlike the one that sent General Marshall off in a vain effort to reconcile irreconcilables in China) does not appear to have resulted from anything resembling low government conspiracy but rather from something closer to high public innocence, colored by ignorance of Korea and by the hangover of faith in United States–Russian co-operation long after the fact of it had vanished.

One business of the United States Occupation therefore was to sell a coalition of pro- and anti-Communist parties to South Korea. Its first effort was an Interim Legislative Assembly, for which free elections were held in 1946. Forty-three anti-Communists and two pro-Communists were elected—clearly no coalition. In an attempt to create one, the Occupation authorities themselves appointed to the Assembly forty-five more persons of varying views, most of them at least tolerant of Communists. In terms of present Western practice the election was not ideal; family heads voted for village leaders, village leaders elected provincial leaders, and so on in somewhat the manner of earlier Western democracy. But the arbitrary United States appointment was worse; it aroused the ire of Korean anti-Communists, made Communism the big political question of South Korea, and upset persons who wanted some sort of elected government. The United States forfeited in Korea the solid position it achieved in Japan by holding elections and operating through the government chosen by it. The only possible excuse for this forfeit was that it aimed at keeping Russia from becoming more troublesome.

Meanwhile, the Russians proceeded with their own plans in North Korea. Their zone became in effect a police state run by Russians through Korean intermediaries, many of whom had received special training before the occupation in Siberia or in Communist China. At elections 99.9 per cent of the voters dropped ballots into supervised black-and-white boxes; conscription began of men between seventeen and twenty-five into the Russian-trained army, which in 1947 already numbered more than 100,000 men, and which had as its core the Koreans who had fought with the Chinese Red Army. The Russians themselves lived off the land; they gave little economic aid that was not geared to the creation of the army in the North and to support of communist groups in the South. Their economic moves were essentially political; they called in all Korean currency in their zone, for instance, exchanged it for scrip, and used the money to finance men and parties in the United States zone.

Few facts on actual political conditions in the North came to light. The unpopularity of the Russian Occupation was evident from the constant flow of emigrants to the South. (It was underlined some years later when the United States forces in their fight back up the Korean peninsula received a more cordial welcome in Communist Pyongyang than in Seoul.) But it would be a mistake to underestimate what support the Russians did receive. They were able to form a government and an army which went on obeying Russian dictates even after the Russian Army had left the country. For such popularity as there was, the causes were similar, one suspects, to those which produced popular support for the Communists in China—economic and political confusion among a Confucian people anxious for social order; desperateness arising from war-end poverty and dislocation, particularly marked among students and present probably even among rural youth; dictation through native intermediaries; an existing body of trained professional Korean Communists; a will to power on the part of old-style politicians; an efficient system of eradicating any outward evidences of dissatisfaction; and a skilled use of the political lie.

The lies were monstrous. They had to do not only with sanguine pledges for future peace and plenty but with distortions of obvious political fact. Yet not a few North Koreans, even some Americans, believed them. At the precise time that the United States was seeking all possible avenues for co-operation with its co-occupier, Russian news agencies charged that the United States was refusing to co-operate, a charge echoed at the time by not a few American publicists. And at the time when the United States was attempting to load the Interim Legislative Assembly with persons tolerant of Communists, the Russian news sources cried out that the United States was backing reactionaries. This cry was also echoed by certain American publicists, even by certain Americans in the occupying force, and it appeared from time to time in United States newspapers and magazines.

In Korea the American heard voices speaking words that he would never know. He walked past a hostile people called by Westerners "The Irish of the Orient," a people supposed to be given to political outbursts and violence, and he knew not what they thought. He looked at Confucian shrines set beside Japanese-built Western office buildings, at rows of wooden houses with sloping roofs, at squalid farm villages; and the sight of the life that would be forever hidden increased his apprehension and did not satisfy his wonder. He listened to the pattern of Korean speech and unconsciously speculated: Can this be a language? Can they be really talking? Can they be scheming something? Even when the curtain of not-knowing was pierced by interpreters, themselves Korean, there was the bewilderment of not knowing where to turn and whom to trust. The Koreans were not obsequious like the Japanese. Not wanting Americans in their country, they did not strive to put them at ease. They did not act toward an American as if impressed by his superiority. Life in Japan, buttered by the enthusiastic deference of the Japanese, could be comfortable, and the dirt and poverty of the country could be dismissed as quaint. But what was quaint in Korea?

The fear was hidden; therefore the fear grew. Some men struck at their servants. Instead of conferring with Korean subordinates some issued orders to them. Some, perplexed by the records the Koreans kept or the actions they took, settled on the imperial rule of playing one off against the other in an effort to ensure honesty. The American complained to himself that Korea was the end of the line (as indeed it was), that nobody cared (as few did). Like the majority of his fellows, he bent his efforts to schemes for going home. In such a situation it was not difficult to develop that peculiar variety of isolationism that was ready to let Russia take on the problems of foreign poverty and perversity.

For two years United States policy toward Korea did not change; it simply muddled along. This muddling was encouraged by the tendency among persons in the War and State Departments to justify the policy of co-operation with Russia not simply as an opportunistic maneuver but as international morality. Consequently, it became customary among many Americans in Seoul and among some in Washington to apply to Koreans who disliked the policy of co-operation a term of moral opprobrium, "extreme rightist." Unfortunately this term took root in the political lexicon of the United States Occupation, and it was not uprooted during the whole course of the Occupation. Koreans who did not mind dealing with both Communists and anti-Communists were called centrists, Communist sympathizers were known as moderate leftists, while the extreme left was reserved for the simon-pure.

This political relativism, which made Communism the point of observation for the political universe, was hardly realistic. Syngman Rhee, head of the "extreme rightists," formally favored more freedoms than the Bill of Rights and the Atlantic Charter, and believed in the nationalization of all but small industry. South Korean parties by and large endorsed the same political program; trusteeship and Communism were such large issues that the parties had insufficient chance to develop varying attitudes towards strictly domestic problems. The parties were separate in their individual desires for power or a share of it, in their varying feelings of cold and warmth for the Occupation, in their varying emotions toward Communism, and in their composition; there were even special groups of intellectuals, students, union workers, and women.

Korean politics, complex, became confused both to Koreans and to Americans by being oversimplified through United States emphasis on coalition with Communism. Kimm Kiusic, a sincere, scholarly man, not unlike Henry Wallace, amenable to a variety of political colorations, was considered by most Americans in Korea a centrist or a moderate, and for a time enjoyed more tacit support from the Occupation than any other politician. There was no evidence, however, that he had wide popular support, and certain Americans in Washington and in Seoul tried to convince themselves that there was a group now outside politics that was soon to come forward in Korea, perhaps in much the same way that it has always been supposed to be about to come forward in the politics of almost all democratic countries.

On this scene walked two chief actors. The first, General Hodge, was authority in South Korea. An able soldier, an excellent negotiator with the Russians, he was neither by experience nor by predilection a politician. He did not like to issue overmany orders, but he talked in tones that made it seem at times that he did. In public address to Koreans he often lectured, and he looked upon some Koreans who disagreed with United States policies as troublesome obstructionists. The second actor was Syngman Rhee, a lifelong professional agitator for Korean independence with a long record of disagreement with the State Department. He disagreed over the prewar policy of tolerating Japan; he disagreed during the war when the State Department declined to recognize a free Korean government. Here was a man not unlike General Hodge: holding many American ideas; convinced in his views and loud in his statement of them; strong in principles; as opposed to Communism in Korea as General Hodge would have been in the United States; altogether a man of considerable force with a readiness of his own to consider those who disagreed with him as obstructionists. Furthermore, he functioned as a politician and was as much concerned with the mind of the potential electorate as General Hodge was concerned with the smoothness of the administration of military government.

These discordant personalities, after jostlings over the issue of trusteeship (Rhee: the United States should get out), clashed so hard over the question of the coalition policy (Rhee: no truck with Communists) that, without viewing each other as enemies, they continued to view each other with distrust. Indeed, many Americans in Seoul labelled Rhee a rightist obstructionist, and upon this theme officers and officials wrote variations to their own tastes; some even charged him with having too strong an orientation toward American ideas. General Hodge, of course, would have hooted at any such charge. Yet while banking in the last analysis on its style of democracy as a model for the government of Korea rather than on Russian-style Communism, the United States Command was at odds with the Korean who managed to be probably the most prominent politically and at the same time the most American ideologically. Obviously the United States could recognize no nonelected leader; but just as obviously it should not have quarreled with any possible friend.

To be sure, Americans in Korea were not ill-intentioned. They were well-intentioned, aware of it, and bewildered to learn that the little children recited a nursery rhyme that, when translated, says:

> Birdies, birdies, fly away home.
> Do not sit on the pea vine, for
> If you do the flowers will fall,
> And many people will cry. . . .

This, in effect, told the Americans to get out of the country. The problem was not one of intention but of information. Before they arrived in Korea, few Americans knew anything about the Far East, let alone the country to which they were sent. Courses for military-government men in Korea were inadequate. Almost no Americans spoke Korean, although it has an easy-to-learn alphabet. There was no foolproof system of finding out what the people thought. G-2 could read letters and collect private opinions; each American could listen to the Koreans around him, but whom should he trust? What was to be made of this ancient country, what of these men in the straw hats, what of these people silent one moment and noisy in demonstrations the next?

The Occupation ran polls, but it tended to distrust them because they turned up answers that did not fit the artificial ideological grid that alone seemed to make Korea understandable. A poll indicating popularity for a separate government for South Korea was called into question because there were loud outcries from certain political groups. The accuracy of the polls, of course, was probably low; an opinion survey in a foreign and Oriental country is not easy. But other devices of intelligence were still rougher, and the American in Korea and the American in Washington wandered amid the sands of conflicting ideas, notions, rumors, propaganda, and guesses—out of which it was difficult to make sense without imposing upon them a preconceived framework of judgment.

At length United States policy began to change. It changed first towards Russia about the beginning of 1947, when it became clear that the hope for just-around-the-corner co-operation was empty. Various possibilities for Korea were considered. It would have been possible, despite Cairo and Moscow commitments, to complain that it was impossible to do business with the Russians and pull out of Korea altogether. Such a step would have appealed greatly to the nationalistic sentiments of Koreans (though hardly to their sense of security), and it would have generated great Korean pressure for a Russian departure. But a police state is proof against considerable pressures, and a United States withdrawal would very possibly have encouraged Russian intrusion even more prominently into the South Korean scene. It would also have been possible to suggest joint withdrawal, which would put harder-to-resist pressures on Russia, for were she to refuse, she would have borne all the not-inconsiderable onus for both her own and the American occupation among a people, in both North and South, whom she wished to addict to her way of thinking. From the United States point of view, however, this suggestion would have been foolhardy if Russia were unwilling to disband the North Korean conscript army. Even then, Russia would only have to step a few feet over her border. The United States would have to step eight thousand miles and at a time when the economic condition of South Korea remained weak.

Besides, however much foreign withdrawal might have

met Korean desires to be alone in their country, it would have weakened the United States in the collision diplomacy that was being carried on with Russia throughout the rest of the world, except in China, and thus in the long run would weaken Korea also. It was too late to call upon fellow trustees, China and Britain, except for formalities. Furthermore, the United States did not wish to admit failure. Admissions of failure, however profitable in the life of morals, appear to spell bankruptcy in politics. It seemed for a time that the only possible course in Korea was for the United States to forget Russia and do her best in her own zone.

Consequently, the State and War departments made ready a plan to spend $540,000,000 to meet the specific economic needs that earlier detailed surveys had uncovered. In April 1947 the plan was ready for submission to Congress. It appeared to be proof against unpleasant surprises: the Russians, of course, could promptly suggest joint withdrawal, but withdrawal would not mean abandonment of the program which could easily be turned over to a United States financial mission. This being the case, there was doubt whether Russia would propose withdrawal at all. There was doubt, too, whether Russia, who controlled ten million of Korea's thirty million people and was not insensitive to the opinion of the rest, would sabotage the United States program, by pulling switches on the power she was sending to the South. Were she to pull them, everyone in Korea would know whose hand had done the work; no amount of propaganda could hide it or its aims. The State and War departments decided to go ahead. They believed they could convince the Koreans that Americans meant very well after all.

When policy changed in regard to Russia, it had to change also in regard to South Korean politics. The one clear fact that had always emerged from the Korean political imbroglio was that the Koreans wanted to run the country for themselves. The authors of the $540,000,000 program—in particular, Assistant Secretary of State John H. Hilldring and Assistant Secretary of War Howard C. Patersen—held closely to this fact. They avoided the naïveté of assuming that recipients of gifts are usually thankful and attempted to meet Korean distrust of the United States by deciding upon an elected, not appointed, government of the South, which could, if the Russians continued un-co-operative, eventually speak in the name of all Korea. Clearly, once it was decided to cease buttering the Russians, it became unnecessary to make them a present of a synthetic coalition of pro- and anti-Communist parties. Gestures had already been made in the direction of the fervent Korean nationalism: Americans had been removed from the main building of state in Seoul, and Koreans had been moved in. Now it became possible to look for a genuine South Korean government.

News of this change of policy spread to Korean groups in Washington, and from there made its way to Seoul, where it was met with enthusiasm. Russia promptly prepared counter-moves. At the foreign ministers' meeting in Moscow in April 1947, at which Secretary of State Marshall was the United States representative, Molotov agreed new joint meetings for a final setting up of a united North–South Korean government. (He also, with unapologetic illogicality charged the United States with illiberalism for not agreeing that the Communists made up the only democratic party in South Korea.) United States policy fell into the trap. The consequence of its blunder was the first of a series of fatal missteps for the United States in Korea. The program of aid was not submitted to Congress; the South Korean election plan was called off for a time. The joint meetings convened, deliberated at length, collapsed. The United States did not, however, resurrect the aid program. It made, in fact, no mention of the program at all, and handed the political problem to the United Nations Assembly, which appointed a committee. Russia refused to let the committee enter her zone, and in

February 1948 calmly set up her own puppet government. A year had passed and the United States position in Korea was worse than it had been.[1]

By the end of 1947, in fact, the United States had lost its chance to strengthen South Korea. For the failure to go ahead with the aid program and with free elections, there are a variety of reasons, one of the most important of which is what might be called a policy lag. When substantial numbers of experts are examining an area in terms of an old policy, it requires time before it is possible for them to see the area in terms of new policy. While the men then in executive positions in the State Department did not look at Korea through the fictitious political grid created during the coalition period, they were dependent for their information on men who went on looking through that grid. The men on the field and the men in subordinate positions in Washington described Korea in the terminology in use a year earlier, and the mutual distrust of Syngman Rhee and John Hodge survived the policy that originally provoked it. The temper and language of an earlier situation continued.

In any case, after 1947 the United States was able to do no more than counter Russian moves. After the Russians had set up their government in the North, free elections were at last held in the South, and a Korean government was installed. Dr. Rhee, not surprisingly, emerged as president. The next Russian step was to remove their own troops, leaving behind, of course, government "advisors" and the North Korean Army. This step was followed by the United States withdrawing its troops also. American advisors, to be sure, remained in small numbers. But the United States left no army comparable to that left by the Russians.

The policy of strenuous effort to be friendly to Russia had ended in making Korea a particularly tempting area for Russian military adventurism. Three years after the United States gave up its plan to aid South Korea—the one plan that might have created enough strength to give pause to Russian expansion—the United States was in fact at war with North Korea and, in effect, at war with China and Russia.

As it concerned American policy, the Korean war was a series of shocks that raised for review the principles that had been deduced from the years of war, civil war, and occupation when the United States had been the chief agent in the cultural meeting of East and West. The first shock, of course, was Russia's actual recourse to arms through the agency of one of her captive states. The second shock was realization of the need to rush assistance to South Korea, previously struck off the War and State Department maps as an indefensible area. It was suddenly and acutely evident in Washington and in the U.N. that although Russia had chosen to strike at the weakest point along the non-Communist periphery, that point would have to be contested: to fail to root out aggression in any country of the world was to fertilize the soil for a fear amongst other countries that aggression against them would not be stamped out. Korea, therefore, would have to be saved, and the unity of the non-Communist world buttressed.

As the line of battle moved up and down the Korean peninsula, there came additional shock. Korea was being saved at the cost of the lives and livelihoods of some millions of Koreans, cast adrift amid ruins. Furthermore, the non-Communist world was taking the lesson that aggression does not pay in a manner that did not bespeak over-great confidence in the United States. What had started as a limited police action and as such was greeted with general though grim enthusiasm, stretched out into a campaign which certain countries, themselves fearful of aggression, came to suspect as a waste of resources and as a danger of a spread of war. And then there came the shock, the great shock, of full-scale Chinese Red Army intervention. This intervention not only created new problems of war; it also prompted fresh division of counsel at the United Nations and acrimonious debate all over the world. Where should American aid be given—East or West?

It had been largely through the eyes of the Americans active in China during the decade between 1937 and 1947 that the rest of the world had seen China. Not two years before Chinese intervention in Korea, the United States had told the world in a special White Paper that China's Central Government was basically at fault for China's troubles. Previously the American Government had tried to believe that the Chinese Communists were something else, and it had made the point that China was too weak and too unimportant to be strengthened. And then late in 1950 the Chinese Communists presented themselves not only as an active military force, operating with considerably more effect than American military men had thought Chinese armies capable of, but also as an active bargainer for international advantage. The Chinese Communist Government demanded in effect that Korea be left to the North Koreans, that Formosa, the seat of China's Nationalist Government, be left to them, and that they be given the seat of that government at the United Nations.

The State Department was faced with the final debacle of its China and Korea policies precisely at a time when it was highly difficult to frame a new policy that would not involve the spread of war, and when it was highly difficult to discuss policy out loud without drawing fresh attack from political opponents at home. Pressure, furthermore, was being brought by various countries abroad to arrange a truce on terms favorable to the North Koreans who had launched the original attack on South Korea and to the Chinese Communists who had followed it up—an arrangement which could have given encouragement to further Communist aggression in Asia and would probably have propagated among Eastern nations fear more intense than the original United Nations action aimed to forestall.

This was the great dilemma which the State Department

confronted during the winter of 1950–51. It could not by its
very nature be resolved in terms of policy. It was the ultimate
consequence of the cultural conflict between East and West,
a conflict that had now become the property of all nations.
What had long been tangled was not easy to unravel; furthermore, it could be rewoven only with the hands of dozens of
other countries upon it. In part this dilemma resulted from
the ability of Russian Communists to push stratagems of war
and politics with fairly exact knowledge of how far they could
go without risking general war, knowledge of a sort that was
not available to the United Nations, whose stratagems were
held back. But the basic quandary involved an old question,
the apportionment of military effort, a question very hard to
solve in a state of semi-paralysis brought on by fear of unlimited war. The question was emphasized by Truman's dismissal
of MacArthur. The tragedy was that no government and no
substantial body of citizens were able to urge unlimited liability of every part of the United Nations for every other part,
and to propose a balanced apportionment of supplies between
East and West. So far as Asia was concerned, the American
Government had a policy of aiding Europe; so far as Europe
was concerned, the Republican opposition had a political
proposal for aiding Asia, a proposal not without call on public
sympathies, since several hundred thousand Americans were
fighting there.

President Truman argued that policy in the Far East had
not been changed, but it remained evident that policy itself
—confused for almost a decade and a half—had not yet been
untangled. It would not be untangled fully until the basic
cultural collision between East and West—the root of Asia's
noises and alarms—would be sensed by the imagination, en-
compassed by the emotions, understood by the mind.

15

Outward West and Inward East

HISTORY IS *now:* IT IS A FLEETING INSTANT WHOSE FORM has been compressed and shaped by eons of time, and whose own small weight will help to shape instants yet to come. In the Far East, the essence of *now*, the essence of today's fleeting instant, is a cultural collision which has erupted into armed conflict. The reality of the instant remains in large part the reality of a tyrannous decade of confusion and error, just as the reality of the decade was the reality of the centuries that went before it. Between East and West there was not enough common ground where men of varying inward drives could meet and talk, not enough community of mind where separateness and difference could be put aside.

Is there then nothing in the present except what was molded by the past? Can there be nothing but separateness, difference, collision? It is clear that the good will of Easterners and Westerners has been strong, but that the particular ways in which they thought and felt and acted have been stronger. To Easterners nature was a bamboo clump to be gazed at emptily, while to Westerners it was an outward force to be controlled and put to work. To Easterners the facts of outward social life were less real than personal relationships within families, while to Westerners such facts were the primary

raw material from which to mold a more abundant life.
Easterners, poor missionaries of their own culture, left with
Westerners little more than a spectacle of poverty and confusion. Westerners, no better missionaries, left a spectacle of
superiority and might. Confronted by a West impelled toward the production of more and more things and the elaboration of bigger and bigger systems of government and
industry, Easterners fell into an uncertainty of mind in which
envy could not overcome distaste. Confronted by an East
indifferent to the countable, the logical, the tangible—confronted, in short, by an inward East—the Westerners fell
back involuntarily upon rationalized myth to explain the
East's strangeness away.

Is this strangeness the continuing and inevitable consequence of the past? If it is, and if the cultural conflict of East
and West is merely a reproduction, painted in higher and
more obvious color, of the separateness and strangeness by
which all groups, perhaps all persons, keep themselves apart
from one another, then there no longer remains hope for any
effective sort of joint social action, for there would then be
no hope for the understanding between individuals upon
which social action depends. The only possible lesson to take
from such hopelessness would be for individuals to retire into
their personal concerns, contemplate such eternal truths as
they privately believe in, shun the world, and await a pre-
ordained decline and fall of empires and governments, industries and exchanges, arts and sciences.

Such a decline and fall would be sudden rather than ·slow.
It is clear that history in the middle of the twentieth century
does not permit cultures to collide, recoil, and fall apart quietly and gracefully. It does permit them to collapse before
dynamic and messianic Russia, manipulating and imposing
dogmas of thought that permit of no question, forcing upon
life itself a measured, organized system of tyranny, which is
self-admittedly the most mendacious, probably the most effi-

cient, undoubtedly the most active, and perhaps the most extreme known in history. Russian Communists, hawking the opposite of liberty, the nadir of equality, together with fraternity of the sort that exists in a concentration camp, has still managed to give many people a feeling of being brought together in mighty and meaningful works. Men and women of various classes, countries, and cultures have even besought the new inquisitors to take away their freedom and to give them in exchange not even bread or security but a sense of purpose in life. The power of the Russian system is essentially a testimony to faith—a faith that is false to all persons who believe in a relatively unfettered search for scientific, social, or religious truth, but yet faith powerful enough to impose itself upon peoples whose own faith has weakened. Therefore, if cultural conflicts be inevitable, the unavoidable consequence is acquiescence to the Russian system or participation in it, whether in the form of Russian nationalism or, what is perhaps more grotesque morally, in the form of another nationalism that adopts Russian methods of total tyranny.

To assume, however, that there is nothing in the present except what was put there by the past and to deduce that cultural conflicts are inevitable and unreconcilable is to overlook, first of all, the important fact that there is a basic unity among cultures that overrides the multiplicity of different cultural forms. Governments differ, but men everywhere deal with the problem of government; ideas about man's individuality differ, but men everywhere face the problems of self; conceptions of time and space differ, together with the mathematics that arise from them, but men everywhere count and measure, put up bridges and buildings, and devise calendars. And there are forever the basic facts of eating, sleeping, working, laughing, sorrowing, loving, talking, begetting children and rearing them, coming into life and

dying, along with tilling fields, making things, and transporting and selling goods. That men have elaborated different
cultures does not mean that they lack common experience.
Indeed, if attention is given to cultural similarities rather
than differences, there are many areas in which peoples removed from each other in time or space draw very similar
conclusions from similar experiences: the ceremonial bath
of the Chinese is not unlike the handwashing of the Jews,
the sacrifice of bullocks not unlike the sacrifices of the
Greeks; socialism in ancient China was attended by many of
the arguments that attend socialism in present-day Britain;
feudalism in Japan called forth a code of behavior comparable in some respects to that called forth by feudalism in
Europe; and the teachings of a philosopher like Lao-tze do
not clash but rather join with those of Jesus, Isaiah, and
Gautama Buddha. It would seem that there is in fact a common ground of experience shared by cultures as dissimilar
as those of East and West, a ground broad enough to make
interchange of ideas possible.

The possibility emerges, therefore, that the cultural collisions of East and West—or, for that matter, the collisions
within the West itself—are the result not of a basic hostility
inevitable in the meeting of any two separate groups, but
rather of the particular manner in which the meeting took
place. It is possible, in other words, that conflict arose not
from the situation but from the way the situation was handled—and mishandling is an error that conceivably can be
corrected. Indeed, there have already been certain correc-
tions of the nineteenth-century mistakes of extreme Western
condescension towards Easterners and of colonial exploitation. If the intensity of the collision of East and West can be
attributed to mistakes of such order, then any argument of
inevitability loses force, and hopes of a coming together of
cultures gain.

The important question to ask, therefore, is what went wrong in the meeting of East and West. In attempting an answer it is important to note instances of cultural contact which led neither to perplexity and confusion nor to continuing and repeated collisions, as for instance the peaceful and mutual interchange of ideas between China and India or the interchange that often takes place between groups in the framework of a single culture. Such interchange, which works slowly and inconspicuously, means, in effect, an open-mindedness towards new ideas and an unconcern for selfish economic advantage.

Another and very different sort of cultural contact works openly, quickly, and, in terms of the moralities of most peoples, wickedly. It suppresses cultural collision by the outright conquest of one culture by another, by the subsequent suppression of the culture itself, and by the extermination of dissidents: a procedure often used in the ancient world and used today by Communist Russia, whose foreign policy consists essentially of strategies to effect total cultural conquest of other countries, as for instance China and the nations of Central Europe.

What went wrong with the West's penetration of Eastern cultures is typified by the confusion and perplexity it generated throughout Asia. It was identifiable neither as total conquest nor as peaceable interchange. The use of unlimited violence to enslave alien peoples was contrary to the accepted general morality of the West, and an openness to alien ideas was contrary to the accepted belief in the moral and technological superiority of Western culture. What is more, the development of rapid and relatively certain transportation in the nineteenth century made for sudden and dramatic contacts between cultures. Under these circumstances, a cultural collision could have been headed off only if the West had approached the East with as much interest in receiving

as in giving new cultural ideas and with as much concern for
giving as receiving material benefits: an interest and a concern obviously impossible for nineteenth-century Westerners, whose notions of the eternal rightness of their particular
ideas served as justification for their taking such benefits as
they could put their hands on.

This smug rationale did not, of course, survive by more
than a few years the century that gave it birth, but a semiconscious conviction of the superiority of things Western did
survive. During the past twenty-five years the contact of East
and West has been attended not so much by obvious economic exploitation as by hidden mental condescension. This
condescension took the form of a one-way communication of
ideas, a type of communication that usually fails unless it is
backed by force. Whenever persons or peoples are free to
learn or not to learn, new ideas gain currency as the result
of contagion, not dictation; of conversation, not monologue.
To teach Easterners effectively, Westerners would have had
to be willing to go to school to the very persons they were
teaching. In the absence of such two-way communication,
furthermore, the teacher could not know his pupils; his
guesses as to what they were thinking had to be based largely
on what he was thinking himself: hence the stereotypes
which fitted the people who believed them more exactly than
they fitted the people they were supposed to describe, and
which interposed an additional barrier to mutual interchange of ideas. The simplest thing in the world—a give-and-
take conversation between friends and equals—was one of
the rarest things during more than a century of East-West contact. Westerners remained convinced that their role in Asia
was to impose so far as possible the standards that prevailed
within their own culture.

The closest approach to any sort of mutual interchange
during the past decade was a supposed mutuality of selfish
interests. China needed ideas of technology and weapons of

war; Japan needed tools of industry; Korea needed national
liberation. The West, on the other hand, needed friends in
war and in peace. In this mutual relationship, Western
interests seemed, however, to predominate. It was tacitly
assumed that, so long as the West pursued a course of enlightened selfishness, all countries would benefit. It was assumed,
for instance, that it was to the advantage of China to be
treated not simply as a country in itself, a country of special
needs, sufferings, and hungers, but as an adjunct to the American war effort and to the American plan for peace, which for
some years centered on the hope of Russo–American co-operation. It was assumed also that it was to the advantage of
Japan and Korea to be treated as adjuncts to American foreign policy. Yet this treatment stirred among the peoples of
the Far East humiliation and confusion, along with the conviction that it is given only to the mighty to walk with pride.
This reaction in turn stirred bitterness and apathy among
Westerners in Asia, so that it even became difficult to respond
to the deep poverty and suffering of Eastern peoples with a
sense of tragedy.

In short, the mistake that threw the cultural meeting of
East and West into an intense cultural collision was the mistake of treating Eastern peoples not straightforwardly as persons who are valuable in themselves but rather as units of
population which can be used as means to some greater end:
the reform of governments and the conduct of trade, the procedures of war and diplomacy, or simply the expression of
Western superiority and an urge to dominate. Under these
circumstances, many Easterners attempted, usually with little success, to use Westerners as means to their own particular
ends. The mistake was a mistake of attitude, a mistake in the
way one person approached another person.

This mistake of attitude is not irrevocable. The mistake will
disappear as soon as the attitude finally changes, and the

attitude itself has been changing slowly for almost a century. The attitude will change finally when a sufficient number of persons grasp a profound, simple, but very taxing fact of human experience: the use of other persons or other peoples as devices to make oneself feel superior provokes hostility and leads to emotional or cultural collision. Other persons, whether they be of one culture or another, must be treated as ends in themselves, not as means to some other end. Once this fact is grasped, two-way conversations between men of different habits and backgrounds of thought and emotion become possible, and way opens to a quiet and unnoticed amalgam of ideas of various cultures. This amalgam cannot be brought about. No outward schemes of war or economics will by themselves produce it. It can only happen. Cultural problems are located in the hidden as well as in the exposed layers of the human personality; they can be solved only out of the semiconscious stirrings of people numbered in the hundred millions.

Receptivity to other cultures does not mean loss of faith in one's own traditions. It does not mean acquiescence to tyranny or to violence. It means rather the recognition that various persons and various cultures stand on a common ground in a free search for truth, however variously they seek it and define it. It means a faith that this common ground is in the long run more solid than empires, tyrannies, systems of rigid organization, and techniques of lying; and that this ground is the only base for the eventual liberation of peoples now enslaved. The contemporary denial that there is such a common ground of truth is essentially a denial that there is anything meaningful in human life. It is a denial of that which is creative in men and of that which has at times made men seek unity with one another. It would seem likely that persons or groups aid themselves only by aiding others, teach others only by being taught themselves, and that they keep themselves alive and their spirits fresh only by taking part in the paradox of gaining by losing. The only alternative to an annihilation alike of separate persons and separate cultures through their constant and now-increasing collision may well be a community of persons and cultures in a unifying search for truth.

Notes

1. The quotations from Lao-tze used throughout this book are taken from the translation by John C. H. Wu, published in 1939 in the magazine *T'ien Hsia* under the title of "Lao Tzŭ's The Tao and Its Virtue." Most of the translation can be found, although not in its original order, in *The Old Fellow,* by Herrymon Maurer, New York, 1943. Mr. Wu's translation has the virtue of catching not only the ideas but the impact of the original. His annotations, which compare the mood of certain passages of Lao-tze with writings of Western authors, provide a helpful bridge from West to East.

2. The lively translation of Lin Yutang is the source of the quotations from the Confucian classics and from Sze-ma Chien's *Life of Confucius.* This translation, originally published in 1938, has the virtues of crisp, succinct English prose and of wide availability. It is included in The Modern Library under the title, *The Wisdom of Confucius.*

The picture of Confucius in the present study is drawn without making distinction between what may be fact about him and what may be fancy. The Confucian teaching, in common with the teachings of other philosophers, was undoubtedly quite flexible in its earliest period. Sze-ma Tan, in the second century B.C., was the first person to divide Chinese philosophy into schools, i.e., Confucian, Taoist, Legalist, and so on. That there was an important degree of intercourse between the earliest philosophies is suggested also by the interaction of the various schools throughout Chinese history and by their tolerance of each other.

3. Some scholars suspect Confucius of having a sense of humor and assert that he laughed at himself over the way rulers failed to make use of him. A disciple said, "Here is a beautiful piece of jade, kept in a casket and waiting for a good price for sale." Confucius remarked, "For sale! For sale! I'm the one waiting for a good price for sale!" Here one suspects not so much humor as bitterness.

The life of this early-day scholar was hardly joyous and certainly far from easy. He was born, out of wedlock it is said, in the small country of Lu and claimed descent from a duke of Sung, another principality. His father died when he was young. As a child he played at sacrifices and ceremonies. His first work was as a granary and cattle clerk, whence he rose to be minister of public works. He began to take in students, and he went on a ritual-research trip to the capital city of Chou. When he was thirty-five years old his own country fell into disorder, and he went forth to serve as secretary to Baron Chao Kao in Chi, where he learned the ancient symbolic dance music, *Hsiao*. (He was so excited by it that "for three months he forgot the taste of meat.") But just as he was beginning to gain the favor of the Duke of Chi, a plot was stirred against him, and he departed for home. There, however, barons presently usurped the authority of the Duke of Lu, and, in the words of the historian Sze-ma Chien, "The country was therefore plunged into a state of moral chaos, from the lords down to the people, and Confucius decided not to go into the government, but retired to study or edit the books of poetry and history and ritual and music." Disciples flocked to him. Subsequently he was given position, destroyed the citadels of usurping barons, and rose to be Chief Minister. After he had been three months in office, ". . . butchers did not adulterate their meat, and men and women followed different lanes in the streets. Things lost on the streets were not stolen. . . ."

Thereupon, enemies sent Lu a present of eighty dancing girls, who so preoccupied the first baron that he missed the Sacrifice to Heaven and absented himself from his duties three days. In any case, Confucius fell out of favor. He left his native country and took to wandering about. Here began a long series of misfortunes that kept him almost always out of office and almost continually on the road. These wanderings, always in company with disciples, went on for fourteen bitter years, at the end of which he returned in 484 B.C. to his home. He was sixty-seven then. He wrote, it is said, a bare chronicle of events in the kingdom of Lu, taught his disciples and died in 479 B.C.

(The above sketch is drawn from the writings of Sze-ma Chien, an early historian who flourished about 100 B.C., but who did not hold a sufficiently fine balance between fact and fancy to convince moderners of the exactness of what he wrote. What is important for a study of the inward content of Chinese culture, however, is not so much what Confucius actually was as how he looked to the generations that followed him.)

4. Fan Chung-yen was a scholar who came from a poor family and became one of the great leaders during the Northern Sung Dynasty. He was responsible for reforms in finance and education during the decade between 1041 and 1050. His remark on the responsibilities of scholars, frequently quoted ever since, is set down by Ou-yang Hsiu in the twentieth chapter of Ou-yang Hsiu's *Collected Works.*

5. These injunctions on etiquette occur in the *Li Chi,* a classic of diverse sources, much of which is given over to a discussion of how to hold funerals. The full quotation runs as follows: "Do not roll rice into a ball, do not leave rice on the table, and do not let soup run out of your mouth. Do not smack your lips, do not leave a bone dry, and do not persist in trying to get a particular piece of meat. Do not turn rice about to let it cool off, and do not take porridge with chop sticks. Do not gulp the soup up, do not stir the soup about, do not pick your teeth, and do not add sauce to the soup." Later on the *Li Chi* advises, "Bite off boiled meat with your teeth, but do not bite off cured meat with your teeth."

6. During the 1930's and 40's Chinese educators and social workers drew attention to the social advantages that would arise from a system of foster-home placement of underprivileged orphaned children. Chinling Women's College, which made a particular study of the problem, found that, although the system of adoption was in wide use, any attempt to introduce a foster-home relationship of nonrelated persons would break upon the hard rock of family centeredness.

7. Confucianists have always disdained the ideas of the legal-

ists. The exception is Hsun-tze, a contemporary of Mencius, who believed human nature was bad but improvable by correction. It was impossible to find a middle ground between his ideas and those of Mencius, and Hsun-tze was later considered heterodox. Just as Confucianism never took to nationalism and drum beating, so too it rejected the idea of a state based on legal restraints.

The *Fa-chia,* the school of law, on the other hand, put first emphasis upon war and punishment. The maintenance of a strong state through agriculture and planned commerce, an idea which attracted some members of the school, together with the expansion of the state through war, constituted the chief function of a ruler. Since the people could not be expected to understand these aims, such Legalists as Han Fei-tze and Shang-tze argued that they must be directed to them by force. Shang-tze, the more extreme of the two, wrote: "Concentrate the people upon warfare, and they will be brave; let them care about other things, and they will be cowardly. . . . A people that looks to warfare as a ravening wolf looks at a piece of meat is a people that can be used. In general, fighting is a thing that the people detest. A ruler who can make the people delight in war will become king of kings."

(The translation is by Arthur Waley; it appears in his *Three Ways of Thought in Ancient China,* London, 1939. Mr. Waley points out that Shang-tze twice suggests that the way to take advantage of an enemy is to do things that the enemy would be ashamed of doing.)

The Legalists rejected both tradition and Tao and made out to argue from hard facts. While their theories contained a mélange of the ideas of the dominant schools, particularly a twisted and corrupted form of Taoism, their specific proposals were unique: the stamping out of all other schools of thought, organization of the people into groups with individuals forced into espionage against other individuals, detailed laws and rigorous punishments, and an eradication of all classes intermediary between rulers and people. The Legalists were in fact responsible in part for the final ending of feudalism in China, and their ideas were politically dominant for almost a century. It was the legalist Li-sze who directed the conquest of all China by the State of Chin and who, in effect, seated the Prince of Chin as Shih Hwang Ti, First Emperor.

The fact that social changes that the Confucianists and the Taoists could not effect were effected by the Legalists is not without bearing on China's history more than twenty centuries later. Furthermore, there are certain evident similarities between Legalist methods and the methods of Communism currently employed in China. While it is well to be wary of exact parallels in history, it perhaps should be noted further that the Legalists could not budge the fundamental Confucianist and Taoist roots of the Chinese mind, and that Legalist teaching survived only as an episode of concern to scholars of history.

8. Dr. Sun's sentiments on moulding together the heap of loose sand are quoted with approval by Chiang Kai-shek in *China's Destiny,* New York, 1947.

9. Dr. Hu Shih has given an interesting single-sentence description of Chiang in his October 1950 article in *Foreign Affairs:* "Chiang was a prodigal son turned Puritan Christian at a mature age, and the world must try to understand him in that light." It might be noted further that Chiang acted somewhat as if he were the only Puritan Christian-Confucian in the country. He was willing to take more responsibility than any man could carry; he became head of countless organizations, party and government bodies, schools, banks, military institutes, and what not. Having the head of the government as head of an organization shielded the latter, of course, from criticism and impeded the development of the idea of public accountability. Furthermore, although this practice aided the unity of the country, it involved Chiang in overmuch activity and strengthened his habit of getting things done—when politically possible—by issuing peremptory orders. Once he ordered that the Western system of dating the years in terms of the Christian era be dropped from Chinese newspapers. A prominent liberal wrote to Chiang, taking him to task for issuing orders, and in the course of the protest mentioned the order on year-dating as evidence. Chiang neglected the homily on orders, immediately issued another order reinstating the Western dating system.

10. The quotations from Chiang Kai-shek in this chapter are taken from *China's Destiny,* New York, 1947, and from *The Collected Wartime Messages of Generalissimo Chiang Kai-shek,* New York, 1946.

11. One of the most important of the past revisionists of Confucianism was Chu Hsi (A.D. 1130–1200), who anticipated a type

of pragmatic study of literature, and who combined with orthodox ideas new contributions from Buddhism. Almost all of the
liberal scholars during the period that followed the Chinese
Renaissance in 1917 were engaged in effect in revisions of Confucianism.

NOTES TO CHAPTER 4

1. John C. H. Wu's "Lao Tzŭ's The Tao and Its Virtue." See
Note 1, Chapter 3.

2. The quotations from Chwang-tze in this chapter are taken
mainly from translations by Lin Yutang. The stories of the man
who would have nothing to do with the well sweep and of Knowledge's search for Tao are taken from *The Wisdom of China and
India,* New York, 1942. A comprehensive collection of scriptures,
folk tales, essays, poems, and jokes. The remaining quotations are
taken from *Musings of a Chinese Mystic* by Herbert A. Giles
("Wisdom of the East Series"), London, 1920. These quotations
include the story of Prince Hui's cook, the account of Wen Wang
and the fisherman, and the comment on "death and life, preservation and destruction."

3. Tradition and the historian Sze-ma Chien hold that Lao-tze
was an early contemporary of Confucius. Latter-day scholars have
not always agreed. Many of them hold that Lao-tze is more properly the name of a book than the name of a man, and there is
disagreement even upon the time the book was written: Arthur
Waley believing that it appeared after the writings of Chwang-tze;
Fung Yu-lan holding that it appeared before Chwang-tze but not
before Yang Chu; and Henri Maspero insisting that it appeared
before Yang Chu.

In an article printed in Shanghai in 1935 and reprinted in
December 1937 in the *Harvard Journal of Asiatic Studies,* Hu
Shih takes issue with this date-shifting in a detailed and extremely
valuable discussion of methods of literary research, "A Criticism
of Some Recent Methods of Dating Lao Tzŭ." This essay is one
of the first reactions against the more extreme methods of the
"higher criticism" to which students of ancient texts have been
devoted. Dr. Hu points out the dangers in arguing from ideas,
analogies, and styles to prove that only works of a certain precise
sort occurred at a given time, and in so doing erects a series of
laws of literary evidence. He concludes that the traditional date

for Lao-tze should be at least tentatively accepted. It perhaps should be added that historian Sze-ma Chien, main source for the traditional date, was two thousand years closer in time to Lao-tze than our latter-day scholars.

4. Of Lao-tze himself almost nothing is known. What, after all, can be known of a man who believes in "no-names" and who refuses to talk about himself? Clearly, he was one of the first prophets or philosophers to applaud man's inner awareness and to decry man's outward egotism, but the outward Lao-tze, manifested in a few unlikely legends and in the decaying forms of a religion that more and more departed from his teaching, has none of the importance of the spirit of Taoism, to which Lao-tze's small book of five thousand characters, known from the early years of the Christian era as the *Tao Teh Ching,* is the first great contribution.

In his history, Sze-ma Chien set down Lao-tze's name and his birthplace, reported that Lao-tze had a meeting with Confucius, and concluded:

"The practice of Lao-tze was the Tao and the virtue. His doctrine emphasizes the hiding of self and not having names.

"He lived for a long time in the state of Chou, but, foreseeing the decay of the state, he departed and came to the frontier. The officer of the frontier was of the name Yin Hsi.

"He said, 'Sir you are about to withdraw. I beg you, compose a book for me.'

"Lao-tze then wrote a book of a first and second part, discussing the concepts of Tao and of virtue, and he wrote five thousand and some characters. Then he departed.

"No one knows where he died."

(Translation by Herrymon Maurer, *The Old Fellow,* New York, 1943.)

5. The connection between literacy, the lack of which has been repulsive to Westerners, and popular culture seems to be involved in paradox, not only as concerns China but also as concerns other countries. So long as most of the people are unlettered, popular culture draws its strength and even its spoken forms from classical, philosophical literature. When the people become lettered, popular culture deluges them with comic books, ladies' magazines, best sellers, and sensational articles in the daily press. (The equivalents of these began appearing before the 1930's in China's

port cities.) In America literacy has been a necessity for large-scale industry. It has given persons the chance to read *The Yale Review, The New York Times,* the Hundred Best Books, and the philosophy of Albert North Whitehead. At the same time, the average literate person has been cajoled into paying less and less attention to the printed word and more and more to the word spoken on the radio or to the scene shown on television. Whether as a cause or as a coincidence, literacy has been connected with the divorce of popular culture from the culture of ideas, literature, music, art.

It is even arguable that literacy makes it more difficult in certain countries for a people to know what is going on. The men who made up the transportation system in China made up the news system also; the tea houses in which they stopped to rest were the places from which news was broadcast. To be sure, it required several weeks before rumor and exaggeration could be sifted out of the reports on any given event. But even farmers in small hamlets or in the remote hill country had a moderately exact grasp of the more important current events. This system was one by which the people themselves decided what the news was: there was no other way for them to be told. But when literacy provides a way for them to be told, the old channels of information dry up, and the possibility presents itself of telling lies systematically.

The consequence of literacy is not, of course, simply the telling of lies. Systems of indoctrination can lie with some effectiveness to illiterates. But it would seem that Western antipathy toward illiteracy in China resulted more from the persistence of Western prejudices than from the existence of Chinese facts.

6. Lieh-tze's story of Old Man Fool appears in Lin Yutang's *The Wisdom of China and India.*

7. Liu Ling was one of seven philosophers famous during the so-called "Decadent Period." As a form of protest against Confucian ritual and propriety the seven took to carelessness in dress and to the drinking of wine to intoxication. Liu Ling's famous statement is set down in his biography in Chapter 49 of the *Tsin Shu.*

8. During the Sino–Japanese war, Minister of Education Chen Li-fu saddled the universities with a tutorial system, designed,

among other things, to provide teacher investigation of possibly dangerous student thoughts. At certain universities the faculties met solemnly to discuss the venture; with equal solemnity the professors invited their charges to tea at their homes or to conversation in their offices. Then with great earnestness, they would ask some such question as, "Are any of you thinking dangerous thoughts?" The students would say No in unison, and the teacher would write a tortuously worded report, whereupon the talk would turn to other matters.

9. Two of the lines of poetry which were adduced against Su Tung-po in his trial for slander of the government run as follows (translated by Lin Yutang):

> A lone stork does not have to sound alarm at midnight,
> It is difficult to tell the sex of black crows.

The lone stork, Dr. Lin points out, "refers to an ancient passage where a distinguished man in a company of petty men was compared to a stork standing alone in a poultry yard of ducks and chickens. The implied meaning was that those at the court were just common fowl; and crying at midnight was supposed to be a function of the stork. The last line was even more offensive, because there are two lines in the *Book of Poetry* which assert, 'Everybody is saying I am a saint, but who can distinguish a male from a female crow?' The court consisted, therefore, of no more than a pack of black crows in which there was no way of telling which was good and which was bad." (The quotation and the translation are from *The Gay Genius, The Life and Times of Su Tungpo,* New York, 1947.)

Nine centuries later, Liang Chi-chao, for whose opinion all China waited when Yuan Shih-kai sought to make himself emperor in 1915, completed the ruin of Yuan's prestige by means of a single highly oblique literary essay.

10. The remark on the similarity between the will of Heaven and the will of the people appears in the *Shu Ching,* the date of whose composition is unknown. The translation is by James Legge as amended by Lin Yutang, who in his introduction to the *Shu Ching* (in *The Wisdom of China and India*) gives a trenchant essay on the authenticity of ancient texts.

11. In his recent work, *The Western World and Japan,* New York, 1950, Sir George Sansom observes that a distinguishing

feature of the typical Asiatic culture as contrasted with the typical European culture is a self-contained agrarian economy composed of a settled peasantry and a ruling class, antagonistic toward change, which wants to keep the peasant a peasant. This
observation has very great bearing upon the caste system in India
and upon the system of duties to overlords in Japan; it has bearing, too, upon China's self-containment. But in China, cultural
ideas were not the monopoly of a single class, except, of course,
such modern ideas as required knowledge of Western languages;
and it would seem that the cultural choices of the Chinese were
made essentially by Chinese of all sorts, Lao-tze and Confucius
alike giving expressions not so much to the ideas of rulers but to
the hidden drives of the people.

12. Buddhism appeared in China at least as early as the first
century A.D. and spread widely thereafter. It gave China two
particular conceptions theretofore absent: a definite picture of a
future life and a sense of compassion, in which was contained a
belief that ultimate reality is not unaware of human suffering.
Responsible for these contributions was Buddhism in its Mahayana (greater vehicle) form, not in its Hinayana form, which is far
closer to the original teachings of Gautama. Hinayana proposes
that certain individuals find deliverance from suffering and re-
birth by following the teachings of Gautama. Mahayana pro-
claims that everyone is potentially a Buddha, and that the function of the spiritually enlightened person is not only to seek
deliverance but also to preach and serve. Both forms teach
Buddha's Eight-fold Path of nonattachment, right thoughts, good
deeds, and so on as the avenue toward the conquest of desire
and of the suffering of life. Mahayana Buddhism, however, is
more aware of the mass of the people struggling to live in the
midst of suffering.

This awareness was manifest in China not only in the provision
of occasions and subjects for worship, of popular and colorful
rites, and of a panoply of saints, but also in the composition of
the Buddhist pantheon. To Gautama Buddha (in China called
Shih-chia-mou-ni after the family name Sakyamuni) there were
added other Buddhas, notably Amita Buddha (O-mi-to-fu), the
repetition of whose name ensured salvation, and Yao-shih-fu,
whose function was to help and heal the sick and suffering.
Besides these already delivered worthies, there were Boddhisattvas
—prospective Buddhas with final deliverance within reach who

refuse it until everyone is saved. The most prominent of these remarkable symbols of the growth of religious experience is Kwan-yin, Goddess of Mercy, to whom the masses of people of China particularly looked for their salvation, in the form of offspring and well-being in this life and in the form of a paradise there-after.

The similarities between Taoism and Buddhism were recog-nized early. Buddhist scholars even wrote commentaries on the *Tao Teh Ching*. The Chan sect, in which the similarity is most evident, was founded, probably in the sixth century, by Buddhi-dharma (Pu-ti-ta-mo) who is said to have spent nine years in medi-tation before a blank wall and to have said to Emperor Liang Wu Ti, a doer of many good works, "These are all outward things which are of no benefit. The truly valuable things are attained only by inner purification and enlightenment which comes through quiet pondering and meditation." (Karl L. Reichelt, *Truth and Tradition in Chinese Buddhism,* Shanghai, 1927.)

Buddhism in essence slipped into the already well furnished rooms of the Chinese mind, adding certain missing metaphysical furniture and disturbing nothing already there. Most Chinese were able to be Confucianists, Taoists, and Buddhists all at once, and roadside temples often featured a trinity of Confucius, Lao-tze, and the Buddha. Buddhism reinforced regard for human life, made of the monastery a place of withdrawal in times of social confusion, gave religion wider popular appeal. But neither its rise nor its slow decline into corrupted forms, which has been going on since the Tang Dynasty, altered notably the basic Chinese reactions to life and to history.

13. Chinese parents have generally eschewed direction of the young child—except as regards toilet habits which are taught in very much of a let-it-happen fashion—and have appeared to West-erners to be spoiling the child completely. The child is given toys and red suits, articles that mean sacrifice for all but the well off. He is coddled by his family; adults, known and unknown, make a show over him. Children, in the Chinese view, are natural, simple, undifferentiated, in short, *whole,* one of the great Taoist attributes. (Lao-tze asked, "Have you reached the state of a new-born babe? In washing and wiping your inner vision, have you cleansed it from all dross?") Yet the seemingly spoiled children of China make an early and comparatively effortless adjustment to adult responsibilities. By the time they are six or seven, the

farmer's children start to trot under miniature carrying poles and to weed in the fields; the children of the better-off look seriously upon the ideographs that their teachers direct them to copy. Customs and habits, the way of life itself, have not been drummed into them but rather absorbed by them.

14. This maxim is repeated countless times in *Shui Hu Chwan,* novel of rebellion against the declining dynasty of the Sungs. This work was not put together in its final form until the time of the Mings. It is one of the greatest, and most violent, adventure stories ever written. Pearl S. Buck's translation, called *All Men Are Brothers* (New York, 1933), is an unusually happy joining of the Chinese vernacular style with flowing scripture-like English.

NOTES TO CHAPTER 5

1. Comments in this chapter quoted from Japanese newspapers or from Japanese officials during World War II are taken either from records kept by interned Americans or from reports by official United States radio-monitoring agencies.

2. Chinese reactions to Japanese behavior in the third century are noted by Sir George Sansom in *Japan, A Short Cultural History,* New York, 1943. This book, a work of wise analysis and of skillful description, is the great *sine qua non* of any investigation of Japanese thought. Stimulating and important, also, is Sansom's *The Western World and Japan,* New York, 1950.

3. Dr. Karl Löwith's analysis of the frog-into-pond poem appeared in his article, "The Japanese Mind," *Fortune,* December 1943. The article represents a very remarkable effort to come close to the almost unapproachable complexities of Japanese thought and feeling, Zen Buddhism in particular.

4. The word *feudalism,* of course, fits only particular conditions prevalent in medieval Europe and England. There is a temptation to use it as a handy bridge for Western understanding of Eastern countries. Unfortunately it is sometimes more an obstacle than a bridge. As Sir George Sansom points out, the Tokugawa Shogunate rested not alone on a system of feudal-like loyalties but also upon intricate political and military maneuvers against the fiefs of the daimyo. The more important daimyo were subordinate more in theory than in fact. The Japanese system, of course, is an overlord system, but the term *feudal*—or for that

matter the term *military dictatorship,* as applied to Japanese life under such ruling families as the Tairas—stir connotations which do not entirely fit the Japanese scene.

5. In the seventeenth century, early converts to Christianity were ordered to turncoat on pain of punishment and death. They stood firm; 37,000 of them took refuge in a dilapidated castle near Shimabara and resisted until death; only 105 of them are said to have survived. This tragic and moving heroism provokes speculation: how much of it arose out of Christian zeal, how much of it from an affinity to the sort of religious experience the Jesuit fathers preached, and how much of it from Japanese attachment to ideas of honor and obligation?

6. The story of the tradesman and the Yoshiwara girl is quoted from Sir George Sansom's *Japan, A Short Cultural History.*

7. Ruth Benedict's *The Chrysanthemum and the Sword* (Boston, 1946), is a remarkable *tour de force* on Japanese behavior and a witness both to the penetration of the author and to the value of cultural anthropology as a tool of analysis. The study was written at the request of the United States Government to aid wartime decisions. The author could not visit Japan, but the study is nonetheless sharply pertinent. (Dr. Benedict's quotation on the experience of the young scholar is from Etsu Inagaki Sugimoto's *A Daughter of the Samurai.*)

8. Karl Löwith's discussion of momentariness is quoted from "The Japanese Mind." See Note 3, Chapter 5.

NOTES TO CHAPTER 6

1. Commodore Perry's report on his visit to Japan—like all his reports and investigations, detailed and exact—extends to three volumes, in which very little of what happened is left out.

2. The emperor of Japan was also the inheritor of the divine command of *Hakko Ichiu:* bring the eight corners of the world under one Japanese roof. He was the custodian of three sacred treasures, articles bequeathed by ancient gods, that proved his divinity: the sacred mirror and the sacred jewels used to lure the sun goddess out of a cave and restore light to the world, and the sacred sword found by the brother of the sun goddess in the tail of a dragon. The jewels were kept in the Imperial Palace, the sword in the Atsuta Shrine, and the eight-sided bronze mirror at

the religious center of Ise. Here the emperor personally reported great events to his forebears; here cabinet ministers, ambassadors, and generals bowed in reverence after assuming office.

Shintoism, the agency by which the emperor was made identical with the country in the minds of the people, was dramatized by such means. It relied not on theology or dogma, but on simple acts of loyalty repeated time and again in the schools, in the barracks, and in the homes, and reinforced by the pageantry and pomp of official ceremony. Nine major festivals and countless minor ones each year kept before the country the splendor, the antiquity, and the solemnity of the imperial genealogy.

The Japanese overlords made use of the name of their emperor by making him at least quasi-divine. They had therefore to take steps to keep his name solvent; if his name was used unwisely or used too much, there was danger of using up its prestige. The emperor was insulated, therefore, not only by ritual and ceremony, but by various groups of advisors: palace dignitaries and, in particular, the privy council. This body was founded in 1888 to discuss the constitution; it officially advised the emperor, but its advice was not independent. Its twenty-six members, although appointed by the emperor, were chosen by the premier. Venerable and ancient men, they did not as a group live long enough to interfere with major political changes. Furthermore, they were joined ex officio by all the members of the existing cabinet. Essentially the council had the purpose of preserving the emperor from too mundane connections with government activity and of shielding his name from blame for unsuccessful policies. Many Japanese organizations provided for blame-taking but not responsibility-sharing persons or groups of persons to protect the top rank from the consequences of criticism or failure.

3. Some of the businessmen co-operated so intimately with the Army that they were considered Army men. One of these was Yoshisuke Aikawa, an aggressive man who wore his hair in the short-cropped military fashion and was given to abrupt samurai-like declarations such as, "I am Aikawa of Nippon Sangyo Company," or "I reconstructed Kuhara Mining some time ago." Aikawa anticipated the increasing influence of the military in the 1930's and 40's. In 1937 he tied his holding company formally to Army economic interests in the Manchuria Industrial Development Company and turned it into one of Japan's largest business organizations, almost as big as the Mitsui combine.

NOTES TO CHAPTER 7

1. John Earl Baker's remarks on the problems of industrialization in China appeared in an article, "Industrializing the Good Earth," *Fortune,* November 1945. Dr. Baker, who served as a director and as a consultant for many Chinese economic undertakings, emphasizes the need for a slow, natural rate of industrial increase. His article is a wise and cogent explanation of the Chinese economy and of Chinese psychology.

2. Scientific and technical terms were hardest to translate. Political terms came easier, as for instance public opinion, *yu-lun,* literally public discussion; equality, *ping-teng,* equal grade; liberty, *tze-yu,* self-origin; freedom of speech, *tze-yu-yen-yu,* self-origin speech. Such words moved readily into the Chinese language and into Chinese dictionaries. One of the hardest problems of translating Western social or philosophical ideas into Chinese was that of reproducing the subtleties of language existing in the original. The system of translation that was used prior to the time when there were persons fluent both in a Western language and in Chinese was to have a foreigner explain a passage as fully as possible and to have a Chinese put down in decent prose what he understood the foreigner to say. This system, responsible for the translation of a great many Western books, was responsible also for not a few errors. (See E. R. Hughes' *The Invasion of China by the Western World,* New York, 1938; the standard history of cultural relationships for the century following 1839.)

3. When George III made representations to Chien Lung, Emperor from 1736 to 1796, concerning establishment of foreign trading, Chien Lung replied that his country already had an abundance of all things it needed. Until the later part of the nineteenth century, the balance of trade between China and Western countries tipped so heavily in favor of China that the problem of payments in gold weighed heavily upon Western governments. What finally changed the balance was the introduction of cheap machine-made goods, which at length destroyed ancient home industries. This process, still going on in China and India, was one which was denounced particularly by M. K. Gandhi, who believed that the cultural loss in India had been balanced by no economic gain, and who tried to re-establish the weaving of cloth as a home industry.

4. The war that began in 1839 continued sporadically until 1842. There were a variety of specific complaints leading up to it, and the particular *casus belli* was a Chinese prohibition on further importations of British opium. The opium, then a respectable article of trade in Western countries, was intended to redress the adverse balance of East-West trade; the war itself aimed to force China to do what she would not do willingly, accept Western commerce. The conflict ended, to the surprise of the Chinese, in their defeat, in the ceding of Hong Kong to Britain, and to the beginnings elsewhere of the system of treaty ports and extraterritoriality.

5. Under ordinary conditions, the Taiping Rebellion might well have spelled the end of the Ching Dynasty. The Rebellion was a hodgepodge of many motives; it took into its ranks members of secret revolutionary societies that wanted to restore the Ming Dynasty; it picked up some ideas, rather bizarre, from Protestant Christianity; it demanded reform and a better lot for the common people, the country being less prosperous and more oppressed than a century before; it gave expression to humiliation over the weakness of the country. It was in a sense the first popular reaction to Westernism, but it lacked any program of dealing with Westernism. It soon attracted the dislike of more conservative Chinese as well as the hostility of the reigning Ching Dynasty. When it at length developed antiforeign tendencies and became an obstacle to trade, Western powers helped suppress it.

6. The most ambitious of the post-1911 leaders was Yuan Shih-kai, the second president of the republic. In the second year of his office, revolts broke out in the South, and Yuan countered by ousting from his government the group that had been associated with the disturbance. Later he abolished Parliament and in 1915 proclaimed himself emperor and head of a new dynasty. Yuan Shih-kai had no more of a program to offer than had the Taipings fifty years earlier. Rebellion broke out all over China, and Yuan cancelled his dynasty. He was about to be deposed as president when he died in 1916.

7. The height of uncritical enthusiasm for Western ideas was reached, roughly speaking, in the decade preceding World War I. The writings of the exiled reformist, Liang Chi-chao, during this period stirred great enthusiasm. In 1902, Liang was calling for "a new people" in articles published in Tokyo and smuggled

into China: "Without a new people, although you change a
method today and change a man tomorrow, daub a bit on here
and clean off a bit there, however you knit your brows in learning, I do not see that it can have any effect. We have been talking
of new things for tens of years." To translate talk into action,
Liang Chi-chao advocated Western science and nationalism almost without qualification. Of nationalism he wrote, "From this
has come the principle of national imperialism by which [West-
erners] not only govern themselves but go out to govern other
people. . . . Their strength abounds within their countries and
so overflows outside." The philosophical implications of evolution also made a great impression upon Liang Chi-chao, although
they impressed him most through the writings of one Benjamin
Kidd, who seemed to solve problems that Marx, Spencer, and
Huxley did not. Liang deduced from Kidd that "Whether it be
a struggle between individual and individual or race and race,
the outcome is that the unfit is defeated and perishes while the
superior who is equal to the situation flourishes. This is an unchanging law, and in this movement for evolution *there must be
the sacrifice of the individual for society, of the present for the
future.*" (The emphasis is Liang's.)

When attention shifted, however, to the vast content of Chinese
culture, Liang Chi-chao declared that there was "a whole continent waiting to be discovered," wrote and lectured with enthusiasm, and wrote "Method for the Study of Chinese History" and
"The Political Thought of Pre-Chin Times." This was no chame-
leon change. The importance of Western ideas of science and
nationalism had not disappeared from Liang's mind any more
than from the minds of other Chinese intellectuals. What had
come very strongly into his mind and their minds was the need to
grow Western ideas on Chinese roots.

(The quotations from Liang Chi-chao were translated by E. R.
Hughes. They appear in *The Invasion of China by the Western
World.*)

8. Chinese were highly conscious of the fact that the cultural
collision of China and the West was accompanied by the brandish-
ing and actual employment of arms. They knew that a government that did no more than unite Western and Chinese ideas
was not solution enough; such a government would have to be
strong enough to survive the attacks of native war lords and foreign imperialisms. This problem is noted by Hu Shih in *The*

Chinese Renaissance, Chicago, 1934: "A Chinese scholar once remarked: 'It is easy for China to acquire the civilization of the West, but it is very difficult to master its barbarism. Yet I suppose we must first master this barbarism before we can feel at home in this new civilization.' By barbarism he means the military side of the Western culture, which does not consist of mere up-to-date equipment, nor mere efficient organization, nor mere resourcefulness in man and money power, but which must presuppose the existence of what may be vaguely termed 'the martial spirit,' under which term we may include the love for adventure, the almost primitive delight in competitive combat, the instinctive love and worship of the warrior, the painstaking cultivation of bodily strength, the habits of obedience, and the readiness to fight and die for an impersonal cause."

This martial spirit, to be sure, was something which Chinese culture held barbaric indeed; it was antithetical to the ideas of Chinese thinkers of all schools, except for the Legalists. Furthermore, World War I made it no less unattractive. Alert to Western changes of opinion, Chinese intellectuals were alert to the disillusion that swept the West after the war. They felt particularly the force of Western disillusion with organized Christianity. The Christianity with which they had come in contact was one which had found place in China through the system of unequal treaties that had been forced upon China by armed might; it was a Christianity, besides, replete with the peculiar worldliness of nineteenth-century England and America. Chinese intellectuals had scant opportunity to discover that Christianity is in its essence hostile to the West's particular variety of barbarism.

It may be that one of the greatest tragedies of the nineteenth and early twentieth centuries was Western inability to picture to the East the basic ideas and the basic spirit of the Jewish-Christian tradition, upon which rested whatever was creative and unitive in Western life. It can be argued that Christianity (as contrasted, say, with Confucianism) is a dynamic religion and as such subject to diabolical subversions. It has the force to energize individuals and groups of individuals, and the energy has at times been used in ways fantastically and fanatically contrary to the spirit of Christ. But without the possibility of misuse there would be no possibility of the full use of Christianity. If men are liberated—and liberation has been a basic fact in every surge and resurge of Christian belief—they are liberated to the possibility

both of good and of evil. Had Christianity been presented in
China as a liberating force and not as a group of exclusive dogmas
and a bundle of exclusive Western customs, a genuine cultural
interchange might have taken place, and China might in fact have
done more for the West by reforming Reformed Christianity than
the West could have done for China herself. Such an interchange
could not be. Christianity looked to many Chinese to be a religion
of the mighty; neither the Bible lessons of the Sunday Schools nor
the sermons of the churches nor the compulsory chapels of the
mission schools and colleges created a different impression. Most
young Chinese concluded that their country would have to become mighty, but that it would not have to become Christian.

9. The literary renaissance (*hsin shih chao,* new tide) was itself
an amalgam of Chinese culture and Western ideas. It did not
decry Chinese culture as did some individuals who believed the
language itself was unfitted for a modern society and that it ought
to be either overthrown or radically altered through a system of
phonetics, a step which could have robbed China of the depth of
its culture and would have kept any new culture shallow.

The aims of the renaissance were stated by Hu Shih thus:
"Looking at it generally, the cause of the decline in literary
studies may be summed up in one sentence, 'Matter is the slave of
manner.' This means form and no spirit, appearance at the expense of spirit. To remedy this fault we must direct the emphasis
to meaning in what we say, the matter behind the manner, the
living kernel within the shell, as found in the old saying, 'with
words unadorned and action undelayed.' . . . I want to declare
a revolution in literary studies with eight objects to be achieved:
give up the use of classical quotations and allusions, of conven-
tions of courtesy, of parallelism both in prose and poetry; do not
avoid common everyday words and expressions; set ourselves to
the construction of grammar; avoid unfelt exclamations; do not
take the men of old as a pattern; in all expression there should be
an individual 'I' present. . . ." (E. R. Hughes, *The Invasion of
China by the Western World.*)

This proposal was not simply a sudden brilliant idea. Behind
it were careful study of the old forms of writing and careful
experimentation in new forms, based on the style of the popular
Chinese novels. Hu Shih, for instance, spent some months com-
posing old-style poetry of the sort required in government examinations, concluding that only mechanical ability of a sort was

required for proficiency. The proposal called, moreover, for an immense and radical change; it asked the educated to give up the unique skill of their group. Yet within three years the Ministry of Education—the one China-wide government ministry during the war-lord days—directed even elementary schools to shift to the new way of writing.

10. The comment of Lin Yutang is taken from *My Country and My People,* New York, 1935.

Notes to Chapter 8

1. Permission for underlings to commit the country to war was specifically granted in the Japanese Constitution: "The exercise of the right of warfare in the field . . . as the exigency of circumstances may require, may be entrusted to the commanding officer of the place, who is allowed to take actual steps his discretion dictates, and then to report to the government."

2. Why did Japan seek to expand where she did? She lies in much the same geographic relation to Asia as island Britain does to Europe; yet, unlike Britain, she did not keep free of territorial ambitions on the continent. Her position on the Asiatic side of the Pacific is in some respects the same as the United States position on the American side: she has a twelve-hundred-mile exposed coast line. But she built her naval fleet for aggressive rather than defensive action.

The degree to which this will for expansion resulted from contact and collision with the West is difficult to determine. Several times in her early history Japan tried to invade the continent; several times forces from the continent tried to invade her; all invasions ultimately failed. The straits between Korea and Japan served not so much as a meeting place as a no-man's land. Japan did not even reach out towards the islands immediately to her north and south. Instead she lay in quiet isolation like some giant unicellular organism upon which the stimulus to reproduce has not yet acted.

In 1894 this organism began throwing off shoots, and each shoot produced new ones until Japan was engulfing not only areas upon the continent but also series of island groups. Japan's expansion began by her treating Korea for what it geographically was—an avenue of approach to China and Manchuria. She advanced so quickly that the Chinese sued for peace, giving up

Formosa and the Ryukyus, an island chain that connects Formosa with Japan and effectively blocks the coast of China and protects the southern approaches to Japan.

After 1905 and the defeat of the Russians, Japan took over the Russian lease in the Kwantung Peninsula, half of Russian-owned Sakhalin Island, and the South Manchurian Railway, and in so doing dug herself deeper into the economic and political life of Korea and of China's northeastern provinces. Her next success was in the Pacific; she capitalized on her participation as an ally in World War I by taking over the former German island possessions north of the equator: the Marianas, Carolines, and Marshalls. She also demanded and got German interests in China.

Just as Germany showed an attraction to the "heart land," so Japan felt drawn to China and to Manchuria, which possesses metals that Japan lacks. In 1931 the Japanese Army took over Manchuria and turned it into a center of heavy industry and a laboratory for totalitarian experiments. Controls were set not only upon major economic and political matters but even upon the daily comings and goings of the inhabitants. A spy system was set up inside the Army and the Government. A single political party was created.

At length Japan turned her attention to China proper. Her strategic aim was to make this vast land mass her great continental stronghold (in much the same way as the Germans aimed to make Russia their stronghold) and to develop inland communications secure from an attack by sea.

3. Since Chinese victories over Japan were not the subject of detailed report in the West, it may be well to consider the tactics of a specific action, the third battle for Changsha, which began December 17, 1941, when Japanese forces moved out from the occupied city of Yoyang at the confluence of the Yangtze River and the Hsiang River. The fifty odd miles of terrain separating Yoyang from Changsha was relatively flat; through it flowed three tributaries of the Hsiang River—the Hsinchiang, the Milo, and the Liuyang—each of which ran directly across the Japanese line of advance.

The Japanese force totalled 150,000 men. There were five divisions, two brigades, two tank regiments, one heavy artillery regiment, and two independent engineer regiments. There were one hundred supporting planes. The Chinese force of 300,000 men was equipped only with rifles, grenades, and machine guns; it was supported by a few howitzers of German and Chinese make. This artillery was emplaced on the top of a hill slightly to the west of Changsha. Part of the Chinese force was stationed in towns removed from the battle area itself; the rest was deployed in depth everywhere between the Hsinchiang River and Changsha and concentrated heavily on the Changsha sides of the Hsinchiang and Milo rivers and in front of Changsha itself.

The Japanese began the crossing of the Hsinchiang on December 17 and were able to complete it by the twenty-fourth. Their drive appeared to gain momentum and they drove on toward the Milo River, where in two previous battles for Changsha the Japanese forces had been flanked, encircled, and cut up with casualties of about 35,000 and 48,000. Yet at the Milo, resistance proved to be surprisingly weak and for the next four days Chinese forces melted like butter before a hot poker. When the Japanese forces converged on the suburbs of Changsha, they were satisfied that the battle had been won.

The Chinese retreat, however, was a scheme, a scheme, moreover, planned not to resemble any scheme used theretofore in the defense of Changsha. To the Chinese no less than to the Japanese the battle appeared all but won. Roads, bridges, rail beds, and habitations had been blasted—not only to make the Japanese advance but the Japanese retreat more difficult—and the Milo River forces had been ordered to offer only weak defense. There was a heavy defense around the city itself, installed in ditches and fortresses and backed up with the howitzers on the hill outside the city. Furthermore, the Chinese forces that had appeared to be routed at the Hsinchiang River had moved in a body to the left flank of the Japanese advance. The forces south of the Milo had moved, again to the left flank, to the town of Pingkiang, some thirty miles from Changsha. There were also forces stationed in the towns of Liuyang and Chuchow nearer by. As the Japanese drove closer to Changsha, General Hsueh Yo dispatched word to the commanders of these units, the most distant of which began moving on January 1. On January 4 the various units converged on the rear of the Japanese forces, at the moment confidently battling their way into Changsha's inner defense works. Simultaneously, the defenders of Changsha rose out of their ditches and attacked. The Japanese found themselves confronted not with a simple pincers movement, but with a vise.

They attempted retreat almost at once, but for two days retreat was impossible. The Ninth Brigade, left behind by the Japanese to guard against surprises was annihilated by Chinese forces left behind to surprise the Ninth Brigade. For two days the Japanese were wedged between attacking Chinese forces, and at night large fires sprang up as they burned their dead. Aiming at a breakthrough in order to get back across the Liuyang River, the Japanese called up heavy air reinforcements and concentrated their tank and artillery fire. The Chinese forces again moved to the flanks and grouped themselves on each side of the retreating Japanese, who were forced in effect to run a gauntlet. As the Japanese fled through this corridor, one part or another of their forces would be intercepted and encircled. Between five and six thousand Japanese were drowned in the shallow Liuyang River, and the survivors found their flight across the deeper Milo and Hsinchiang far costlier than their earlier and triumphant crossings. Retreating in many areas more slowly than they had advanced, they took ten days to cover the fifty miles separating Changsha defenses from the Hsinchiang. They reached the base at Yoyang, but for every two soldiers who had departed only one returned.

4. Signatories to the Nine-Power Treaty on principles and policies concerning China, February 6, 1922, were Belgium, Britain, China, France, Italy, Japan, the Netherlands, Portugal, and the United States. The text reads, in part:

ARTICLE I.

The Contracting Powers, other than China, agree:

(1) To respect the sovereignty, the independence, and the territorial and administrative integrity of China;

(2) To provide the fullest and most unembarrassed opportunity to China to develop and maintain for herself an effective and stable government;

(3) To use their influence for the purpose of effectually establishing and maintaining the principle of equal opportunity for the commerce and industry of all nations throughout the territory of China;

(4) To refrain from taking advantage of conditions in China in order to seek special rights or privileges which would abridge the rights of subjects or citizens of friendly States, and from countenancing action inimical to the security of such States. . . .

ARTICLE IV.

The Contracting Powers agree not to support any agreements
by their respective nationals with each other designed to create
Spheres of Influence or to provide for the enjoyment of mutually
exclusive opportunities in designated parts of Chinese territory. . . .

5. It was not known until after World War II that the Japanese would have attacked even if the United States had been willing to make concessions. Captured documents indicate that the
Japanese Government wanted either war or a completely free
hand in Asia.

NOTES TO CHAPTER 9

1. The Japanese attempted to co-ordinate their forces by subor-
dinating air and naval forces to ground forces. The chief function
of the Japanese Navy until the Battle of the Philippines was to
act as a troop carrier or as a troop and supply escort. It was
expected to strike quickly, preferably at night, inflict enough
damage to upset enemy plans, and to retire before being exposed
to too much danger. There is no indication that the Japanese
Navy was seeking battle when it suffered the defeats of Midway
and the Coral Sea. It was escorting land forces sent out·for action
against definite land objectives.

In the earlier days of the war the air force was effective in
bombing and strafing enemy troops, and it had measurable success
with torpedo bombing of ships. But even before the days of Allied
air supremacy, the Japanese showed little inclination to follow an
over-all plan for systematically reducing Allied strength. Rather
they went after enemy opposition whenever and wherever it
seemed to turn up.

Under these circumstances, Japan relied basically on her ground
forces to counter the growing strength of the Allies. Here geography was her greatest help. Between Tokyo and Australia and
between Singapore and Midway lay chains of islands that could
be made into a two-way system of double defense lines. Two
chains of islands stretched east-west and faced Australia; two
others stretched north-south and faced Midway and Hawaii. Each
chain could be used to supply or reinforce the other according to
the needs of the moment. The weakness in this system was that
once a central link was cut off, the chain itself parted.

2. Elsewhere in the Pacific, during the same period, the northern Japanese island of Paramushiro was both shelled and bombed; the southern supply port of Rabaul was blasted practically out of effectiveness; a twelve-ship convoy was shattered north of New Britain island; forces landed on the Green Islands above Bougainville to cut off some 22,000 Japanese and bring practically to an end the campaign for the Solomons. This show of strength impressed the Japanese sufficiently to lead to the discharge of their army and navy chiefs of staff. The bases attacked had all been heavily fortified.

3. It would seem that Admiral Halsey might wisely have left one task group near Leyte instead of taking all his forces north to engage the Japanese carrier fleet. Five American ships might have been saved; more Japanese ships might have been destroyed. History will argue and the United States Navy is already arguing the question endlessly. Memoirs have already been written about it. While the merits of the argument are not a concern of this study, the nature of Halsey's decision is; for the decision to leave a group of jeep carriers to tangle with cruisers and battleships points to the instinctive contempt of Japanese fighting strength which Halsey was occasionally given to display. This contempt led, it would seem, to a reasonably exact estimate of both the United States and the Japanese positions and abilities. Halsey, in preoccupying himself with the destruction of a fleet that might cause damage two months later rather than with the fleet that might cause damage at the moment, was justified not only by the outcome of the battle but by the blow which was dealt to Japanese hopes.

4. The quotations in this chapter on Japanese reactions during the war are taken from translations by the United States agencies that monitored Japanese radio broadcasts.

5. The lack of correlation between bomb damage and declining Japanese industrial production is not stated in the United States Strategic Bombing Survey's reports, but is suggested by a reading of them.

Notes to Chapter 10

1. Jawaharlal Nehru once wrote, "The average European concept of Asia is as an appendage to Europe and America—a great

mass of people fallen low who are to be lifted up by the good works of the West."

2. According to the Buck survey, 54 per cent of Chinese farmers owned all their own land; 29 per cent owned some; 11 per cent owned only their homesteads (and were therefore classed as tenants); 6 per cent owned nothing. According to other surveys conducted on different bases, tenancy ranged from 19 to 29 per cent. Compare these figures with those for Japan: 31 per cent owners, 43 per cent part owners; 26 per cent tenants. Compare them with United States figures: 51 per cent owners, 10 per cent part owners, 39 per cent tenants. Tenancy was more prevalent in the rice areas of South China than in the wheat areas of the North.

The charge of great inequality in land ownership is still made by newspapers and periodicals in China despite the fact that Mao Tse-tung said in April 1948, that "We spend altogether too much time in seeking out the hidden wealth of the landlords. No, comrades, this is not the way. In this the masses are wrong. All the correct opinions of the masses we must carry out loyally, but sometimes they are incorrect. You must understand that some of the middle peasants must be allowed to obtain more land than the average of the poor peasants generally. We do not advocate absolute egalitarianism. Our aim is only to destroy feudal exploitation . . . The whole area where agrarian reform is possible cannot exceed eight per cent of the rural communities, or ten per cent of the rural population." (Quoted in Robert Payne's *Mao Tse-tung, Ruler of Red China,* New York, 1950.)

Such remarks from Mao Tse-tung should not be considered statements of settled policy. Other statements have been at variance with the one quoted above. Mao embraces a flexibility of approach to all but basic questions of strategy, suiting policy to a definite situation as it emerges.

3. In the face of the competition for supplies going on at the time between the United States, British, and Russian armies, it seemed to the United States impossible to meet promises made to the Chinese. In 1942 T. V. Soong begged President Roosevelt for one hundred cargo planes, which would have duplicated Burma Road tonnages. He won his point, over the objection of General H. H. Arnold, but lost most of the planes through a last-minute diversion to Alaska. Such diversions were frequent.

A part of what was decided at the Casablanca Conference, January 1942, was disclosed to Chiang—little aid for China—and he then indicated that six years of war was a long time, and that he could not hold out much longer. T. V. Soong repeated this statement at the first Quebec Conference in August of the same year, but no supplies were forthcoming. The British in particular wished no diversion of matériel from the western Mediterranean.

4. H. H. Kung was moved out of the Finance Ministry (he remained Vice Premier); Ho Ying-chin ceased to be Minister of War (he was sent to Kunming to be the opposite number of Major General Robert McClure); and Chen Li-fu dropped out of the Ministry of Education (he went to a patronage post within the Kuomintang). These three ministers had been the target of severe United States criticism. At the same time, Wang Shih-chieh became Minister of Information and undertook to liberalize the censorship; and Chen Cheng, who was liked by the American military, became the new Minister of War.

In December 1945, Foreign Minister T. V. Soong became Acting Premier. In January 1946, Chiang Kai-shek announced a projected constitutional convention. In May H. H. Kung resigned as Vice Premier; Chiang Kai-shek resigned as Premier. T. V. Soong became Premier, and Wong Wen-hao, China's WPB head and a man of his own mind, became Vice Premier. That same month the Kuomintang Congress agreed to Chiang's proposal for a constitutional convention. The same Congress agreed to take party officials out of the schools and out of the Army, and even undertook to change the nature of the San-min-chu-i Ching-nien-tuan, a little Kuomintang for students. In June the government promised that district and provincial people's councils would be elected throughout Free China. Chiang Mon-ling, liberal President of Peking National University, became Secretary-General of the Cabinet. Many of these changes were more drastic than any change in the preceding eight years of war.

5. The text of the secret Yalta agreement is as follows:
"The leaders of the three Great Powers—the Soviet Union, the United States of America and Great Britain—have agreed that in two or three months after Germany has surrendered and the war in Europe has terminated, the Soviet Union shall enter into the war against Japan on the side of the Allies on the condition that:

(1) The status quo in Outer-Mongolia (the Mongolian People's Republic) shall be preserved;

(2) The former rights of Russia, violated by the treacherous attack of Japan in 1904, shall be restored, *viz:*

(a) The southern part of Sakhalin as well as all the islands adjacent to it shall be returned to the Soviet Union,

(b) The commercial port of Dairen shall be internationalized, the pre-eminent interests of the Soviet Union in the port being safeguarded and the lease of Port Arthur as a naval base of the Soviet Union restored,

(c) The Chinese-Eastern Railroad and the South-Manchurian Railway, which provide an outlet to Dairen, shall be jointly operated by the establishment of a joint Soviet-Chinese company it being understood that the pre-eminent interests of the Soviet Union shall be safeguarded and that China shall regain full sovereignty in Manchuria;

(3) The Kuril Islands shall be handed over to the Soviet Union.

"It is understood, that the agreement concerning Outer-Mongolia and the ports and railroads referred to above will require concurrence of Generalissimo Chiang Kai-shek. The President will take measures in order to obtain this concurrence on advice from Marshal Stalin.

"The Heads of the three Great Powers have agreed that these claims of the Soviet Union shall be unquestionably fulfilled after Japan has been defeated.

"For its part the Soviet Union expresses its readiness to conclude with the National Government of China a pact of friendship and alliance between the U.S.S.R. and China in order to render assistance to China with its armed forces for the purpose of liberating China from the Japanese yoke."

A current argument is that the Yalta pact was justifiable in terms of the conditions existing at the time. Sumner Welles writes, "While a few were questioning the wisdom of some of the Far Eastern agreements made at Yalta, those who were not motivated by purely political partisanship were generally willing to concede that if these agreements would tend to prevent postwar controversies between the major allies, make for co-operation between Moscow and Washington as well as between Moscow and Nanking, and promote the rapid pacification and recovery of a devastated sector of the globe, the concessions by China that they involved would be justified in China's own highest interest. . . . No reasonable man could have been so ingenuous as to assume in September 1945 that the infinitely complicated machinery of rehabilitation was going to function smoothly without many a breakdown. Yet he would have seemed equally unrealistic had he anticipated all that has since taken place."

Mr. Welles presents as evidence the fact that although certain of President Roosevelt's advisors had reached the conclusion that Japan was in effect defeated already, the Army and the Joint Chiefs of Staff did not share these conclusions and recommended that Russia be brought into the final battle against Japan.

He suggests that some of the President's representatives in the Far East "served him in ill stead" and sent him "inaccurate information," despite which the President did not swerve from his fundamental aim for a strong and united China. "He held that the best assurance of this would be a firm agreement between Moscow and the Chinese Nationalist Government guaranteeing Stalin's support of the government of Chiang Kai-shek and his non-interference in China's internal affairs." Mr. Welles notes that in wartime conferences with the Russians, sufficient co-operation was shown in order to reach agreements, and sums up his argument with the question, "In view of Russia's record during the war, was there any reason why President Roosevelt should have assumed that the Yalta agreement would be reached only 'on paper'?"

It is evident of course that Russia engaged in duplicity in her carrying out of the Yalta agreement. Noteworthy is the firmness with which Stalin insisted that he would carry it out in good faith. On May 28, 1945, almost three months after Yalta, Harry Hopkins cabled the following report to President Truman of a conversation with Stalin: "By August 8 the Soviet Army will be properly deployed on the Manchurian positions. . . . [Stalin] made categorical statement that he would do everything he could to promote the unification of China under the leadership of Chiang Kai-shek. He further stated that this leadership should continue after the war because no one else was strong enough. He specifically stated that no Communist leader was strong enough to unify China. . . . He stated categorically that he had no territorial claims against China and mentioned specifically Manchuria and Sinkiang, and that in all areas his troops entered to fight the

Japanese he would respect Chinese sovereignty. . . . He agreed
with America's "Open Door" policy and went out of his way to
indicate that the United States was the only power with the
resources to aid China economically after the war. . . . He agreed
that there should be a trusteeship for Korea under the United
States, China, Great Britain, and the Soviet Union."

Apart from serious misjudgment of Japan's military potential,
the question is whether the duplicity of Russia could have
been foreseen at the time of Yalta or before. It would appear
strange, to say the least, that the American Government did not
have in mind that recent event, the Stalin-Hitler pact, and that
record of avowed attachment to duplicity, Soviet descriptions of
Soviet foreign policy. Four years of wartime history are not a
substitute for knowledge of the years that went before. Why then
was the American Government so innocent of history at Yalta?

This innocence is difficult to understand without reference to
the atmosphere in Washington at the time. There were indeed
persons who warned against risking plans for peace on the expectation of co-operation from Russia; there were persons who
specifically questioned the wisdom of increased Russian influence
in Manchuria; and not all of these persons had political axes to
grind. But there were many, many more persons, very sincere and
patriotic, who felt a strong sense of mission to defend American–
Russian co-operation as the great hope for the postwar world.
Except by officers of the armed services, Manchuria was a very
freely discussed topic during the last months of 1944—the President was even quoted in private as to how far he was willing to go
at the coming Yalta Conference in making concessions to Stalin—
and a very great deal of zeal was expended in focusing government
opinion toward recognition of the value of Russian co-operation
in the Far East. At this time, the Chinese Communists were still
widely considered an independent revolutionary force whose good
will could be won for the United States, and it was in fact believed
that the Chinese Government, weak and corrupt, would benefit
from coalition with them. The overwhelming weight of the argument emphasized the value of Russian influence in Manchuria
and of Communist influence in China. Persons who embraced
such views were, relatively speaking, the moderates. Persons of
more extreme views, but by no means of Communist convictions,
were insisting that recognition should be taken away from Chiang
and given directly to Mao. In short, by far the greater part of the

American Government had forgotten history, had fallen prey to wishful thinking, and had assumed that Stalin would not tell lies.

(The quotations from Mr. Welles are taken from his book, *Seven Decisions That Shaped History,* New York, 1951. The quotations from Mr. Hopkins' cable are taken from Robert E. Sherwood's, *Roosevelt and Hopkins,* New York, 1948.)

NOTES TO CHAPTER 11

1. The poem by Lermontov is quoted by Nicholas Berdyaev in *The Russian Idea,* New York, 1947.

2. Lenin's statement was made on December 24, 1920. It is quoted in David J. Dallin's very helpful source work, *The Rise of Russia in Asia,* New Haven, 1949.

3. The Sun-Joffe agreement is quoted from the *China Year Book, 1924–25.*

4. The statement concerning the Comintern views of the rightist members of the Kuomintang is given in Dallin's *The Rise of Russia in Asia.* It was part of the instructions sent from the Comintern in February 1927, and quoted by Stalin in a speech on April 1, 1927.

5. The Chinese Communist party was attempting to create insurrections both in Hankow and in Shanghai. An antiforeign attack in Hankow failed when the British consul handed the British Concession over to the insurrectionists and ordered British nationals onto a gunboat in the Yangtze River. J. B. Powell's *My Twenty-five Years in China,* New York, 1945, contains interesting data on this period, as concerns both Hankow and Shanghai.

6. The criticism of Li Li-san is taken from *The Rise of Russia in Asia.* Mr. Dallin there quotes the Comintern publication *Strategiya i Taktika,* Moscow, 1934.

7. Mao's criticism of "ultra-left" policies is made in *Turning Point in China,* New York, 1948. The Comintern's criticism of Mao's criticizers is quoted from *Strategiya i Taktika* in *The Rise of Russia in Asia.*

8. Mao's statement of strategy appears in "The Chinese Revolution and the Communist Party of China," written in 1939. It appears in the *China Digest.*

9. The Communist slogans were reported by Edgar Snow in *Red Star Over China,* New York, 1938. Dr. Hu's comment on the Communist strategy of retreat appears in his article, "China in Stalin's Grand Strategy," *Foreign Affairs,* October 1950.

10. The Chinese Communist denunciation of a united front with the Kuomintang against Japan is quoted from David J. Dallin's *Soviet Russia and the Far East,* New Haven, 1948, a volume which, although it was published a year earlier, continues the story of Chinese-Russian relations from the point where *The Rise of Russia in Asia* leaves off.

11. *Izvestia's* denunciation of the Sian kidnapping is reported in *Soviet Russia and the Far East.* Mr. Dallin quotes the editorial of December 14, 1936, as follows: "Under whatever slogans and program the Sian insurrection be conducted, this move . . . represents a danger not only to the Nanking government, but to all of China. It is clear that despite Chang Hsueh-liang's anti-Japanese banner, his move can benefit only Japanese imperialism. So long as the Nanking government conducts a policy of resistance to the Japanese aggressors, the united popular front against Japan is understood by all its participants to mean not a front against Nanking, but a front together with Nanking."

12. *The Tactical Line of the Chinese Communist Party* was published originally in Yenan, probably in 1937.

13. The belief that Chinese Communism was an independent movement was abetted by the Communists themselves. In 1939 Mao Tse-tung told the late Joy Homer, "Probably you remember that as a group we were once very anti-Christian and committed atrocities against your missionaries. Now we are grateful for the help you give us. It is more than politics, this gratitude. We consider your way of life and thought closer to our own than any other single philosophy." (*Dawn Watch in China,* by Joy Homer, Boston, 1941.)

14. The statistical information given by Mao Tse-tung to the Seventh Congress of the Communist party is contained in "On Coalition Government," published in Yenan in 1945.

NOTES TO CHAPTER 12

1. Changes in the minds of scholars are reported in detail in Derk Bodde's *Peking Diary,* New York, 1950.

2. *On the People's Democratic Dictatorship* was published in Peiping in July 1949. The excerpts from it are taken from Dr. Bodde's *Peking Diary*. Mao's article appears in complete form, but without a title and with slight editorial differences, in the State Department's *United States Relations with China*.

3. The Soviet-like remarks in this paragraph were culled from the Chinese press and were quoted by T. F. Tsiang in a statement to the General Assembly of the United Nations on November 21, 1950.

4. There appears to be general consensus of opinion that graft and corruption were general in wartime China. This consensus, however, was based essentially on supposition and hearsay, not on fact that could be subjected to laws of evidence. The writer must therefore state that he believes but that he cannot prove that corruption was rife. He must also point out that hearsay, which often says more than it hears, can lead readily to exaggeration. A Chinese proverb says: "One dog barks at his shadow; a hundred dogs bark at the barking."

5. *Turning Point in China* is the report by Mao Tse-tung to the Central Committee of the Communist party of China on December 25, 1947. It was published in New York in 1948.

6. The comparison between Japan and the United States was made by Lu Ting-yi, Chief of the Propaganda department of the Chinese Communist party in the November 4, 1946, *Emancipation Daily*. It is quoted in H. Arthur Steiner's valuable discussion, "Mainsprings of Chinese Communist Foreign Policy," *The American Journal of International Law,* January 1950.

7. Silence is a traditional refuge of Chinese who believe themselves unfairly attacked. Whether from some subtle dependence on Confucius' *Li* or Lao-tze's *Tao,* men will often keep quiet even when their life is at stake—if they are certain they are in the right. Such quiescence seems natural to the Chinese mind: Why put out propaganda after all unless you have something to hide?

8. The reasoning behind the Marshall Mission was stated on May 25, 1946, by John Carter Vincent, head of the State Department's China desk, as follows: "Our efforts to bring about peace and unity in China are not altruistic. They are in furtherance of clear national and international interests. . . . We must stand

for the independence and territorial and administrative integrity
of China. But we cannot again place our sole reliance upon the
self-denying principles of the Open Door and the Nine-Power
Treaty. We must make positive efforts to bring about a strong
unified China. . . . The alternative to the policy of working for
unity in China by the peaceful means advanced by General Marshall is, it seems to me, unqualified support of the existing government in the hope that unity can be achieved by force; but that
carries the unwelcome possibility that China would be divided
into two opposing camps and thus seriously handicap any constructive policy in the Far East."

NOTES TO CHAPTER 13

1. The constitution was first proposed by General MacArthur
to the Premier, Prince Higashi-Kuni, head of the first post-surren-
der government. Very little happened. As soon as the Shidehara
government appeared, MacArthur took the problem up with the
new Premier. After considerable discussion with the government
and within the political parties, a partial draft was put together
in January 1946. Its great defect was its reluctance to break
sharply with totalitarian controls.

MacArthur thereupon offered to Shidehara the research facilities and suggestions of SCAP's Government Section, headed by
Brigadier General (later Major General) Courtney Whitney. After
further discussion a draft was completed, and the Japanese made
ready to show it to the Emperor, not without misgivings, for the
document not only stripped him of his formal sovereignty but also
of his actual wealth. The Emperor was pleased. He talked with
MacArthur (who described him as the most liberal man in the
Japanese government) and took the unprecedented step of propagandizing the merits of the constitution to the government that
had created it.

After the spring elections of 1946, which had been arranged
for a public argument about the constitution—it never developed
—there were two months of free debate in the Diet. Thirty-three
articles were amended, three deleted, and one added. It was during this period that SCAP refused to have any views on the document. On October 7, 1946, the House of Representatives passed
the constitution with only five Noes.

NOTES TO CHAPTER 14

1. At Moscow, Secretary Marshall handed Molotov a letter which pointed to the need for a united government of Korea but emphasized the readiness of the United States to take independent action to strengthen South Korea. Molotov promptly made a concession that Russia had been refusing to make: discussion of the formation of a united government with non-Communist Korean politicians. It may have been that the State Department did not expect this concession, and that it had in mind no course but the very honorable one of putting all cards on the conference table. It may also have been that the State Department had concluded that the large aid program it had been planning did not represent the best use of American resources in a world that was becoming increasingly contentious, and that it was better to make another try at Russian-American co-operation and to pass the Korean problem to the United Nations if co-operation proved impossible. In any case, after the new Russian-American talks foundered, aid for Korea, although it passed from Army hands into those of the E.C.A., did not increase. It stayed practically at relief levels. (The abandoned $540 million program was intended to be in addition to minimum-survival grants.)

Selected Bibliography

The list of books and articles that follows does not include all the written material consulted in the course of the current project. It includes materials of which the writer has made use and also such materials as he recommends as of use to persons desiring further reading.

Allen, George Cyril. *Japanese Industry: Its Recent Development and Present Condition.* New York, International Secretariat, Institute of Pacific Relations, 1939.

———. *A Short Economic History of Modern Japan.* London, Allen and Unwin, 1946.

Baker, John Earl. "Industrializing the Good Earth." *Fortune,* 32: 148–57 (November 1945).

Benedict, Ruth. *The Chrysanthemum and the Sword; Patterns of Japanese Culture.* Boston, Houghton, 1946.

Berdyaev, Nicolas. *The Origin of Russian Communism.* London, G. Bles, 1937.

———. *The Russian Idea.* New York, Macmillan, 1948.

Bisson, Thomas Arthur. *Japan in China.* New York, Macmillan, 1938.

Bodde, Derk. *China's First Unifier.* Leiden, E. J. Brill, 1938.

———. *Peking Diary.* New York, Schuman, 1950.

Brewitt-Taylor, Charles Henry, trans. *San Kuo.* Shanghai, Kelly & Walsh, 1925.

Buck, John Lossing. *Chinese Farm Economy.* Chicago, University of Chicago Press, 1930.

Buck, John Lossing. *Farm Tenancy in China*. Chengtu, 1944. Pp. 455–66 *Of Economic Facts*, No. 33 (June 1944).

———. *Land Utilization in China*. Shanghai, The Commercial Press, 1937.

Buck, Pearl S., Trans. *All Men are Brothers* (*Shui Hu Chuan*). New York, Day, 1933.

Buss, Claude Albert. *War and Diplomacy in Eastern Asia*. New York, Macmillan, 1941.

Byas, Hugh. *Government by Assassination*. New York, Knopf, 1942.

Chamberlin, William Henry. *Japan over Asia*. Boston, Little, 1937.

Chang Kia-ngau. *China's Struggle for Railroad Development*. New York, Day, 1943.

Chiang Kai-shek. *China's Destiny*. New York, Macmillan, 1947.

———. *The Collected Wartime Messages of Generalissimo Chiang Kai-shek*. New York, Day, 1946.

Creel, Herrlee. *The Birth of China*. London, J. Cape, 1936.

Cressy, George B. *China's Geographic Foundations*. New York, McGraw, 1934.

Dallin, David J. *The Rise of Russia in Asia*. New Haven, Yale, 1949.

———. *Soviet Russia and the Far East*. New Haven, Yale, 1948.

———. *Soviet Russia's Foreign Policy, 1939–1942*. New Haven, Yale, 1942.

Embree, John Fee. *The Japanese Nation, A Social Survey*. New York, Farrar & Rinehart, 1945.

———. *Suye Mura, A Japanese Village*. Chicago, University of Chicago Press, 1939.

Fahs, Charles B. *Government in Japan*. New York, International Secretariat Institute of Pacific Relations, 1940.

Fung Yu-lan. *A History of Chinese Philosophy;* trans. by Derk Bodde. Peiping, H. Vetch, 1937.

Giles, Herbert Allen. *History of Chinese Literature*. New York, D. Appleton & Co., 1901.

———, trans. *Musings of a Chinese Mystic*. London, Murray, 1920. ("Wisdom of the East Series")

Goodrich, Luther Carrington. *A Short History of the Chinese People*. New York, Harper, 1943.

Grajdanzev, Andrew Jonah. *Modern Korea*. New York, Day, 1944.

Grew, Joseph Clark. *Ten Years in Japan*. New York, Simon and Schuster, 1944.

Griswold, Alfred Whitney. *The Far Eastern Policy of the U.S.* New York, Harcourt, 1938.

Hearn, Lafcadio. *Japan, An Attempt at Interpretation*. New York, Macmillan, 1904.

Holcombe, Arthur N. *The Chinese Revolution; A Phase in the Regeneration of a World Power*. Cambridge, Harvard University Press, 1930.

Holtom, Daniel C. *Modern Japan and Shinto Nationalism*. Chicago, University of Chicago Press, 1943.

Homer, Joy. *Dawn Watch in China*. Boston, Houghton, 1941.

Hommel, Rudolf P. *China at Work; An Illustrated Record of the Primitive Industries of China's Masses, etc.* New York, Day, 1937.

Hu Shih. *The Chinese Renaissance*. Chicago, University of Chicago Press, 1934.

———. "A Criticism of Some Recent Methods of Dating Lao Tzŭ." *Harvard Journal of Asiatic Studies*, 2:373–97 (December 1937).

———. *The Development of the Logical Method in Ancient China*, Shanghai, Oriental Book Co., 1922.

———. "China in Stalin's Grand Strategy." *Foreign Affairs*, 29:11–40 (October 1950).

Hughes, Ernest R. *The Invasion of China by the Western World*. New York, Macmillan, 1938.

Isaacs, Harold Robert. *The Tragedy of the Chinese Revolution*. London, Secker & Warburg, 1938.

Latourette, Kenneth Scott. *The Chinese, Their History and Culture*. New York, Macmillan, 1934.

———. *A History of Christian Missions in China*. New York, Macmillan, 1929.

———. *The History of Japan*. New York, Macmillan, 1947. (Revised edition of *The Development of Japan*).

Lin Yutang. *The Gay Genius, The Life and Times of Su Tungpo*. New York, Day, 1947.

———. *My Country and My People*. New York, Reynal & Hitchcock, 1935.

———, ed. and trans. *The Wisdom of Laotse*. New York, Modern Library, 1948.

———, ed. and trans. *The Wisdom of China and India*. New York, Random House, 1942.

Lin Yutang, ed. and trans. *The Wisdom of Confucius*. New York, Modern Library, 1938.

Lory, Hillis. *Japan's Military Masters; The Army in Japanese Life*. New York, Viking, 1943.

Löwith, Karl. "The Japanese Mind." *Fortune*, 28:132–35 (December 1943).

McCune, George McAfee. *Korea Today*. Cambridge, Harvard University Press, 1950.

McGovern, William Montgomery. *The Early Empires of Central Asia*. Chapel Hill, University of North Carolina Press, 1939.

MacNair, Harley F. *China in Revolution*. Chicago, University of Chicago Press, 1931.

Mao Tse-tung. "The Chinese Revolution and .the Communist Party of China. *China Digest*.

———. *New Democracy*. New York, New Century Publishers, 1945.

———. *Turning Point in China*. New York, New Century Publishers, 1948.

———. "Strategic Problems of China's Revolutionary Wars." *China Digest*.

Mei Yi-pao. *The Ethical and Political Works of Motse*. London, A. Probsthain, 1929.

Norman, E. Herbert. *Japan's Emergence as a Modern State*. New York, International Secretariat, Institute of Pacific Relations, 1940.

Oliver, Robert T. *Korea, Forgotten Nation*. Washington, Public Affairs Press, 1944.

———. *Why War Came in Korea*. New York, McMullen, 1950.

Payne, Robert. *Forever China*. New York, Dodd, Mead, 1945.

———. *Mao Tse-tung, Ruler of Red China*. New York, Schuman, 1950.

Powell, John B. *My Twenty-Five Years in China*. New York, Macmillan, 1945.

Price, Willard. *Japan Rides the Tiger*. New York, Day, 1942.

"Red Star Rising." *Fortune*, 34:106–11 (July 1946).

Reichelt, Karl L. *Truth and Tradition in Chinese Buddhism*. Shanghai, The Commercial Press, 1927.

Sansom, Sir George B. *Japan, A Short Cultural History*. New York, Appleton-Century, 1943.

———. *The Western World and Japan*. New York, Knopf, 1950.

Selle, Earl Albert. *Donald of China*. New York, Harper, 1948.

Sherwood, Robert E. *Roosevelt and Hopkins.* New York, Harper, 1950.

Snow, Edgar. *The Battle for Asia.* New York, Random House, 1941.

———. *Red Star over China.* New York, Random House, 1938.

Stein, Sir Mark Aurel. *On Ancient Central-Asian Tracks.* London, Macmillan, 1933.

Steiner, H. Arthur. "Mainsprings of Chinese Communist Foreign Policy." *The American Journal of International Law,* 44:69–99 (January 1950).

Sugimoto, Etsu Inagaki. *A Daughter of the Samurai.* New York, Doubleday Page, 1926.

Sun Yat-sen. *Memoirs of a Chinese Revolutionary.* London, Hutchinson, 1927.

———. *San Min Chu I, The Three Principles of the People.* Trans. by Frank W. Price. Shanghai, China Committee, Institute of Pacific Relations, 1927.

Suzuki, Daisetz T. *Zen Buddhism and its Influence on Japanese Culture.* Kyoto, The Eastern Buddhist Society, 1938.

Trotsky, L. D. *Problems of the Chinese Revolution.* New York, Pioneer Publishers, 1932.

U.S. Department of State. *United States Relations with China, 1944–1949.* Washington, Government Printing Office, 1949. ("Far Eastern Series No. 30")

Waley, Arthur. *An Introduction to the Study of Chinese Painting.* London, E. Benn, 1923.

———. *Three Ways of Thought in Ancient China.* London, Allen & Unwin, 1939.

———, trans. *The Analects of Confucius.* London, Allen & Unwin, 1938.

———, trans. *Monkey,* by Wu Ch'êng-ên. New York, Day, 1944.

———, trans. *The Tale of Genji,* by Lady Murasaki. Boston, Houghton, 1935.

———, trans. *The Way and Its Power.* London, Allen & Unwin, 1934.

Welles, Sumner. *Seven Decisions That Shaped History.* New York, Harper, 1951.

Wu, John C. H., ed. and trans. "Lao Tzŭ's The Tao and Its Virtue." *T'ien Hsia,* 1939.

Wu Yi-fang and Price, Frank W., eds. *China Rediscovers Her West.* New York, Friendship Press, 1940.

Index